AF292521

THE GREAT TRAMWAYS CONSPIRACY

THE GREAT TRAMWAYS CONSPIRACY

THE COVERT CAMPAIGN THAT KILLED OFF THE BRITISH TRAM

MICK HAMER

PEN & SWORD TRANSPORT

AN IMPRINT OF PEN & SWORD BOOKS LTD.
YORKSHIRE – PHILADELPHIA

First published in Great Britain in 2026
Pen & Sword Transport
An imprint of
Pen & Sword Books Ltd
Yorkshire – Philadelphia

ISBN 978 1 03614 334 3

A CIP catalogue record for this book is available from the British Library.

Typeset in 11/14 Palatino by SJmagic DESIGN SERVICES, India.

Printed and bound in India by Replika Press Pvt. Ltd.

The Publisher's authorised representative in the EU for product safety is Authorised Rep Compliance Ltd., Ground Floor, 71 Lower Baggot Street, Dublin D02 P593, Ireland.
www.arccompliance.com

For a complete list of Pen & Sword titles please contact

PEN & SWORD BOOKS LIMITED
George House, Beevor Street, Off Pontefract Road, Hoyle Mill, Barnsley,
South Yorkshire, England, S71 1HN.
E-mail: enquiries@pen-and-sword.co.uk
Website: www.pen-and-sword.co.uk
or
PEN AND SWORD BOOKS
1950 Lawrence Road, Havertown, PA 19083, USA
E-mail: uspen-and-sword@casematepublishers.com
Website: www.penandswordbooks.com

CONTENTS

ACKNOWLEDGEMENTS

The research for this book has been carried out at a large number of archives and libraries over the past seven years. I owe a big debt to their staff, people who know their collections inside out and who have generously nudged me in the right direction.

I would also like to thank Caroline Warhurst, Helen Grove and Simon Murphy at the London Transport Museum Library and Hannah Bales and Laura Waters at the National Tramway Museum for all their help. Joan Francis of Unite granted me access to the archives of the Transport and General Workers' Union at the University of Warwick and Kath Shaw at Living Streets allowed me to trawl through the archives of the Pedestrians' Association. Martin Sanders helped me to navigate the University of Warwick's impressive collection in the Modern Records Centre and Melissa McGreechan of Transport for London Corporate Archives helped me study some of the rarer records belonging to Transport for London.

The staff at a host of other archives have diligently helped with my queries. They include: the Bodleian Library, my local library in Brighton and Hove, the British Library Newsroom, the East Sussex Record Office, Hampshire Archives, the Hartley Library archives collection at the University of Southampton, the Institution of Civil Engineers, the London Archives, the London School of Economics, the National Archives, the Royal Archives, the Royal Society for the Prevention of Accidents, Southampton City Archives and the University of Sussex. I'm grateful to all these archivists and librarians for their unstinting help.

I am also grateful to the following people for allowing me to reproduce images: Ben Goodwin of Alstom, Caterina Tiezzi, at the London Transport Museum, Elisabeth Lee at Lambeth Borough Archives, Gareth Prior at British Trams Online, Jon Day, of the National Motor Museum, Mike Sutcliffe, Nick Higton of the Railway and Canal Historical Society, the Bus Archive, Brighton's Step Back in Time, and the Transport Library. Special thanks go to Peter Waller of the Online Transport Archive, who helped me find several suitable images, and to Ed Douglas who took time off from his busy schedule to take photographs of his local trams.

I would particularly like to thank Megan Sullivan at Gale Cengage, who granted me unfettered access to Gale's collection of newspapers at home, so I could pursue my analysis of astroturfing in the national press during the COVID lockdowns.

I am also indebted to the National Tramway Museum for allowing me to quote from historic documents in the museum's library and to Transport for London for allowing me to quote from unpublished records that are TfL's copyright.

I am grateful to Stephen Joseph for reading an early draft and for his very helpful comments. Finally, I'd like to thank John Scott-Morgan, for commissioning this book and for helping to find photographs.

Every reasonable effort has been made to trace copyright holders of material reproduced in this book. If I have inadvertently overlooked anyone the publishers would be glad to hear from them.

INTRODUCTION

The tram jolts as it rounds the bend, hurling Johnny sideways against Pat who is sitting next to him.

Johnny is a sailor on shore leave in London and Pat is his date for the evening. It is Pat who breaks the silence in the awkward moment that follows.

'I'm sorry,' she says.

'That's alright,' says Johnny.

'There won't be any trams soon, they're scrapping them all,' says Pat.

Pool of London, directed by Basil Dearden, is a gritty thriller shot in London in 1951 and this scene appears half an hour before the end. It deals with social themes in docklands, smuggling, petty crime, interracial love – Johnny, played by Earl Cameron, was black and Pat, played by Susan Shaw, was white – and the coming end of London's trams.

At the end of this scene an unspoken question hangs in the air: Why?

A few months later a similar conversation was taking place in a car a few miles away on the South Circular Road. A young boy asked his father about the trams.

'They'll be getting rid of them soon,' said his father.

'Why?' asked the boy, in the irritating way that small children have.

That boy was me. And my father, who worked in the transport industry, was something of an authority. I don't remember his precise words but his reply was on the lines of trams were slow, old-fashioned and held up the traffic.

The answer didn't satisfy me then. It doesn't now.

There was always something odd about the decline of the British tram. In the years before the First World War, trams provided the cheapest-ever form of transport for millions of people in Britain's towns and cities. For most city dwellers, a gong warning of an approaching tram was a more familiar sound than the whistle of a steam train. The tram continued to flourish until well into the 1920s. And then the rot set in. By the 1960s, trams had virtually vanished from the streets of mainland Britain.

Britain was not the only country to scrap its trams. Several others, including France and the United States, also tore up most of their tramlines. But some countries in

Western Europe, notably Germany and the Low Countries, kept them and today modern trams glide along the streets of cities like Amsterdam, Brussels and Cologne.

So why was there this difference?

Fast forward to 1985 and I was one of hundreds of journalists who descended on Blackpool to cover the Conservative Party conference. While I was there, I thought I would also write about the centenary of Blackpool's trams, the first electric trams in the country, which had begun running along the promenade in 1885.

Blackpool had the only surviving street tramway in mainland Britain. And it owed its survival partly to the party conferences. Politicians of all persuasions enjoyed taking a tram up the prom during the conference and this well of political sympathy helped to ward off any threats of closure.

There was a new age of the tram in the offing, I wrote in *New Scientist*, 'As Blackpool's trams clank up the prom into their 101st year, their prospect is less lonely than it once was.'[1] And so it turned out. Trams returned to the streets of Manchester in 1992. Two years later they came back to Sheffield. A total of six urban areas in Britain now have trams.

The resurrection of Britain's trams was part of a worldwide revival. In the US, dozens of cities have reintroduced streetcars. Los Angeles, for example, which famously scrapped its streetcars in the 1960s, opened its first new light rail line in 1990. In Paris, trams disappeared in 1938. They returned to the northern suburb of Saint-Denis in 1992.

How to explain these changing fashions? One factor was plainly technological change. At the start of the twentieth century, the electric tram had a clear edge over the primitive and unreliable motorbus with its open top, solid rubber wheels and smelly petrol engine. Thirty years on, the tram's superiority was less marked. Bus technology saw major advances in the 1920s. Pneumatic tyres made buses quieter and more comfortable. The introduction of covered tops meant that passengers no longer risked a drenching in bad weather. And diesel engines slashed the cost of running a bus. It was easy to portray a 25-year-old tram as antiquated and out of date when it was standing alongside a gleaming new bus.

Another factor was investment in public transport. Before the First World War, Britain had made a huge investment in infrastructure, in tramways and railways. After the war, things began to change. Trams were the first to go, followed by the trolleybuses that had replaced many of them. Finally, many railways were torn up. Large sums of money were still invested in transport, but this was to build roads, principally to benefit motorists and lorries.

A key turning point in the fortunes of the tram came with the publication of the final report from the Royal Commission on Transport in 1931. Trams, it concluded, were 'in a state of obsolescence'. After that damning verdict the British tram went into a precipitous decline.

One hundred not out: Blackpool built these new trams for the centenary of its electric trams in 1985. (Tony Stevenson)

I first came across the commission's report in a second-hand bookshop about forty years ago. Official reports are never riveting reads, so I skimmed it, made a mental note of some interesting passages and stuck it on my bookshelves for later.

A few years ago I took the report off the shelf and looked at it again. On closer examination, the section on trams seemed flaky. My curiosity aroused, I decided to delve a bit deeper. The minutes of evidence given to the commission, amounting to more than a thousand pages, are no longer easily available. But when I eventually found a copy, the plot thickened. Dozens of different witnesses had given evidence, including representatives of railway companies, tram operators, motorists, trades unions and civil servants as well as interested individuals.

The commission obsessively taxed these witnesses about trams being obsolete. Tramway officials denied the claim, as did the trade union representing tram workers. Two men from the ministry also refuted the suggestion. The commission asked a specialist transport economist, a rare breed back then, to give expert evidence. He also denied that trams were obsolete.

So why did the commission reach its apparently perverse conclusion? Why did the commission discount the evidence of the experts?

The debate on the future of the tram was essentially a political argument. Should the tram rails be ripped up and antiquated trams replaced with more flexible and cheaper buses? Or should trams be modernised? The weight of evidence favoured modernisation, at least in the major cities. So why were trams condemned? A key part of the explanation was that the commission's members were mostly keen motorists and wanted to keep their roads free of any obstructions that held up their cars, from pedestrians to trams.

There have been thousands of books about British trams, mostly lamenting their decline and examining tramway engineering. This book is different. It is an investigation into the clandestine political shenanigans that sealed the fate of the British tram. And packing the Royal Commission with petrol heads was only part of the story.

Anyone who starts out on a major investigative piece of journalism like this always entertains some preconceptions. I already knew about the congressional antitrust hearings in the US, back in 1973, when a young attorney pointed to a conspiracy between the motor industry, big oil and tyre makers to buy up and close down street railways and replace them with buses. The conspiracy resurfaced more recently as a sub-plot in the 1988 motion picture *Who Framed Roger Rabbit?* It is a story that has been hotly disputed over the years, not in the least by General Motors.[2]

One of my preconceptions was that a similar conspiracy was impossible in Britain, because tramways were mostly in the hands of local authorities, not private companies, so it was the ballot box and not shareholders' meetings that would decide the fate of the tram.

How wrong I was.

In the course of my research, I visited dozens of archives, trawling through unpublished records of the major organisations, as well as looking through the personal papers of the Minister of Transport who set up the Royal Commission, to tease out the behind-the-scenes manoeuvring, the stories that never saw the light of day.

I spent many hours trawling through digitised newspaper archives, which have only recently become available, looking for patterns. I uncovered a trail of dirty tricks and deceit, a classic tabloid crusade replete with lashings of fake news and – to my great surprise – early examples of a public relations tool known as 'astroturfing'. Today astroturfing is closely associated with social media. Vested interests create the appearance of a grassroots campaign – hence the name – using fake identities to plant false news stories and so mould public opinion.

A hundred years ago the correspondence columns of newspapers were the equivalent of social media. Paid letter writers, often concealing their identity behind pseudonyms, created the impression of a widespread hatred of trams in the letters pages. 'Special correspondents' repeated and amplified the message in editorial columns. Some newspapers colluded in this deception.

The effect of this covert campaign was to establish a widely accepted, but largely false narrative, that trams were obsolete and they should all be scrapped.

Who was behind the propaganda? My quest to uncover the truth behind the demise of the tram had turned into a whodunnit. The most likely source of the propaganda was the tram's pneumatic-tyred rivals. So I wasn't surprised to find evidence of bus companies lobbying against trams. But the source of the astroturfing was more difficult to pinpoint. Eventually I stumbled on a trail leading back to big oil.

And then events took an utterly bizarre turn with a chance discovery. I was lying on a beach in Corsica reading a book about spooks in the roaring twenties when I came across a familiar address. This was the place I had regarded as the headquarters of the astroturfing campaign. It turned out to be an MI5 safe house. How could this possibly be connected to the anti-tram campaign?

Chapter 1

THE ROYAL SEAL OF APPROVAL

Vast crowds of people lined the streets of South London, straining to catch a glimpse of the Prince of Wales as he opened London's new electric tramway. The ceremonial tram had been painted white for the occasion, decorated with Prince of Wales feathers and adorned with palm leaves. It was the first municipal electric tram in the county of London and the spectacular turnout completely eclipsed controversies about the technology and the cost to ratepayers, at least for the moment. This was the royal endorsement not only of electric trams but also of the broader social aims of the London County Council. It was less of an inauguration and more a triumphal progress. And the crowds, said the reporter from the *Daily Telegraph*, were 'unmistakable testimony to the popularity of the latest municipal enterprise'.

The morning of Friday 15 May 1903 was unpromising. It was dull and overcast, and a stiff breeze made the day feel unseasonably cool. Shortly after 3 pm the Prince of Wales, accompanied by Princess Mary and their two eldest sons, Edward and Albert, dressed in sailor suits, left their home in the Mall in a horse-drawn carriage. They drove over Westminster Bridge to Saint Thomas's Hospital, where 2,500 guests were waiting in a handsome canvas marquee that the LCC had erected in the hospital grounds, adjacent to the terminus of the new tramway, where the electric trams began their journey to Tooting.

John Benn, chairman of the highways committee, said how pleased the council was by the Prince's support. London, the hub of the British Empire, lagged behind the rest of the world in developing trams. He was sorry that the Prince and his family couldn't have come by tram but the council's attempts to be allowed to run trams over Westminster Bridge had been repeatedly blocked by parliament, most recently by a single vote.

Benn said the council intended to buy out the remainder of the privately operated trams in its area, improve conditions for the workers and replace the old horse trams with new electric ones. The tram, he declared, was 'the people's motor, at the modest fare of half a penny'. The minimum fare on the LCC's trams was half that of privately operated trams. At this point, Benn's speech was punctuated by a steam tug on the river tooting in apparent approval.

The LCC was controlled by the Progressive Party, the name the Liberal Party used in London. But the ceremony witnessed an outbreak of cross-party consensus. Gerald Balfour, the Conservative President of the Board of Trade, pointed to the rapid growth of electric trams. Back in 1897 the country had 40 miles of electric tramway. Now there were 900 miles and trams were very popular. The only hint of criticism came when Balfour pointed out that these electric trams drew their power from overhead wires. The LCC had chosen a different method. Instead of overhead wires, which were often criticised as unsightly, the LCC adopted a different and controversial technology. Its trams drew their power from a live rail in a small tunnel, or conduit, buried under a slot in the road surface.

The London County Council's specially decorated tram about to set off from Westminster Bridge Road for Tooting on 15 May 1903. The Prince of Wales is doffing his top hat to a guard of honour from the London Fire Brigade. (London Borough of Lambeth Archives Department)

The Prince entered into the spirit of the occasion. He had brought four halfpennies with him to pay for the family's tram fares. 'We do not want to begin by defrauding the council,' he said. 'We are very happy to have this opportunity of identifying ourselves with this great scheme which will so materially benefit the working classes in whose welfare we take the deepest interest.'

The Princess and his two sons, said the Prince, were very much looking forward to their tram trip to Tooting. The rest of his speech came close to being a manifesto not only for electric trams but also for the council's social policy. In Tooting, the royal party was due to inspect workers' cottages that the council was building. It was impractical to expect a worker to live in Tooting and work at Westminster, said the Prince, reported in the *Daily News* the following day:

It is an absolute necessity and not a luxury that he should have a conveyance. And what is true for this district applies equally to all parts around London.

We are not dealing only with locomotion; it is also a question of health. By giving cheap facilities of access from the heart of the capital to the suburban districts you are removing the working classes from the scene of their daily toil and from what are still too often insanitary dwellings to healthy districts where light, air and cheerful surroundings are obtainable.

Mr Benn tells us that our great Empire City is behind the times, but let us hope that such great undertakings as these with which we today are associated will gradually make up whatever may be the leeway.

And with the audience's loud cheers ringing in their ears, the royal party left their pavilion and climbed into the special tramcar. The weather too cheered up. The clouds cleared and were replaced by a spell of warm sunshine. The Prince of Wales released the brake and set the tram in motion before handing over to an LCC driver. Benn assumed the role of conductor, took the family's fares and issued them with souvenir tickets.

The original intention was that the royal party would travel inside the tram. The lower deck had been fitted out as a drawing room with comfortable antique armchairs instead of the normal benches. But the two young princes, Edward, aged 9, and Albert, 7, had other ideas. They wanted to go on the top deck of the tram. So Edward and Albert scampered upstairs followed by their parents. Princess Mary and three future kings sat on the slatted wooden seats at the front of the tram. A convoy of trams followed the royal tram carrying the rest of the guests.

The Prince of Wales was taken aback by the extraordinary throng along the route. He had expected no more than a bit of crowd at either end of the line. Hundreds of thousands of Londoners lined the streets all the way to Tooting. A reporter from *Municipal Journal* even put the crowd at two million and it was certainly on a similar scale to the number of people who had watched the coronation of his father Edward VII the year before. Shops were closed, there was festive bunting everywhere and people hung out of almost every window amid scenes of public rejoicing. 'Everywhere it was evident the people were making holiday,' said the reporter.

The huge turnout came as a delightful surprise to the Prince, who acknowledged the cheers by raising his top hat above his head for much of the five-mile journey to Tooting, prompting one observer to note that the heir apparent didn't have much hair apparent.

The carnival atmosphere continued for the entire journey. The tram stopped at a school in Kennington Road and a choir of 1,200 boys and girls sang *God Bless the Prince of Wales*. At Clapham the cheers rose to a crescendo and the Prince stood up to acknowledge the crowds. It was by all accounts a very smooth and comfortable journey.

'Nowhere along the line of the route were the crowds denser or the welcome more enthusiastic than at the terminus of the system at Tooting,' reported the *Daily Telegraph* the following day The road was packed and such was the crush that several people fainted and had to be treated by St John's Ambulance crews.

The royal party left the tram and went to inspect the model workers' cottages that the LCC was building on the Totterdown Fields Estate. It was a taste of the country.

Hundreds of thousands of people lined the streets to see the LCC's inaugural electric tram and its royal passengers. The photo, taken from the first floor of the Plough Inn, shows the tram in Clapham High Street on its way to Tooting. (Author's collection)

Unlike the overcrowded tenements of central London, you could still hear birdsong and the lowing of cattle in Tooting. The royal couple were impressed with the neat and tidy two-storey cottages. Each house had a garden and they all had electric lighting. The estate had been designed sensitively and the council's architects had kept mature trees and planted privet hedges.

A terraced house could be rented for 7 shillings a week. The royal couple met the first tenant, a nurse, who had just moved in. Princess Mary took a keen interest in the house telling officials that there needed to be more shelves in the kitchens and sculleries for people to store their pots and pans.

As the tram started its return journey, the Prince stood to acknowledge the cheers. 'In popular demonstrations the return journey was a repetition of what had taken place before. If anything, the crowd was even greater in Clapham and Kennington,' said the *Daily Telegraph*. Festivities at an end, the royal party took their carriage home and the public service began. Such was the press of people wanting to travel on an electric tram that the police had to control the crowds.

Back home the prince asked his secretary to send a note of heartfelt appreciation to the LCC:

> It was a matter of great satisfaction to their Royal Highnesses that they were able to take part in the inauguration of so important a scheme conceived and now being carried out by the London County Council. Their Royal Highnesses much enjoyed their journey to Tooting and back and were touched by the enthusiastic reception given to them throughout the whole route.

The ceremony made a lasting impression on the royal couple and fifty years later Queen Mary, as she had become, still remembered the occasion with affection.[3]

However, two newspapers were intent on spoiling the party: the *Daily Mail* and its stablemate the *Evening News*. Both papers were owned by Alfred Harmsworth, a keen motorist who, in common with other members of the wheeled classes, had developed a pathological loathing for trams, partly because they occupied the middle of the road, the natural habitat of the road hog. Early in the twentieth century, the *Daily Mail* decided that the LCC's trams were being wastefully run and the paper launched a wider crusade against trams which was to last for decades.

At the *Daily Mail*, a reporter's job was to 'find an angle quickly, regardless whether it was justified by the full facts or not,' wrote one commentator on Fleet Street. Almost every story had to support the anti-tram crusade, facts had to be massaged or suppressed so that they didn't contradict the editorial line.[4]

The day before the Prince opened the tramway to Tooting, the *Daily Mail* printed a lengthy spoiler. It alleged there was a £500,000 black hole in the LCC's accounts and the Tooting tramway had cost more than twice as much as the LCC had said it would. The *Mail* had a point – of sorts. The conduit system of electrification was more expensive than overhead wires. But the paper's report considerably overegged the financial impact. In a long and detailed reply, larded with statistics, which few readers would have had the stamina to digest, Benn disputed the *Mail*'s sums. The cost, he concluded, was only slightly more than the original estimate.

The *Evening News* was similarly quick to find fault, comparing the LCC's tramcars unfavourably with those run by the London United Tramways, a private company in West London. 'The wooden seats, thinly protected by a strip of carpet… are not nearly as good as those on the West London tramways,' grumbled the paper. London United Tramways had a network of lines radiating west from Shepherd's Bush and Hammersmith. Its first electric trams began running two years earlier in April 1901. It too celebrated the achievement with an opening extravaganza, although it was on nothing like the scale of the LCC's.

Back in 1901, the *Mail* had been on the side of progress. It strongly supported electric traction, even urging readers to vote for Liberal candidates in the LCC elections. 'One of the strongest reasons for acquiring a Progressive council today is that the whole of the London tramway system may be altered from horse traction to electric traction.'[5] Electric traction meant cheaper fares and better trams. The election saw the Moderates, or Conservatives, lose eighteen seats, giving the Progressives a comfortable majority, which they used to take over the private tram companies within the council's borders.

By the time the tramway to Tooting opened in 1903, the *Mail* had completely changed its tune. It was now anti-LCC and anti-tram.

What had caused this change of heart? To answer this question, we have to go back to the days when horses first started to drag trams around the streets of London, to the days when powerful enemies tried to drive trams off the streets and to the outbreak of internecine warfare between private tram operators and their council counterparts.

Chapter 2

TRAMS VERSUS TOFFS

George Francis Train was the man who brought trams to Britain. Citizen Train, as he liked to call himself, was an eccentric, larger-than-life American entrepreneur. An atheist, a romantic revolutionary, a supporter of Irish independence, and a champion of votes for women, but not for Black people, Train was by turns endearing and infuriating. His first commercial success was to set up a shipping line, with clippers sailing from Liverpool round Cape Horn to California. He then reinvented himself as a railway magnate. Train made and lost several fortunes. He was also a traveller of some note and with some justification claimed to be the real-life model for Phileas Fogg in Jules Verne's novel *Around the World in Eighty Days*.[6]

Citizen Train never shied away from rubbing up the authorities the wrong way. In Ireland he was jailed after landing at Queenstown in 1868 with a stash of Fenian propaganda. Two years later he was jailed in Marseille for backing the revolutionary communards. Back in the United States he was jailed yet again. This time his crime was to defend the maverick feminist Victoria Woodhull's reporting of an adultery case, arguing that the bible was far saucier than Woodhull's report. They were both jailed for obscenity. But his first taste of jail began in Britain when he was put behind bars for the heinous crime of injuring the public highway.

Train opened his first horse-drawn tramway in Birkenhead in August 1860. He then turned his attention to London, where the Commissioners of the Metropolis Turnpike Roads allowed him to lay a tramway a little over a mile long on the Bayswater Road on the north side of Hyde Park. The first horse tram started trundling along the metals on 23 March 1861.

For the grand opening, Train laid on a lavish lunch for 300 influential guests. It was one of many similar events, with Train calculating that a bit of American pizzazz would see his tramways floating to success on a tide of Moët and Clicquot.

Trams quickly became embroiled in party politics. The Liberal *Daily News* approved of them and the paper's founder, the author Charles Dickens, was said to be among the spectators who witnessed the enthusiastic reception for the London opening. 'Perhaps none of our great thoroughfares are better adapted for the favourable working of the tramway than the Bayswater Road,' said the paper.

But the former – and future – Conservative MP, Alexander Beresford Hope disagreed. Beresford Hope, who lived opposite Marble Arch, could see the works from his front window. The rails stuck up out of the road. 'Such rails would be highly dangerous and treacherous to carriages and horses passing over them.' Carriages could not cross the tracks and trams would monopolise the road. Beresford Hope took Train to court and the magistrates fined Train one shilling.

The two protagonists in this opening skirmish were like chalk and cheese. Train habitually trampled on establishment sensibilities. Although born into a Methodist family, he had no time for the church. Beresford Hope on the other hand was a pillar of High-Church conservatism. He had a condescending attitude towards the working class, who he believed should accept a 'little direction from the Church and their social superiors'.

The two men were also diametrically opposed over events in America as that country slid towards civil war following the election of President Abraham Lincoln in November 1860. Train was strongly pro-Union, despite his opposition to giving Black people the vote. He made speeches to raise money for the cause and used his shipping contacts to try and prevent gunrunning from Britain to the southern states.

Beresford Hope was firmly on the Confederate side. His home was a safe house for Confederate agents in London. 'The Confederate nation,' he said, 'had passed the Red Sea, in God's name let us give them a helping hand to reach the promised land.' There was no shortage of sympathy for the Confederates among the British establishment. Train's politics marked him out as an outsider.

Despite these differences, there can be little doubt that the main cause of the difficulties faced by these early tramways stemmed from Train's choice of rail. Known as a step rail it stuck up as much as one inch above the surface of the road, which could wreak havoc with the wheels of horse-drawn carriages when they crossed the tramlines. Undeterred, Train opened two further lines in London and three in the provinces.

A more serious challenge to the Bayswater tram came when Beresford Hope led a deputation to the turnpike commissioners. His petition, signed by the great and good, was a litany of grievances about accidents, the effect on traders, and the impact of trams on omnibuses.

This last complaint was the nub of the petition, for the deputation had been organised by John Bradfield, a parliamentary lobbyist whose clients included several turnpike trusts and the London General Omnibus Company, the city's foremost bus operator. Bradfield had put together a coalition of malcontents to support the bus company. As if to underscore the point about trams endangering other traffic, three days later a London General bus collided with the Bayswater tram. With a fanfare of publicity, the bus company announced it would prosecute Train.

In the meantime, Train applied to extend his Bayswater Road tramway west to Notting Hill. The commissioners not only refused to allow the extension but told Train to remove his existing tramway.

A packed public meeting called on the commissioners to think again, saying the trams were a vast improvement on buses. An 8,000-strong petition called on the commissioners to save the tram. But there was no reprieve and workers began lifting the track in September 1861.

The London General's prosecution came to court in December. The company said its bus had got stuck on the tramway and the accident had caused £9 of damage to its bus. The magistrates threw out the case, blaming the bus for deliberately ramming the tram.

Train's grand plans finally fell apart in south London, when he was prosecuted for making the road dangerous. The core of the case was the number of accidents. The tram passengers may benefit from the smooth ride given by rails, commented the *Field* – the country gentleman's newspaper – in May 1862, 'to all others they are snares and stumbling blocks. No one who has ever experienced it will easily forget the severe jolt which a phaeton or gig receives in passing over the rails of Mr Train's tramway.'

The case was of such significance that it was heard by the Lord Chief Justice. A petition signed by 11,500 people was produced supporting the trams. The opponents could only muster a flimsy petition on 'a wretched-looking sheet of paper'. However, the jury convicted Train and the court told him to remove his tramway.

Train faced a bill of £500 for costs. He refused to pay, pleading poverty, and ended up in a debtors' prison. It was public posturing, designed to highlight his

People power: the popularity of the new trams was no match for London's wealthy and influential carriage owners. (Barry Cross Collection/Online Transport Archive)

cause, for Train was not short of money at the time. After a few weeks, the debt was mysteriously paid and Train returned to America to a resounding chorus of 'good riddance' from the establishment.

Train blamed his failure partly on the conservative establishment, partly on his support for the Union and partly on the bus industry – 'an unrelenting foe'.[7]

But the interest in trams didn't go away. The reason was simple. The friction between the metal wheel of a tram and a rail was far less than that between the wheel of a bus and what was often a very rough road. This gave a tram a huge practical advantage. It was far easier for a horse to haul a tram. As a rule of thumb, a horse could pull twice as many passengers in a tram as in a bus. So, trams were normally cheaper than buses, with fares within the reach of poorer people.

In 1865, the tram promoters returned to the fray with a new type of rail with grooves. This rail, the precursor of the modern tram rail, could be laid flush with the surface of the road and at least in theory would not endanger other traffic. Trams, claimed a promotional pamphlet, would be 'first class carriages at reduced fares'.

It was the opening salvo in a pamphlet war. Bradfield countered that trams would be 'mischievous and dangerous obstructions and nuisances'. Bradfield described himself as a 'parliamentary agent acting in opposition to the tramway and street railway schemes'. The tram promoters' riposte was to pillory Bradfield as 'conductor of the omnibus opposition' and as a mouthpiece for the London General.[8]

For a brief moment, the tide of history was running in favour of trams. Investors could see handsome profits in the new technology. However, promoting a private bill in parliament to build a tramway was expensive and time-consuming, especially if there were objections. The Board of Trade sympathised with the promoters' plight and decided to cut the red tape and create a simpler alternative.

In its original form, the Tramways Bill of 1870 would have enabled companies simply to apply to the Board of Trade for an order allowing them to build a tramway. The *Economist* in March 1870 thought the bill had the balance right. Tramways 'are matters of local interest…and parliament after laying down general rules, may very safely wash its hands of the matter.'

But the bill was severely mauled in its passage through parliament. Instead of giving companies virtually free rein to build tramways, the act handed local authorities sweeping new powers over the companies.

Three far-reaching measures in the Tramways Act would hamper the future development of trams. Under the Act, councils could veto new tramways. In cases where the rails ran through more than one local authority, promoters needed to secure approval for the tramway from authorities covering more than two-thirds of its length. This 'two-thirds rule' gave councils a lot of leverage. Many of them saw tramways as cash cows and would present companies with a shopping list of sweeteners. If companies didn't pay up, they risked having their plans vetoed. It was effectively blackmail, observed one former minister.

Secondly, the act obliged companies to compensate councils for future damage to the roads. Companies had to maintain the surface of the road between the tram rails – and for a distance of 18 inches on either side of the rails. Initially, the promoters acquiesced in this obligation, believing that this subsidy for councils' road maintenance bills would mean that they were less likely to veto their plans. Finally, councils were given the right to buy out tram companies after 21 years, opening the door to municipal control of tramways.

To some extent, parliament's caution was understandable. MPs were 'still shocked by the rapacious history of water supply and gas monopolies'. The continual digging up of streets by rival companies to lay drains and mains often left roads unsafe for weeks.[9]

Birmingham was quick to get in on the Act. England's second-largest urban area was a good prospect for trams and several companies had been sniffing around even before the legislation reached the statute book. In 1871 the Corporation decided that it would build the tramways and lease the lines to a private company to run the trams. Instead of promoting its own private bill, the Corporation opted for the simplified procedure and asked the Board of Trade for a provisional order. The new procedure worked smoothly and Birmingham's first trams began to run in 1873.

If Birmingham was a good place to build tramways, London, the world's largest city, was even more attractive. Towards the end of 1870, ten rival companies drew up plans for more than 100 miles of tramways. Tramways would crisscross central London and the wealthy residents of elegant Georgian squares faced huge disruption by having their streets dug up to lay tram rails.

The *Daily News* backed the plans, saying the tram was one of 'the greatest improvements made in the locomotion of London'. The paper's paean of praise emphasised the tram's superiority over 'that old familiar rattle-trap', the omnibus.

But the sheer scale of the plans outraged residents. The protesters were well-heeled, well-organised and well-titled. Throughout December 1870 they turned up in force at council meetings to argue against the trams.

The prospects for tramways in London were complicated by the structure of local government in the capital. After sweeping away rotten boroughs in the Great Reform Act of 1832, the government streamlined the system of local government to cope with the growth of urban areas during the industrial revolution. Most towns had one council, which set the rates – the property tax that financed most municipal works – and maintained the roads.

However, the Reform Act did not apply to London. In London, the only significant change in local government had been the creation of the Metropolitan Board of Works, a response to the last great cholera outbreak of 1854. Its crowning achievement, and that of its chief engineer Joseph Bazalgette, was to create a sewage system that rid the capital of the scourge of cholera.

Road maintenance was in the hands of vestries, so called because the parish council meetings were originally held in the church vestry. Even by 1870 some vestries still kept religious links. The upshot was that in London, new technology was confronted by a system of local government that had its roots in the Middle Ages.

The patchwork of local authorities in the capital was a major stumbling block for tramway promoters. They not only needed the consent of the Metropolitan Board of Works but also from vestries covering at least two-thirds the length of the route. From the outset, the Board of Works saw its role as fashioning a sensible network of tramways from the promoters' plans. The spectre of 'tramway mania', was raised by Bazalgette who warned that promoters' plans should be 'carefully controlled'.[10]

In the face of the outcry from the more fashionable parts of the capital, the board decided to restrict trams to main roads, those roads that were already bus routes. In January 1871 it approved thirty-one separate tramways, including one along Oxford Street. Beresford Hope, who was back in parliament again, still lived in his handsome Georgian townhouse by Marble Arch. If these plans went ahead, he would have the Oxford Street tramway in front of his house, and another one running along the side.

Given the continuing controversy, the Board of Trade asked one of its railway inspectors, who was familiar with trams in America, to produce a report in an attempt to inject some rationalism into this polarised debate. He said trams would be beneficial and vestries should not be allowed to veto them.

London was always going to be the key battleground in the fight over trams. The focus of almost all national newspapers was on London, and MPs who could be calm and rational about trams in the provinces rushed to the barricades when the discussion came round to laying tram lines in central London.

The company promoting the Oxford Street trams adopted a belt-and-braces approach, introducing a private bill for the tramways as well as getting the Board of Trade to grant a provisional order. In June its private bill was thrown out after being 'hotly opposed' by Beresford Hope. The vote was decisive and put tram opponents in a strong position in the coming battles.

Beresford Hope denounced the 'evils' of tramways in a letter to *The Times*, claiming that parliament hadn't known what it was doing when it approved the Tramways Act. Under pressure from MPs, the government referred the central London schemes to a select committee.

The tram's opponents lined up to denounce the tram in their evidence to the select committee. Beresford Hope's contribution reeked of the carriage folk's prejudices. 'A lady who is very much accustomed to drive herself through the crowded streets of London', he claimed, strongly opposed trams. The tramway promoters, he said, characterised the contest as being between 'the upper ten thousand and the rest of the world now I say distinctly that is not the case'. Few dispassionate observers doubted that Beresford Hope was among the upper ten thousand.

The Oxford Street shopkeepers said there were a 'great many carriages of ladies shopping standing at their doors…you will often see 12 to 20 carriages standing in a row'. Trams would drive away both carriages and trade. The powerful railway companies joined the bus companies in attacking the tram plans. An engineer who helped build the Metropolitan Railway, the world's first underground railway, called for a ban on trams in central London. His evidence was scarcely disinterested. The railway didn't want any competition from trams.

The select committee's report, published in June 1872, was a damp squib, concluding that schemes should be judged on their merits. However, the tram opponents enjoyed the political momentum and intended to capitalise on it by erecting new stumbling blocks for tram promoters.

In August, the powerful Ways and Means Committee of the House of Commons announced a new standing order, the rules that govern its proceedings. This standing order extended the two-thirds rule to cover private bills. Any bill for a new tramway needed the approval of local authorities for at least two-thirds of its length. However, this rule had a sting in its tail. In the absence of this approval, MPs would not be allowed even to discuss a bill. Getting approval for a tramway from a slew of different vestries in London was a nightmare. The vestries now enjoyed a virtually unassailable veto on trams in central London.

The prospect of trams that ran on steam caused fresh foreboding among the carriage folk. In 1876, the Wantage tramway, a rural line in Berkshire, was permitted to try steam trams. As the move towards mechanisation gained momentum, a London Carriage Owners' Protection Society was formed 'to protect the proprietors of vehicles against tramway companies'.[11]

Despite the opposition from carriage owners, by the early 1880s the shares of many tramway companies were doing well, and dividends of 8 or 9 per cent were common. 'Growing rich and prosperous,' said one pundit, the companies 'are pushing out their lines in all directions'. The profits prompted the companies to look afresh at central London. The crowds that thronged the city streets would be guaranteed to fill their trams.

On Tuesday 7 November 1882, Edmund Tattersall, scion of the family of racehorse auctioneers, placed an advert in the *Morning Post*. Headed 'opposition to proposed tramway lines for Kensington, Westminster and Belgravia', the advert appeared on the front page of the next day's paper and gave notice of a protest meeting to be held on Friday at Tattersall's auction house in Knightsbridge. It was a clarion call for the carriage folk. Tramways 'would destroy all the roads for the use of carriages and

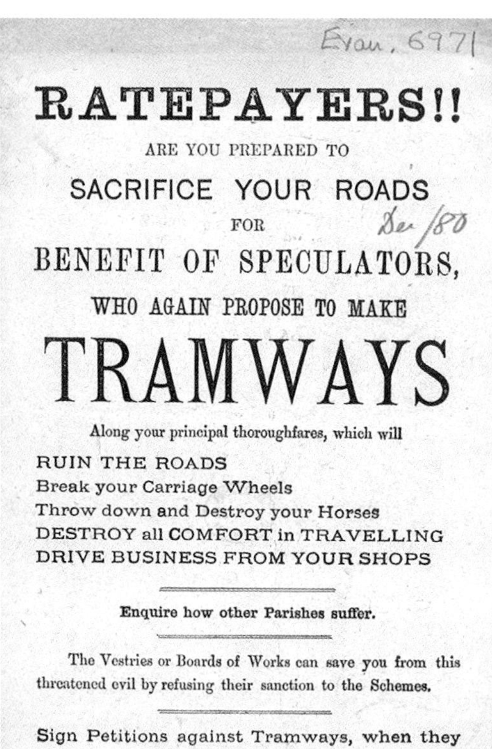

Left: **Ratepayers' revolt:** local authorities, or vestries, had the power to block new tramways. When acting together they effectively wielded a veto on tramways in central London. The handbill dates from 1880. (British Library Collection)

Below: **Don't frighten the horses:** the introduction of steam trams on the rural Wantage tramway and the prospect of them spreading to London horrified the capital's carriage owners. (Jeoffry Spence Collection/Railway & Canal Historical Society)

would injure to a very alarming extent the value of all house property and be most injurious to…trade in the district as it would drive the wealthy inhabitants of the mansions, their best customers, away from their doors.'

What had prompted Tattersall's ire was an ambitious plan to build a 'missing link', with trams running across Westminster Bridge, and through the fashionable centre to link up with tramways in west London. The route would take trams past the front door of Tattersall's, the scene of regular bloodstock sales, events where toffs rubbed shoulders with sleazy sporting characters.

Tattersall told the meeting that while tramways may be useful in some districts – a nod to those wealthy residents who had invested in lucrative tramway shares – they 'would be a great nuisance' and threaten house prices. The upshot of the meeting was to set up the West End Tramways Opposition Association, which soon eclipsed the carriage owners' society. The London General, which had a long-standing policy of supporting tram opposition, took a keen interest in this new organisation and provided seed funding to help this influential group get started.[12] For the rest of the century, Tattersall's association spearheaded the fight to keep trams out of central London.

The carriage folk believed they had a hereditary right to the roads. Tramways, wrote society journalist George Sala, 'are utter ruin and discomfiture to the art of driving'. The whiff of snobbery was never far away from the forces massing to oppose tramways. Tram passengers came from working families. They commuted by tram and cheap fares allowed them to enjoy excursions on their days off. A plan to extend tramlines into deepest Hampstead provoked a squeal of outrage from one bookseller, writing to the *Hampstead and Highgate Express* in January 1882. 'If trams are permitted they will bring crowds of the most objectionable classes to disperse in the midst of our town with all the noise, drinking and other unseemly behaviour of many Sunday excursionists. This will be a very grave evil.'

By the closing years of the nineteenth century, the battle lines were established. On one side were the tram companies. On the other side was an array of formidable foes, the carriage folk, wealthy property owners and the vested interests of the bus and railway companies.

Chapter 3
'A MOMENTOUS INTRIGUE'

At the dawn of the twentieth century, Britain's tramways were in a state of flux. Many of the leases granted under the original legislation were falling due. At the same time other countries were witnessing wholesale technological change, with electric trams replacing the old horse cars. These trends created considerable tension. Companies near the end of a lease were reluctant to modernise their trams. The result was that Britain was slow to go electric. Out of more than 1,000 miles of tramway in 1896, only 80 miles were operated by electricity. Yet in America more than eight out of ten trams were electric.

No wonder some commentators viewed the Tramways Act as 'the most disastrous legislative experiment which has been attempted in England during the last half-century'.[13]

The assumption underlying the 1870 legislation had been that private companies would operate tramways. The system began to break down in 1882 when the Yorkshire woollen town of Huddersfield built a network of tramways but then couldn't find a company to run the trams. The impasse forced the Board of Trade's hand. Rather than leave miles of unused tram rails rusting in the road, the Board allowed the corporation to run the trams.

Huddersfield's first lines, operated by steam trams, opened in January 1883. Free of the burden of paying shareholders' dividends, Huddersfield set a high standard for municipal operations. The fares were modest, the services good, and working conditions were vastly better than those on privately operated trams. On top of that, the Huddersfield trams turned a modest profit.

This success prompted widespread interest. Should trams be run for private profit or public benefit?

'The public now has an unparalleled opportunity,' wrote the Fabian socialist Sidney Webb. 'The tramway companies only received their concessions on condition that the local authority should have the power to take over the whole concern at the expiration of 21 years from the time when the promoters were empowered to construct the line.'[14] In 1889, Liverpool asked the Board of Trade for permission to run its own trams, Glasgow followed suit in 1890 and the following year the London County Council decided that it too wanted to run its own trams.

Glasgow was the role model for municipal tramways. In 1894 the city started running its trams, after a bad-tempered handover between the old company and the corporation. The private company was obstructive and forecast that running trams would quickly bankrupt the corporation. To help make sure this prediction came true it refused to sell its horses and tramcars to the corporation – and it started its own bus company to compete with the corporation trams. So, the corporation not only had to start afresh it also had to fend off competition from the company's buses.

The company's trams were a source of frequent complaints. They were 'rather small, rather dirty and rather infrequent, and the fares were high'. From the start of municipal operations, the corporation improved the conditions of tram workers, cut their hours, raised their wages, gave them free uniforms, slashed fares and made the trams more frequent and more reliable. And on top of that the Corporation trams made a healthy profit for the rates. The municipal service was everything the company service was not.[15] The only losers from the changeover were the company's shareholders, who had been enjoying handsome dividends for several years.

The struggle between private enterprise and municipal trading was a turning point in the story of the tram and one that irredeemably damaged its long-term prospects. The breach permanently divided the industry and over the ensuing decades the campaign against municipal-owned trams evolved to become a campaign against all trams.

Vocal opposition to any extension of municipal enterprise came from the Liberty and Property Defence League, a small-state pressure group. The league was a curious collection of railway companies, ship owners, licensed victuallers, music hall proprietors, pawnbrokers and most importantly landowners. Self-help and not state help were its watchwords and it pledged to combat 'the general inroad of state socialism upon individual liberty, private enterprise and the rights of property'.

The move towards municipal trams was part of a more general trend towards municipal trading. The Liberal mayor of Birmingham, Joseph Chamberlain, had been dismayed by the activities of the city's two rival gas companies, which were continually digging up the city's roads. So, Birmingham bought out the companies, bringing order to street repairs and making a modest profit to boot. The city later took over the water companies to ensure a supply of clean water.

Birmingham and Glasgow were practical demonstrations of the benefits of municipal trading. But this cut no ice with the Liberty and Property Defence League. 'All reasoning and all facts,' claimed the League in its 1892/3 Annual Report, 'show that municipal management is…costly, inefficient, and more or less corrupt.'

The battle between the forces of private property and public interest reached a climax in 1902. The leading private company was British Electric Traction, which had been registered in October 1896. Its aim was to take over horse tramways, convert them to electricity and build new lines. The changeover from horse to electric trams was an expensive business, although one that was potentially very profitable. Electric trams could carry twice as many passengers as a horse tram, but they were far heavier, so that meant digging up the road and laying sturdier rails and foundations as well as wiring up the network for electricity.

It was no coincidence that BET was founded in 1896. It was the year of the new Light Railways Act, legislation designed to make it easier to construct light railways in country areas and so boost the rural economy. BET and the London Chamber of Commerce had shaped the new act, which curbed the power of councils to block rural lines. Unfettered by the old legislation, BET was intent on spreading electric tramways into the suburbs and then sitting back to rake in the profits.

But BET's ambitions soon attracted the attention of an investigative journalist – Robert Donald – the founder and editor of *Municipal Journal* and a staunch supporter of municipal enterprise. BET's ambitions went far beyond suburban trams. It wanted to control electricity supply and distribution as well. Despite its name, said Donald, BET was not so much a traction company but more of a promoting company.

It was an octopus with tentacles spreading all over the country. It bought up horse tramways and converted them to electricity. It promoted light railways and turned them over to subsidiary companies in a complex series of financial manoeuvres that netted BET, and its directors, fat promotion fees. By 1902 BET had more than eighty subsidiary companies and controlled the tramways in at least seventy-five towns, from Accrington to Yarmouth.

Robert Donald, the investigative journalist and founder of *Municipal Journal*, who exposed British Electric Traction's aggressive strategy of expansion. He became editor of the *Daily Chronicle* at the start of 1904. (Author's collection)

British Electric Traction bought up a series of horse tramways around the turn of the last century. In Gravesend BET's electric trams replaced horse power in 1901. The two trams are pictured only yards apart, with the same shops in the background. (Author's collection)

Donald's exposé uncovered a network of interlocking companies supplying electricity and running trams with their operations orchestrated by a tightly knit band of directors. Foremost among these was Emile Garcke, BET's managing director, who was on the board of at least forty BET companies. Donald dubbed him 'Oligarcke'.

Garcke was the puppet master pulling the strings behind the scenes. He was a workaholic who in his early days kept a bed in his office so that he could work late. His colleagues used to dread a dinner invitation, not because Garcke was a poor host, but because dinner was inevitably followed by lengthy late-night business meetings.

Municipal trading was a direct threat to BET's ambitions. 'The agitation against municipal trading can be traced to the London Chamber of Commerce and more particularly the Electrical Trades Section and the Anti-Municipal Trading Committee of it,' wrote Donald in the *Westminster Gazette* of 22 May 1900. BET directors were the most prominent members of these groups.

BET's real aim, said Donald, was to create an 'electric trust', a vast sprawling monopoly of power stations, electric lighting and tramways. Donald's use of the word 'trust' was deliberate. It referred to John D. Rockefeller's notorious Standard Oil Trust, which had been devised to circumvent American state rules on monopolies by creating a network of seemingly independent concerns that were in practice controlled by Rockefeller. This scheme became illegal after the United States passed the antitrust legislation in 1890.

The 'electric trust' was more than a simple case of imitation. The source of the money behind BET was a bit of a mystery. The Liberal press believed that the American financier John Pierpont Morgan was the financial muscle behind BET. So, was an American-style trust controlling British trams and power stations? It was a logical deduction. Certainly, Pierpont Morgan underwrote a BET share issue in 1901, and at the same time he was trying to gain control of the London Underground.

The anti-municipal campaign stepped up a gear in August 1902 when *The Times* started to publish the first in a series of articles about 'municipal socialism' which appeared under the byline of 'a correspondent'. Many of the pieces were little more than tendentious tittle-tattle, denouncing municipal fever hospitals, swimming baths, sewage farms and free libraries.

Municipal trams were one of the prime targets in this series. In addition to examples of municipal extravagance, the anonymous correspondent raised the cry of 'rate-aided competition'. It was a familiar refrain among railway managers. Slow suburban steam trains might have outpaced horse-drawn cars, but they were no match for the new trams. Electric trams were quicker over short distances and much more likely to take passengers to where they wanted to go. But railway managers

The friendly camaraderie of workers on this BET tram in Devonport seems far removed from the machinations of the people behind the company. (Barry Cross Collection/Online Transport Archive)

clung to the belief that municipal trams were unfairly subsidised out of the rates and taking passengers that were rightfully theirs.

The London and North Western Railway had seen a drop of more than 400,000 third-class passengers in the last half of 1901. 'As the falling off is mostly in regard to penny fares, it is accounted for by the working of tramways, and particularly electric tramways near the great cities.' It was all the more galling, claimed *The Times*, because this company paid rates in no fewer than forty-six towns with trams, so the railway company's rates were subsidising the competition.[16]

The Times articles had the hallmarks of an orchestrated campaign. The first was plugged by a self-important editorial in the same issue. The articles, it claimed, would 'fill thinking men with grave apprehension' and alert the public to the dangers of the collective state. The subject was so important that it was worth six more editorials – from September to November – as the series progressed and dozens of mostly supportive letters. A London evening newspaper also reprinted the articles.

The campaign gained further traction with a paper given to the economic section of the prestigious British Association by an expert from America, the Hon. Robert P. Porter.

Porter said that municipal enterprises had failed in the United States and that there was one word for municipal trading – socialism. Porter concluded his talk by quoting extensively from *The Times* editorial that began the series. The next day *The Times* repaid the compliment, praising Porter's 'exceedingly interesting' paper in its editorial. It was hard to escape the suspicion that Porter, *The Times*, and its anonymous correspondent were all hand-in-glove.

It wasn't long before the series piqued the attention of inquisitive journalists. Who was behind all this, they wondered? *The Times* articles, as the *Daily News* acidly observed on 20 October, 'did not read as if they were entirely without motive'.

The whole point of the campaign, said a *Daily News* columnist, was 'to induce a reactionary House of Commons to crush progressive local authorities, beginning as always with the London County Council.' Property owners, in the shape of the Liberty and Property Defence League, and BET were behind the campaign. '*The Times* has allowed itself to be made the catspaw of [a] ring of capitalists.'

The *Morning Leader* had also been sniffing around the story. 'Who is the Hon. Robert P. Porter, who is fighting so largely in the anti-municipal campaign in England and whose paper read before the British Association is receiving such wide and forced publicity?'

The answer to this rhetorical question did nothing to enhance Porter's credibility. 'He is not known in the United States as an authority on municipal government.' Although normally termed an American, Porter had been born in England and went to America as a teenager. He had a wide circle of friends and associates, including the writer Mark Twain. Porter became a newspaper proprietor whose paper supported Benjamin Harrison in his successful presidential bid in 1888. His reward for this support was to be made superintendent of the US Census.

'Why he is called honourable we have never been able to discover,' continued the *Morning Leader*. However, there was much more to Porter than just a phoney honorific, the paper revealed.

Mr Porter is known on the continent in quite another capacity than that of an economist. He is known as one of the able and well-paid ambassadors of the Standard Oil Trust. He has acted for it in many ways. He has also been the agent of another American trust. In England he associates entirely with company interests, more particularly electric tramway interests.[17]

The *Daily News* was also hot on the scent. It was 'a momentous intrigue…so elaborate in its ramifications, so audacious in its strategy,' it trumpeted, 'that our story would be incredible were it not substantiated at every point by facts of an indisputable character.' The series of articles in *The Times* – there had been fourteen of them by the time the *Daily News* published its exposé – 'deliberately and venomously slandered the municipal life of the whole country'. The paper pinpointed the source of the articles as being a new free-enterprise pressure group, the Industrial Freedom League, acting in cahoots with BET.

These were effective and accurate hatchet jobs. For Porter was no disinterested bystander. He was on BET's payroll. On 18 September, five days after his paper to the British Association, Porter was put on a monthly retainer for his services. The heading in the board's minute book is 'Industrial Freedom League'.[18]

The first public sighting of the Industrial Freedom League was in a letter to *The Times* in February 1902. The letter, signed by one 'Dixon Hy Davies' of Manchester, claimed local authorities were 'degenerating into…state-aided monopolists'. After a run-of-the-mill tirade about municipal trading, Davies solicited backing for a new Industrial Freedom League, which was being set up to oppose 'this unscrupulous trading policy' and asked supporters to contact the league at 37 Norfolk Street, off the Strand.

So, who was Davies and what was his link to an off-Strand office? Although the letter in *The Times* didn't acknowledge any association, Dixon Henry Davies was the Great Central Railway Company's solicitor. The office off the Strand was occupied by Sydney Morse, BET's company solicitor. His office was handy for BET, which had its headquarters a couple of doors further down Norfolk Street

The groundwork for the Industrial Freedom League was laid on 31 October 1901 when the key figures met at London's Trocadero restaurant. The event was publicised as a 'complimentary dinner' given to the Hon. Robert P. Porter by the London Chamber of Commerce's municipal trading committee. This committee had been set up at the prompting of BET, which was deeply concerned by the municipal threat to its electricity supply plans. Porter was billed as a 'United States Commissioner'. Amongst the people who turned up to dine and listen to Porter's words of wisdom were Garcke, Morse, and Dixon Henry Davies.[19]

Municipal ownership was vanishingly rare in the United States. Out of the 150 principal cities in the US, only two or three owned their own gas works, about a dozen had their own power stations and none had tramways. 'State or municipal ownership deadens enterprise there can be no sort of doubt,' said Porter. Not a mile of the 20,000 miles of street railways was controlled by 'a town clerk – though some of it may be in the hands of a receiver – better that, I hear you say, than on the rates.'

Porter was playing to two audiences. In Britain, he aimed to stop municipal trading dead in its tracks. But he was also playing to the folks back home. Glasgow's successful takeover of the city's trams had sparked considerable interest on the other side of the pond and Porter wanted to prevent the contagion of municipal trading spreading to America.

The first meeting of the Industrial Freedom League took place at the Westminster Palace Hotel in April 1902. The main reason for founding the League, said Alexander

Henderson MP, who chaired the Great Central Railway Company, was to combat 'the grave and growing evils of municipal trading'. Local authorities, said Henderson, should not run gasworks, power stations or tramways.

Garcke and a long list of other luminaries from BET were on the League's ruling council. BET's support for the League fitted comfortably with the company's political leanings. In its early days, BET had a policy of reserving one or two seats on its board for Conservative politicians.[20]

Municipal electric trams threatened both suburban steam trains and privately owned trams. So, the railway companies and BET formed an alliance against a common enemy – the municipal tram. The *Daily News* said that the League was acting on behalf of an electric trust 'composed of a small ring of Anglo-American capitalists'. The *Railway News* emphasised the benefits of the league to railway shareholders. For investors, railway shares were a safe source of reliable dividends. The league was a 'railway shareholders' protection association'.

According to the League's publications, it was 'an association to free private enterprise from undue interference and from rate-aided competition [and] will endeavour to carry out its objects by keeping the press well informed of the trends of municipal socialism.' Among the list of the league's prominent supporters was the name of Charles Moberly Bell. Bell was ideally placed to ensure that the press was kept well informed of trends in municipal socialism as the manager of *The Times* and he used that paper as a megaphone for the Industrial Freedom League.

Several Fleet Street newspapers followed up the *Daily News* revelations, asking BET, Moberly Bell and the Industrial Freedom League for an explanation. None of them would comment. The Liberal magazine *Truth* – the Edwardian equivalent of *Private Eye* – said the story had 'thrown an agreeable light on *The Times* campaign… But apparently the cardinal fact that the manager of *The Times* is actively associated with the trust-begotten league of freedom is to go unchallenged.'

The response to the revelations came in the form of a letter, not to the *Daily News* but to *The Times*. The letter, signed by 'the writer of the articles' claimed that the *Daily News* exposé was 'a cock-and-bull' story and denied any link with the Industrial Freedom League or an electrical trust.

So, who was the 'writer of the articles' and what weight should be attached to this denial?

Months after the brouhaha had subsided, *The Times* carried a letter from one Edwin A. Pratt lauding the series for establishing that municipal trams were subsidised from the rates. It took nearly eighty years for the identity of the writer to emerge, when an enterprising historian asked *The Times*' archivist to lift the cloak of anonymity. It was no wonder that Pratt thought so highly of the articles; he wrote them.[21]

Pratt had joined *The Times* in 1890. He was Moberly Bell's first appointment and stayed on the paper for ten years. He was never less than conservative in his views. He penned another series of articles for the paper vilifying unionised labour for causing a 'crisis in British industry' because it wanted a 48-hour week. Pratt subsequently worked in public relations for the Railway Companies Association. He also wrote pamphlets arguing against railway nationalisation.

Robert P. Porter, the other anti-municipal protagonist of 1902, was also an acolyte of *The Times*. Two years after his foray into economics at the British Association, Moberly Bell gave him a job at *The Times*. He went on to become the paper's Washington correspondent.

Chapter 4

THE DEPARTMENT OF DIRTY TRICKS

The Times articles were the tip of a very large iceberg. British Electric Traction, working hand-in-glove with the Industrial Freedom League, maintained an inventive and well-financed propaganda department, mostly staffed by renegade journalists. Their job was to organise a dirty tricks campaign. Its objective: to kill off municipal trading and in particular the council tram.

Hundreds of articles appeared in the provincial press under fictitious or misleading bylines. Deceitful letters appeared in local papers, apparently from members of the public, with the identity of authors concealed by pseudonyms. In reality, these letters were the products of a department of dirty tricks.

The web of deceit didn't end with these journalistic enterprises. BET and the Industrial Freedom League also used ratepayers' associations as fronts, setting up new associations or infiltrating established ones. These fronts too bombarded editors with letters opposing municipal trading.

In April 1901, a curious article appeared in the *Hendon and Finchley Times*. 'A very valued correspondent sends us some figures as to the loss on electric light schemes.' The article listed nearly two dozen local authorities that were losing money on municipal electric lighting. The 'valued correspondent' pointed out that the London borough of Hendon was sparsely populated and 'if places like Bath, Bedford and Cardiff…cannot make it pay what possible hope can there be of it paying in Hendon?'

What prompted this article was Hendon's plan to generate its own electricity. At the same time, two BET companies had just gained the right to supply electricity for lighting and trams over a large part of north London. Furthermore, BET was negotiating to take over the local horse trams and convert them to electricity. So BET wanted to stifle Hendon's plans to supply electricity and prevent municipal competition from eating into the profits of what promised to be a very lucrative monopoly.

Two months later the *Tottenham and Edmonton Weekly Herald* and other papers in the area carried identical letters about Hendon's electricity plans from someone using the pen name 'True Progressive'. 'Hendon…is quite unsuited for municipal trading in electricity,' claimed True Progressive. The council should leave private capital to take the risk or else, the letter writer said, ratepayers faced another 3d on the rates.

It didn't take long for the story behind these letters to unravel. When True Progressive's epistle arrived on the editor's desk it was accompanied by a handwritten covering letter on the notepaper of the Electrical Power Distribution Company, a major part of the BET group. The covering letter made it plain that the company would pay handsomely for the publication of True Progressive's letter.

'Dear Sir,
'If you care to insert the enclosed in your next issue, you may charge us at the rate of 2d per line.
'Please put me on your quarterly subscription list and charge to the company.'

The covering letter was signed 'T. C. Elder'. The enclosure was the letter from True Progressive. The scrappy handwriting of the covering letter betrayed the fact that T. C. Elder had copied out the same letter a large number of times.

The letter 'was intended to be taken as the contribution of a local ratepayer', wrote Robert Donald, the editor of *Municipal Journal*, and was part of BET's aim 'to secure an absolute monopoly of electric light and tramways' in North London.[22]

Truth was equally scathing. It was an attempt to 'humbug the readers of local newspapers with an expression of opinion from a true progressive ratepayer,' commented the magazine, which wanted to know 'how many local papers have earned their 2d a line by co-operating in this fraud on their readers.'[23]

BET was not just a pioneer in electric light and tramways, it was also a pioneer in the duplicitous public relations technique now known as astroturfing.

In an age before commercial broadcasting, the printed word had an enormous impact on public opinion – there was no other source of information. BET's paid letter writers used the correspondence columns of newspapers to spread fake news.

True Progressive was certainly a prolific correspondent, writing to dozens of papers in North London in an effort to secure BET's monopoly. His alter ego T.C. Elder was Thomas Elder, a jobbing journalist. He was hired by BET in early 1901 to organise its campaigns.

It was plainly a substantial operation because a year later, Elder and two other scribblers were hard at work producing letters to the press from True Progressive and other pseudonyms as well as articles from Special Correspondents, Contributors, Experts, and other misleading pen names.

Another sample of the output from Elder's typewriter appeared in the *Kilburn Times* and dozens of other papers, again signed by True Progressive. 'Simultaneously with the success of a great commercial organisation in obtaining an act of Parliament empowering it to supply electric current over an area of 300 square miles, several of

ALL COMMUNICATIONS TO BE ADDRESSED TO "THE COMPANY."

THE ELECTRICAL POWER DISTRIBUTION COMPANY, LTD.

TELEGRAMS
PEGAMETER,
LONDON.

SURREY HOUSE,
NEAR TEMPLE STATION,
VICTORIA EMBANKMENT,
LONDON, W.C.

June 19/0[?]

Dear Sir,

If you can to insert the enclosed in your next issue, you may charge us at the rate of 2d. per line.

Please put me on your quarterly subscription list; & charge to the company.

Yours faithfully
T. Creed [?]

Astroturfing: letters in local papers praising the work of private companies and pretending to be from members of the public were actually paid for by British Electric Traction and written by company employees. The covering letter says that the Electrical Power Distribution Company, part of the BET group, will pay newspapers 2d a line for printing its letters. (Municipal Journal/British Library Collection)

the lesser local authorities…are plunging into the business on their own account on a small and therefore uneconomical scale.'

The letter issued a dire warning that ratepayers 'will be faced by the ugly alternative of either abandoning their expensive little generating station and buying electricity from the big company which can supply at much lower rates or else of maintaining their own system and paying a considerably higher price for current.'

Curiously, the letter did not name this benevolent organisation which was going to supply limitless cheap electricity. The warning that ratepayers could lose money came from an expert named John S. Raworth, while the letter quoted a magazine called *Electrical Investments*, which was unlikely to be regular reading around the breakfast tables of North London. 'Under the stress of open competition progress is affected by the survival of the fittest and the consumer derives the utmost advantage thereby. If, however, a community is tempted to [municipalise] the electricity supply prices must be maintained above the competitive level and consumers cannot but suffer,' concluded the letter in a Darwinian take on electricity supply.

For those in the know, there were clues aplenty as to who was behind the letter. BET's fingerprints were all over it. The big company was the North Metropolitan Power Distribution Company, a BET subsidiary. John S. Raworth was a BET director. And *Electrical Investments* was BET's company magazine.

The following year, Elder even wrote a letter under his own name to the national press. Describing himself as 'one of the few persons who have made a study of municipal electric light accounts,' Elder claimed that several councils were losing money on electric lighting.

Elder's letter was written from his home address. But the subterfuge didn't last long. The next day, the *Daily News* outed him. 'Mr T. C. Elder, who wrote us yesterday from the rusticity of Streatham' is employed by BET. 'Why Mr Elder should have tempted providence by writing to us I do not know,' wrote the *News* columnist, 'He might surely have known that certain exposure awaited him if he tried such an experiment. He did not, of course, offer us 2d a line but I think we have our reward.'

The Industrial Freedom League, which was often indistinguishable from BET, set out to court ratepayers' groups. They were natural allies. No ratepayer wanted to pay more rates. And it was easy to portray municipal investment as frittering away the rates, even if the reverse was true. In Leamington Spa, where the local tramway company had been taken over by BET, the link with the Industrial Freedom League was openly admitted. The Leamington Ratepayers' Association had been set up the previous year. One of its leaders, a baronet, let slip the role of the league at its annual meeting in 1903.

'The Industrial Freedom League, which was largely composed of the chairmen of railway companies and other wealthy men, was willing to act as a central ratepayers association for the country,' said the baronet. The implication was that this association was promoted by the Industrial Freedom League. The baronet didn't mention BET, but two councillors who spoke at the meeting were both directors of the Leamington and Warwick Tramways and Omnibus Company, a BET subsidiary.

Ratepayers' associations were frequently no more than fronts for industrial interests. The chairman of the Great Eastern Railway frankly admitted setting up one ratepayers' association on 'a non-political basis' to 'stem the torrent of socialism'.[24]

A British Electric Traction tram in Stourport. In the early years of the 20th century, BET owned more than one in seven of the country's tramways, including the Kidderminster and Southport Electric Tramways Company. (Barry Cross Collection/Online Transport Archive)

'Ratepayers associations spring up where the BET interests are at stake,' observed *Municipal Journal*. It was a familiar corporate tactic.

On the south coast, one such newly created group was the Hove Ratepayers' Defence Association, set up to support BET in its struggles with Hove council. The Sheffield Ratepayers' Association, which falsely claimed that the council's trams were losing money, had been established to attack council control of the trams. In Birmingham the local Trades and Property Owners' Association was brought into BET's orbit.

While *The Times'* series was still in full swing, an editor of a provincial paper handed the Liberal-supporting *Morning Leader* a scoop. It was a copy of an endearingly frank circular to provincial papers. Written on the Industrial Freedom League's notepaper, the circular offered papers professionally produced free copy, which naturally enough would peddle the league's point of view.

The executive committee of the Industrial Freedom League…propose from time to time, as occasion may arise to have special articles written dealing with various phases of municipal trading. They are anxious to arouse the ratepayers to a feeling of opposition against municipalities going outside their legitimate functions in competing with the aid of the rates against private enterprise.

The articles will be typewritten and sent free of charge. They will be headed "from a special correspondent" and if you agree to publish them every care would be taken that they should not appear in any journal within the area of your circulation. They will, of course, be subject to editorial revision.

I shall be very glad if you will favor (sic) me with an early reply saying if you are willing to accept the articles for publication in your journal.[25]

This circular was part of the League's mission to keep the press well informed of municipal socialism, which the *Morning Leader* observed often meant informing the press 'of facts and figures, which have no existence'.

The first of this series of free articles, headed 'Municipal Trading: its risks and fallacies' appeared in the *Manchester Courier* at the end of September, under the byline 'by a special contributor'. In the *Midland Express* the articles appeared under the byline 'Fairplay'. In all the number of provincial papers carrying this series ran into double figures.

The third article in the series was about trams. Headed 'tramways: a serious outlook' it was 'special to the *Berkshire Chronicle*' and written 'by an expert'. The same piece was equally special to the *Marylebone Mercury* and the *Kent and Sussex Courier* and many other papers. In common with others in the series the article was long on invective and short on facts.

There was a clear connection between these articles and the companion ones in *The Times*. The series in both *The Times* and the local papers ran over three months, finishing in November and were designed to undermine popular support for municipal trading in the run-up to the November deadline for councils to submit private bills – which might include proposals for municipal trading.

Chapter 5

BRIBERY FAILS TO SWING BIRMINGHAM VOTE

The decisive battle in the struggle between British Electric Traction and the forces of municipal enterprise came in Birmingham. The city had originally leased the operation of its tramways to private companies but in 1899 it elected to run its own trams when the leases fell due. Despite this decision, there was a reasonable working relationship between the city council and the City of Birmingham Tramways Company, which had become the main private operator. The company ran mostly steam trams but it also had horse trams and even battery-powered trams.

In the early years of the 20th century Birmingham was one of the last strongholds of steam trams. It was also the focus of British Electric Traction's efforts to create an extensive network of electric trams. (Barry Cross Collection/Online Transport Archive)

In June 1902 the chairman and majority shareholder in the tramways company issued a circular to shareholders saying he had sold his shares to a 'London syndicate' which was planning 'important developments'. The syndicate was BET. Despite Birmingham's avowed intention to municipalise the trams, BET clearly calculated that this would be a shrewd investment because it paid the chairman nearly twice the face value of his shares.

BET's confidence that it could change the council's mind was founded on the local support it had secured. It had the backing of the property owners' association and two of the most powerful figures in the city: Arthur Chamberlain, the younger brother of the former city boss and pioneer of municipal trading Joseph Chamberlain, and John Nettlefold, who was both Arthur's cousin and his son-in-law.

BET's supporters swung into action with the aim of halting the municipal tram in its tracks. The 'hastily formed' Birmingham and District Trades and Property Owners' Association had only been established the previous year. It was, according to one local paper, an association of slum landlords, set up to shield their rental income from municipal interference. The property owners joined BET's anti-municipal campaign hoping to curb the corporation's power and therefore 'gain a further period of security for the dirty and dilapidated dens which are called homes by the poor.'

The Property Owners' Association wrote to every councillor warning them that municipal trading 'in its hideous nakedness' was 'nothing but a stepping stone for revolutionary socialism'. They followed that with a handsomely produced and widely circulated pamphlet, paid for by BET or the Industrial Freedom League – the two were effectively synonymous. The circular told how municipal enterprises in a large number of towns were making losses.

The sheer weight of details in the pamphlet seemed impressive. But it was mostly fake news, or 'the most amazing collection of lies yet put forward,' as the *Clarion* put it. Ten of the points in the pamphlet were lifted from the series in *The Times*. The only other acknowledged source was the *Glasgow Herald*, a long-standing opponent of municipal trading.

Journalists on the *Birmingham Daily Gazette* gathered up copies of the pamphlet and sent them to the places where the trams were allegedly losing money, asking the councils to comment. The replies were uniformly dismissive. 'A more gross, partial, unfair, and exaggerated account it has not been my lot to read for many years,' commented the chairman of Sheffield's tramways committee. It was, he said, 'a travesty of one-sided and inaccurate statements.' Other councils also condemned the references to them.

The campaign against municipal control gathered pace. Towards the end of September, two public meetings were held. One was for municipal control and the other one, against, was convened by councillor Nettlefold. On the morning of the meetings *The Times* ran the eleventh in its series on municipal socialism. The article, which ran for the best part of a page and quoted approvingly the 'Hon' Robert P. Porter's speech to the British Association earlier in the month, was devoted entirely to Birmingham.

Porter was the star speaker at Nettlefold's anti-municipal meeting. It was his first outing since he joined the BET payroll – although that was not public knowledge. Nettlefold began proceedings by praising the articles in *The Times* and Porter gave a rehash of his talk to the British Association. Municipal trading had failed in America and it would fail over here, he claimed. His remarks were reported at length in the next day's issue of *The Times*, while the rival, better-attended, pro-municipal meeting barely rated a mention.

Collusion? There was no shortage of suggestive links. Porter, for example, was on the council of the Industrial Freedom League. So too was Nettlefold. And the League had written to the property owners offering support. 'All trading enterprises entered into by corporations must eventually be failures financially, owing to the inevitable lack of thorough knowledge of the business undertaken,' it claimed. The letter was published in *The Times.*

'The Property Owners' Association may be acting quite independently of the British Electric Traction Company,' said the *Birmingham Daily Post*, 'but it is clear that both are involved in the propagation of the same ideas…and it is further clear that the more those ideas take root in the country the better it will be for the industrial company we have named.'

The left wing *Clarion* was less circumspect in its criticism. 'Who are the promoters of this campaign?' asked its columnist Robert Suthers. 'They are the people who want to get the…tramways' profits for themselves. A handful of dividend hunting shareholders who hope, by lies, by misleading statements, and by fallacious arguments, to frighten the citizens into voting against municipal trams.'[26]

Before the Birmingham Corporation could take over the trams it had to negotiate several hurdles. It needed the approval of ratepayers before it could promote a parliamentary bill. The first stage in this process was to hold a public meeting, where the opposing forces could slug it out.

The meeting, which was held in the town hall on 5 November, was extremely rowdy. The Lord Mayor opened the meeting by saying the bill would 'empower the corporation to work tramways'. The remark was greeted with huge cheers. Nettlefold got no further than saying 'as one who disagrees' before his remarks were drowned out. The meeting decided to hold a local referendum.

The poll was a Dickensian affair. Only ratepayers could take part in this referendum, so the electorate was overwhelmingly male. But some men had more votes than others. Every ratepayer had one vote. However, those owning property with a rateable value of more than £50 got an extra vote for every additional £25 of rateable value, up to a maximum of six votes. This weighting gave the wealthy a much greater say than the workers who were the majority of the trams' passengers. On top of that, there was wholesale bribery and corruption as well as credible reports of gangs beating up shopkeepers who supported the council.[27]

The voting took place over three days. Voters had to choose between voting for, or against, the council's plans. The Property Owners' Association was not short of money. It had committee rooms in various parts of the city and employed some 200 vehicles – from horse-drawn conveyances to modern automobiles – to take people to the polls. At one workshop a man turned up and offered the employees a shilling and a ride to the town hall in his horse-drawn brake if they would vote against the bill.

A reporter from the *Birmingham Daily Gazette* confirmed that voters were being bussed in from the local pubs and that you could smell 'the potations' on their breath:

> They are brought up very much in the way of prisoners in charge of a warder. The latter is a stout dark-whiskered man with a corduroy cap, who says to the men to vote "against" and they do it. Time after time these last two days he had been followed into the town hall by those who for the time being are little more than slaves.

A police officer on duty at the town hall told the *Birmingham Daily Post* that 'he had never before seen so many well-known thieves, pickpockets and gaol birds as he had seen that day at the town hall'. Just about dinner time three illiterates cast their votes against the bill. As one of them received his voting paper from the clerk he said: 'They told us we should have a cold lunch when we had signed this.'

One canny ratepayer turned up at the town hall with his 'carer' telling him in front of officials: 'You pay me and I'll vote, but not before.' Just occasionally a voter became separated from his guardian. One illiterate handed over a form on which his name had been filled in by someone else. The clerk noticed that he hadn't voted for or against.

> 'Did he want to vote for or against,' enquired the clerk.
> 'Will they know if I vote for?' he asked the clerk while looking around to check that his chaperone was otherwise occupied.
> 'No,' said the clerk.
> 'Then mark me for.'

A vicar confirmed the standard bribe was a shilling. 'Working men have been deliberately bribed to vote against the bill. A man known personally to me, who is willing if necessary to come forward and testify to the fact, was offered a shilling on Friday evening to go up and vote against the bill.'[28]

Even the *Birmingham Mail*, which was unsympathetic to the council's policy, was appalled by the scenes. 'No thoughtful citizen could watch some of the incidents of the poll…without becoming sick at heart.' The paper called for a full inquiry into the conduct of the poll and to discover where 'the money was obtained which has been spent so freely in the last few days…there would be little difficulty in ascertaining who the men are who proffered bribes so freely… Moreover, it might be possible to ascertain who controlled these puppets.' In the popular mind, concluded the editorial, 'crooked methods and a bad cause always go together.'[29]

BET was the obvious source of the money. But the Property Owners' Association denied any connection with BET. The *Birmingham Daily Gazette* commented:

> We note there has been no disclaimer to help from the Industrial Freedom League, which is the British Electric Traction Company under another name.
>
> We know that tens of thousands of circulars have been issued to the people of Birmingham against the bill. Who pays for them? We know that scores of vehicles have been hired to bring up grossly illiterate voters to poll against the bill. Who pays for these vehicles? We know that there is far more money being spent in this fight than mere disinterested citizens would be willing to supply. Who provides that money?[30]

As the election reached its climax on Saturday, sandwich board men appeared around the city centre. The placards read: 'Chamberlain against the bill' and 'throw out the bill and stop further municipal meddling'. Several newspapers drew parallels between the American backers of BET and the attempt to import corrupt election practices common in American town halls.

Despite the wholesale bribery, the council won a crushing victory, with 64 per cent of the votes backing the plan to municipalise the trams. The reaction from BET was muted. In the BET magazine *Electrical Investments*, the market report from Birmingham was simply: 'Monday 10th November. City trams have become rather flat.'

BET made one last-ditch attempt to change the council's mind. After its referendum victory in November, the council met in May 1903 to ratify its decision to take over the trams. BET went on the offensive, producing a daily newspaper called *Tramway News*, which was published over nine days in the run-up to the council decision. In an editorial in its first edition, *Tramway News* claimed its purpose was to correct 'many false, many ignorant' statements which 'prejudice the public mind'.

The paper stressed the advantages of BET running the trams. *Tramway News* was priced at one halfpenny, but in practice it was a free sheet. The cover price, said *Municipal Journal*, 'was a fiction – like most of the contents'. The anti-municipal push was important enough for Emile Garcke and dozens of BET's headquarters staff to spend a fortnight in Birmingham producing the paper.

The council was unmoved by BET's stunt and decided to push ahead with its bill by a large majority. The *Birmingham Daily Gazette* predicted that the freesheet would be counter-productive.

If it had any effect at all it should be in the direction of stiffening the determination of the public representatives to have nothing at all to do with Mr Emile Garcke and those who are associated with them, for they represented a type of speculator with whom it was best to have as little to do as possible.

BET, said *Municipal Journal*:

… knew perfectly well when it bought up the Birmingham tramways that it was speculating. It speculated in the hope that it would succeed in inducing or coercing Birmingham City Council to give it an extension of the leases, otherwise it would sustain a heavy loss. Therefore [BET] is going to reap the reward of all speculators.[31]

The battle for Birmingham was over. Parliament approved Birmingham's bill and the city took over the tram lines in stages from 1904 as the leases fell due, replacing the old horse and steam trams with modern electric ones. In the end, BET's activities had little impact on Birmingham. Under municipal control, the city's tram network went on to be the fourth largest in the country, after London, Glasgow and Manchester.

One of Birmingham's last steam trams. After British Electric Traction's defeat in the battle of Birmingham it was the council and not the company that electrified the city's tramways. (Author's collection)

After the rout of BET at the battle of Birmingham the forces of private enterprise were put to flight all over the country. The speed of this reversal in fortune was staggering. As late as 1905, six out of ten trams on the city streets still belonged to private companies, although most of these private trams were clapped-out horse cars. A year later seven out of ten trams were run by local authorities.

There were two basic reasons for the success of municipal trams. The first was that, unlike companies, councils did not have to pay large and sometimes inflated dividends to shareholders. And secondly, it was cheaper for councils to borrow money, because they had a secure source of income in the rates.

Nevertheless, the Industrial Freedom League continued to issue apocalyptic warnings about municipal debt spiralling out of control. It was pure scaremongering. The terms used in the debate about municipal trading were loaded, as Suthers pointed out. To the league diehards, municipal debt was a burden. But if a private company borrowed money to invest in trams, it was known as 'capital' and counted as an asset.

To the League the inevitable failure of municipal tramways was an article of faith. Faced with the obvious success of municipal control, the League resorted to casting doubt on the accuracy of council accounts. This sparked two official inquiries. Were councils cooking the books? The inquiries came to similar conclusions. There were some criticisms, mostly of smaller councils, but the larger municipalities which produced audited accounts emerged virtually unscathed. There was no evidence that councils were falsifying their accounts – although that didn't stop the League from continuing to dispute municipal accounts.

However, the acrimony generated by this vitriolic struggle had a corrosive effect on the future of the tram. BET's antics left a lingering legacy of mistrust. The tramway industry became permanently divided between private and public sectors.

In March 1902, while the battle of Birmingham was still raging, Glasgow invited managers from the largest municipal operators, including Leeds, Liverpool, London, Manchester and Sheffield to a meeting in Manchester to discuss the future of the industry. The critical issue for the managers was who should speak on their behalf in pay negotiations or in talks with the government.

At the time the Tramways and Light Railways Association was the only representative body. BET was the dominant force in this association. It paid hefty contributions to the association's coffers and most of the leading figures in the association had links to BET.[32] So it was inevitable that the burgeoning municipal sector felt the association couldn't represent its views. At Manchester the municipal tramways decided to set up a new group, the Municipal Tramways Association.

Although both associations shared the common aim of promoting trams, there remained a deep-seated and often well-founded suspicion of the private sector's motives. The Tramways and Light Railways Association tried to heal the rift, but it

The Tramways and Light Railways Association organised lavish exhibitions like this one in Islington's Agricultural Hall in June 1900 to promote the electric tram industry. The association was dominated by British Electric Traction. (Author's collection)

was rebuffed. Councils saw the approach as a takeover plot, designed to strengthen the malign influence of BET. The two associations would remain separate and often at odds with each other throughout the electric tram era.

This schism had far-reaching consequences. Unlike the motor manufacturing industry, which from 1902 onwards was represented by a single trade association, there was no single voice representing the tramway industry. The two associations were often more concerned with scoring off each other than with lobbying for the industry they both claimed to support.

A case in point was the long-standing grievance of the local authority veto over new tramways. The private sector wanted parliament to change its standing orders so that MPs were not barred from debating bills for new tramways on their merits if enough local authorities objected, in the same way as they could discuss gas and water company legislation.

But the initiative failed because of opposition from local authorities, which didn't want to lose any of their powers. It was a municipal victory that backfired spectacularly; the tramway undertaking that would suffer most from the use of the veto was a municipal operator – the London County Council.

Chapter 6

THE BATTLE FOR WESTMINSTER BRIDGE

The London County Council's policy, under Progressive control, was to buy up the capital's private tram companies when their leases expired. The council started running its first trams in 1899. As the buy-outs continued, so the council's empire grew. It had tramways north of the river. It had tramways south of the river. But it did not have any council tramlines linking the two parts of its empire. The local authority veto had kept the centre of London free of private trams. Could the LCC succeed where the old private companies had failed?

The LCC had one important advantage over the private companies, and that was the Embankment, a handsome tree-lined thoroughfare on the north bank of the Thames that was easily wide enough to accommodate a pair of tramlines in addition to other traffic. But its suitability for trams was far less important than its ownership. The Metropolitan Board of Works had built the Embankment on top of a major sewer, part of the sewage works that helped to rid the capital of cholera. The LCC inherited the road when it replaced the Board of Works in 1889. It was one of only a handful of highways controlled by the county council.

The London boroughs, which had replaced the old vestries, still had the power to veto tramways on their roads. But they could not veto trams on roads belonging to the LCC. Consequently, when the LCC promoted a private bill to lay a tramway on the Embankment, parliament had to debate it. However, the council still faced an uphill struggle. The Progressives controlled the LCC, but Parliament had a Conservative majority.

The LCC made several attempts to gain Parliament's approval for its plans. But running trams on the Embankment meant laying tracks across Westminster Bridge. And that was politically sensitive. The bridge was on Parliament's doorstep. Its 1898 bill was vehemently opposed by the Earl of Kinnoull, who now headed the West End Tramways Opposition Association. Trams, he said, 'would cause the gravest inconvenience in the important neighbourhood of Westminster and the Houses of Parliament.'

Once the LCC had gained a toehold on the far side of Westminster Bridge, the floodgates would open. There would be nothing to prevent tramways crisscrossing central London, he warned. 'If these results are to be avoided the decisive battle with the tramways must be fought at Westminster Bridge, and on this bill.' The railway companies strongly supported Kinnoull. Of the eight MPs organising opposition to the bill, four were directors of railway companies. The bill was heavily defeated.

The LCC tried again in 1902, sparking opposition from a series of interlinked factions. Wealthy property owners and carriage owners opposed trams in central London on principle. So too did the bus and railway companies. Cheap trams would undercut their profits. Then there were groups like the Industrial Freedom League, which opposed the principle of municipal trading. And lastly there were the motorists, who were taking over the role of the carriage folk. They saw the streets as their rightful inheritance and resented the intrusion of trams.

This time the council's bill for the Embankment trams was coupled with a bill to build a new subway running the length of Kingsway. The subway under Kingsway, a new road that the LCC was creating as part of a slum clearance scheme, was uncontroversial and this was approved. But Embankment trams were a political minefield. The House of Lords threw out the bill.

Next year, the LCC tried again. The bill was broadly supported by the Liberals and opposed by the Conservatives, led by Sir Frederick Banbury, the MP for Peckham and a director of the Great Northern Railway. Banbury was a most conservative MP. A man of fastidious habits, he wore a frock coat and a top hat long after the fashion had passed. Widely known as the great obstructionist, he was lampooned in the magazine *Vanity Fair* as 'the blocker', someone who could be counted on to oppose change, from votes for women to allowing trams over Westminster Bridge.

The bill was debated in the House of Commons in March 1903. The Liberals mounted an ambush, forcing a vote while Conservative MPs were still at dinner. Banbury, who was the acknowledged master of this tactic, was alert to the Liberals' ploy. He sent out messengers to nearby watering holes and separated dozens of MPs

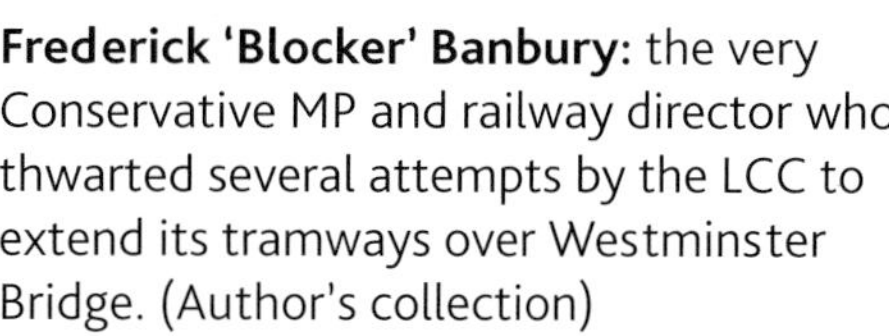

Frederick 'Blocker' Banbury: the very Conservative MP and railway director who thwarted several attempts by the LCC to extend its tramways over Westminster Bridge. (Author's collection)

prematurely from their post-prandial ports. When the vote was taken at 11 pm, 133 MPs voted for the trams and 134 were against. The bill had failed by one vote.

The LCC tried again in the next parliamentary session. The bills, with only small changes, were becoming an annual event, following a course that was every bit as predictable as the Lord Mayor's show. The operators of horse buses felt particularly threatened by the new electric trams. The London Omnibus Owners' Federation claimed that trams would 'extinguish private enterprise and establish a huge rate-aided monopoly', arguing that modern motor buses would supersede the LCC's 'cumbersome electric cars'. Blocker Banbury once again orchestrated the opposition and MPs threw out the bill by a comfortable majority.

The next year the LCC was back again. This time, the bus operators led the fight against the Embankment trams. Trams, claimed the bus owners, would prevent the Embankment from being used as a fast relief road for Fleet Street and the Strand.

'You can safely affirm that these tramways are not self-paying,' claimed the briefing to MPs from Thomas Tilling one of the federation's leading members, which argued that private motor buses would provide a better service.[33]

The claim brought a dismissive snort from the chair of the LCC's highways committee. The council's trams had been entirely self-supporting, he said. And the idea that motor buses could replace trams was palpably ludicrous. There were only twenty motor buses in London at the start of 1905 and although the number rose rapidly, motor buses were extremely noisy and unreliable.

Banbury took more of a back seat in the debate. His reticence was not entirely unconnected to a monster petition from the residents of South London supporting the trams. The petition, nearly 1¼ miles long, had been signed by 110,000 people many of them Banbury's constituents.

John Burns, the Liberal MP and LCC councillor, effectively put the case for the LCC's trams. MPs should not pay heed to the knee-jerk reactions of the bus companies, which had opposed every plan to build tramlines in central London. 'Neither tube railways nor motor omnibuses were so cheap, so clean, or so speedy as electric trams,' said Burns.

It was a finely balanced debate and when the vote came the result was a tie. The speaker voted for the trams and so the bill was sent for detailed consideration by a select committee. The committee heard various objections. The Savoy Hotel claimed that noise and vibration from trams would severely damage its business. St Thomas's Hospital said trams would disturb nurses and patients staying in its new wing on Westminster Bridge Road, while an estate agent said trams would cut the value of property on the route.

The LCC's plans emerged unscathed from the committee hearing and went to the House of Lords. The LCC's plans got a fillip when the Royal Commission on London Traffic produced its report, the day before the crucial vote in the House of

Lords. The Royal Commission had laboured for more than two years to untangle the mess of London's traffic. Its report roundly condemned the congestion caused by trams reversing on the Surrey side of Blackfriars and Westminster Bridges – a consequence of the veto on trams in central London. 'It is difficult to appreciate how such a state of things can have been tolerated for so long.' Tramways, said the commission in 1905, 'are very useful for short-distance traffic.'[34]

The commission recommended a 'large extension of tramways in London' and said high priority should be given to linking up tramways 'across the Thames by Westminster and Blackfriars bridges.' The LCC naturally enough saw the report as 'a great vindication of our tramway policy.'

In anticipation of the report, the City of London, which had long been at loggerheads with the LCC over allowing trams in the City, finally agreed to accept tramlines on Blackfriars Bridge.

Despite the commission's backing, the Lords threw the bill out. Lord Halsbury, the Lord Chancellor and the government's most senior law officer, was hugely influential in swinging the vote. He categorically denied that the Royal Commission was in favour of this plan. Not far short of 100 peers attended the debate and the LCC's bill was lost by a hefty majority of thirty-one.

A fair idea of the forces lined up to fight the trams can be gleaned from the peers who voted down the scheme. There was Lord Avebury, who now chaired the Industrial Freedom League, the Earl of Wemyss, the moving spirit behind the Liberty

Lord Halsbury, the Lord Chancellor, blocked the LCC's attempt to build tramways over Westminster Bridge in 1905, after telling fellow peers that the Royal Commission on London Traffic had *not* recommended allowing trams to cross the bridge. He was fibbing. The commission wanted to see trams cross the bridge. (Edward Linley Sambourne/ Punch)

THE LORD HIGH OBSTRUCTIONIST.

POLICEMAN PUNCH. "HERE ! WHAT ARE YOU PLAYING AT ?"
LORD H-LSB-RY. "I'M HORATIUS ! I'M KEEPING THE BRIDGE ! !"
POLICEMAN PUNCH. "OH ! YOU ARE, ARE YOU ? WELL, THIS ISN'T ANCIENT ROME. THIS IS MODERN LONDON; AND YOU'VE JUST GOT TO MOVE ON."

and Property Defence League, Lord Kinnoull of the West End Tramways Opposition Association and a clutch of railway directors. In other words, the usual suspects.

The vote met with widespread outrage across the political spectrum. Two Conservative MPs publicly regretted the vote. Liberal MPs were less polite. 'It is simply monstrous that 64 persons, responsible to nobody at all, should cause hundreds of thousands of South London toilers to tramp another year across the bridges in all weathers, or spend an extra halfpenny fighting for a bus,' said Thomas Macnamara, a South London MP.

Unnamed members of the Royal Commission said they were 'surprised and disgusted' at Halsbury's claim that they did not favour running trams over the bridges and along the Embankment. They let it be known that they had taken great care with the phrasing of the report on this point so that its meaning was crystal clear: they supported trams on the Embankment.

Only a handful of newspapers supported Halsbury. Cartoonists in both the *Daily Mirror* and *Punch* depicted him as Horatius, the legendary Roman hero, defending Westminster Bridge against hordes of trams. In *Punch*, Halsbury is being confronted by a policeman. 'This isn't ancient Rome, it is modern London,' says the policeman, 'you've got to move on.'

An editorial in the *Daily Telegraph*, with one eye fixed on the inevitable calls for reform of the House of Lords, called the vote 'a regrettable blunder' and accused the Lords of 'unreasonable antagonism'. The LCC called the vote 'high-handed' and 'ill-considered'.

Two days later, Macnamara asked the prime minister if he was aware that the Royal Commission on London Traffic supported the LCC's tram scheme. 'I believe the hon gentleman's interpretation of the Commissioners' report is substantially correct,' replied Arthur Balfour, contradicting his most senior law officer. He went on to drop a heavy hint that parliament should be prepared to consider the scheme again. The LCC duly tabled its bill again, while the City of London sponsored another bill to widen Blackfriars Bridge to make room for the LCC's tramlines.

The political landscape was changing fast. The 1906 general election produced a Liberal landslide, which swept away many of the trams' opponents. Banbury lost his seat. With the change of government, Halsbury ceased to be the Lord Chancellor. Parliamentary resistance melted away.

Vociferous opposition still came from the West End Tramways Opposition Association and the bus operators, who had a profitable business picking up passengers from the tram termini and taking them to places on the far bank.

The bills sailed through the House of Commons in April 1906 and the Lords in July, with barely a hint of the earlier controversies. The LCC's contractors were soon digging up the road to extend the tramlines over Westminster Bridge and onto the Embankment. Next year trams started running along the Embankment.

Westminster Bridge and its iconic trams in about 1910. County Hall on the far bank of the Thames, the future home of the London County Council, is still a construction site. (Author's collection)

The tram in the foreground is turning onto the Embankment from Blackfriars Bridge. The shelter for tram passengers had been hotly opposed by both motorists and the police because it obstructed traffic. (Author's collection)

The Kingsway subway coupled with the crossing of Blackfriars and Westminster bridges allowed passengers for the first time to travel by tram from north to south London and back again. (Author's collection)

'Now that the tramways run along the Embankment, it seems almost unimaginable that any objection could ever have been taken to them,' observed the author Francis Stopford, who hailed the way trams had improved the Embankment. Far from being the fast relief road of the motor lobby's vivid imagination, said Stopford, before the trams started to run 'the Embankment was the abiding place of squalor, vice and misery after nightfall. No one willingly went that way on foot.'[35]

One of the few losers in this saga was a publican in Westminster Bridge Road. His pub was directly opposite the old tram terminus. He told his bankruptcy hearing that extending the trams over Westminster Bridge had ruined his business. A local estate agent confirmed his story, telling the *Daily Mail* that in the evening rush hours, over the three hours up to 8 pm, 300 trams, each containing 70 or 80 passengers, had left the now defunct terminus. 'It was inevitable that these people should take the opportunity of making any small purchases they needed.' Pubs, tobacconists and sweet shops near the terminus had been robbed of half their trade, he said.

Chapter 7
THE WASTRELS

The key recommendation of the Royal Commission on London Traffic of 1905 was that a single body should control the capital's transport. The London County Council thought it was the logical choice to be the new traffic board. After all, it was in charge of the capital's largest network of tramways. And following the Liberal landslide in the general election of 1906, the Liberals controlled both the government and the LCC. There was a good chance, then, that the LCC would be the new traffic board. It was a prospect that seriously alarmed the *Daily Mail*.

'It is an open secret that just now the LCC is moving heaven and earth to obtain this power itself, notwithstanding the very dubious results it has achieved with its tramways, the accounts of which are open to the gravest criticism,' said the *Mail*. The allusion to phoney accounts was a long-cherished mantra of the anti-municipal campaign. But the newspaper went further. The LCC, it said, intended 'to cover London with obsolescent tramways'. This dubious claim marked a significant shift in the political debate, and the *Mail*'s part in it. It wasn't just that municipal trams were bad, or even that the LCC was bad; all trams were obsolete.

For more than two decades the West End Tramways Opposition Association had led the battle to keep trams out of central London. The carriage folk had been the mainstay of the association. However, as the number of horse-drawn carriages dwindled with the seemingly unstoppable rise of the motor car, so the association's influence waned. The balance of power was changing and the motor lobby emerged as the new force to be reckoned with.

The *Daily Mail*'s owner, Alfred Harmsworth, a vocal champion of the cause of motoring, was part of a circle of wealthy and well-connected car enthusiasts centred on the Automobile Club, later the Royal Automobile Club, that included his good friend the motoring MP John Scott Montagu and Mansfield Smith-Cumming, a dare-devil driver who went on to become head of MI6. Harmsworth can claim to have been the Automobile Club's saviour. His generous donations bailed out the club when it was on the verge of going broke.[36]

Early motorists had at first been sympathetic to electric trams. Harmsworth even spoke at a public inquiry in support of a tramway near his home on the Isle of Thanet. But this initial infatuation soon faded and motorists came to loathe trams and Harmsworth's *Daily Mail* launched a virulent anti-tram crusade.

So grave was traffic congestion in central London that the government set up the Royal Commission on London Traffic in February 1903. The magazine *Car*, which was edited by Scott Montagu, later Lord Montagu of Beaulieu, ran a series of articles by William Rees Jeffreys, secretary of the Roads Improvement Association, on the causes of congestion.

A former civil servant in the Board of Trade, Rees Jeffreys knew his way round the corridors of power. He was a key figure in the nascent road lobby. In 1903 he was secretary of the Motor Union, an offshoot of the RAC, the Commercial Motor Users' Association – which represented bus and lorry operators – and secretary of the Roads Improvement Association. Trams on rails, wrote Rees Jeffreys, are 'a perilous obstruction' because they are 'incapable of turning aside in order to pass or be passed by others'. It was a telling turn of phrase. Other vehicles should make way for motor cars, which Rees Jeffreys plainly thought were top of the hierarchy of traffic.

Rather than launch a full-frontal assault on the tram, Rees Jeffreys concentrated his fire on two targets: the termini on the edge of central London where trams had to reverse because the local authority veto had kept them out of the centre and siting poles for overhead wires in the middle of the road. The congestion caused by tram termini, such as the one at Shepherd's Bush 'constitutes a public scandal', said Rees Jeffreys. Companies should buy up nearby houses and demolish them, to create a terminus off the public street.

The article brought a tart response from James Clifton Robinson, the managing director of London United Tramways, who was miffed that Rees Jeffreys had singled out his company's terminus at Shepherd's Bush. Bus owners, pointed out Robinson, 'congest and defile the street'. Does the Roads Improvement Association, he asked, 'tell them they should buy land for their starting places'?[37]

Tramway poles in the middle of the road similarly impeded motorists, complained Rees Jeffreys. 'The central part of the road is wasted and overtaking and passing trams on the right is practically impossible by reason of the short distance between standards.' In 1904, Rees Jeffreys led a deputation to the Board of Trade, which promised a clamp down on these poles.

The tactic of nibbling away at the right of trams to be on the road was applauded by motorists, as part of a wider anti-tram strategy. 'Credit is due to the Roads Improvement Association,' wrote the *Automotor Journal* in a piece that was probably penned by the avidly pro-motorist editor, Stanley Spooner, 'for the determined manner in which they are keeping the tramway nuisance – one might really say tramway scandal – before the public.'

With the Royal Commission's report expected in a matter of months, Harmsworth's *Daily Mail* ratcheted up the rhetoric. The motor show of 1905 sparked a series of articles forecasting a bright future for motor buses. An editorial – Harmsworth often wrote them himself – pronounced the 'doom of the tramway', predicting that buses would soon replace trams. Three days later the *Mail* featured a lengthy article by an anonymous 'expert' claiming that the country had squandered £60 million on 'out-of-date tramways'. Motor buses and electrified railways would make trams obsolete, claimed the expert.

The articles were picked up by local newspapers and in the motoring press. Montagu's magazine *Car* called for a halt to new tramways, because trams 'may become obsolete in the course of a very few years' and would be replaced by motor buses.

Reality was absent in this fantasy world. At the time there were only 124 motor buses in London, the city that had more motor buses than anywhere in Britain. These evil-smelling vehicles were extremely unreliable and broken-down buses littered the roadsides.

The Liberal press was less smitten. 'Will the motor bus last?' asked the *Daily News*. 'The tram runs smoothly. It has none of the vibration which seems certain to bear hardly on the physique of those who work motor buses. It does not break down. Moreover, it earns a handsome profit for the ratepayers.'

Despite the evidence that could be heard the length and breadth of Fleet Street, the *Daily Mail* continued to plug the motor bus as a way of ridding the streets of trams. 'It seems a retrograde measure to introduce the street railway on a large scale in London' when the 'most go-ahead cities' are abandoning trams and replacing them with motor buses.

The two most go-ahead cities were Berlin and Boston. Neither of them had abandoned trams. It was fake news, but it was what the paper wanted to believe, and what it wanted its readers to believe. It was also what Harmsworth wanted to believe. His oft-repeated refrain was 'the motor bus is coming'.

In the run-up to the local elections of 1907, the campaign to oust the Liberals from the LCC gathered intensity. The Conservative party in London had been rebranded for the campaign, with the candidates now calling themselves 'municipal reformers' instead of 'moderates'. The London Municipal Society's manifesto – the Conservative manifesto in all but name – accepted that it wasn't possible to go back to private trams, but it pledged to establish a 'uniform system of municipal accounts and an audit conducted by qualified and independent auditors'. This audit, the Conservatives fondly believed, would prove that the Progressives at the LCC had been cooking the books – an allegation that the Industrial Freedom League routinely trotted out when confronted by successful examples of municipal enterprise.

The *Daily Mail* and the *Daily Mirror* stepped up their attacks on 'the wastrels' – a word used by both newspapers. Harmsworth, who had been created Lord Northcliffe in 1905, owned both papers. 'The Wastrels and socialists of the London County Council today begin their great campaign of misrepresentation…[hoping]

The Conservatives seized control of the London County Council in 1907 after a campaign that successfully smeared the Progressives as 'wastrels', largely because of the council's spending on tramways. (Edward Huskinson/London Picture Archive)

to conceal from the ratepayer their business ineptitude,' claimed the *Daily Mail*.[38] 'For ten years they have wasted the substance of the people of London in every conceivable extravagance. They embarked upon a huge tramway enterprise… The actual result is that, despite cooked accounts, the tramways are today insolvent.'

The voters, said the *Daily Mail*, 'can rid themselves at last of the wastrel incubus…let them use [their power]… to overthrow the arch spendthrifts.' And just in case any readers missed the message about municipal extravagance the editorial repeated the word wastrel no fewer than eight times.

The Progressives, who had controlled the LCC since it was first set up in 1889, were on the defensive. 'The attack of the Municipal Reformers is being delivered with great spirit and enterprise,' said the *Daily Mirror*. 'Its keynote will be the increasing burden of the rate.'

The *Daily Mail* weighed in with a series of articles on how the Progressives would ruin every class of society, as part of a broader campaign against 'municipal extravagance'. The anti-tram propaganda was the main plank in the campaign.

Clerks would lose out because the council had spent millions on trams 'which do not benefit you because you are not classed as a working man'. Workers would suffer because municipal trams had supplanted private trams 'which would have given work to thousands of men'. And lastly, on the eve of the election, the core message: property owners would suffer because of higher rates.

The Municipal Reformers cleverly turned the slogan that Liberals had used against BET back on the Progressives. 'The municipal octopus', screamed one *Daily Mail* headline, 'how it strangles enterprise.'

The message that every class of society would lose if the Liberals continued to control the LCC was hammered home at every opportunity. 'During the last fifteen years we have had a House of Commons to save us from the London County

Council. Now we are looking forward to a new London County Council to save us from the House of Commons,' Lord Elcho told an election meeting held at a London club. Elcho's father, the Earl of Wemyss, was the founder of the Liberty and Property Defence League.

The Conservatives' campaign was wildly successful. The Progressives were swept out of power in a landslide. And the Conservatives would continue to run the LCC for the next twenty-seven years. However, the victory didn't bring major changes. The Municipal Reformers quickly brought in accountants to scrutinise the council's finances, to back up their claims about cooking the books. The accountants failed to find any evidence.

Despite the change in political control, the LCC remained committed to trams, and to expanding the system, although it reined in some of its more ambitious plans. The *Mail*'s campaign had spared the capital from a 'vast extension of the London tramway system,' according to Northcliffe's biographers.[39]

The arguments over the rival merits of trams and buses rumbled on. The chairman of one of the capital's larger bus companies claimed 'that the motor omnibuses are

Edwardian heyday: the change of political control at the London County Council made little difference to its tram policy. (Carpenter Collection/Library of Congress)

affecting the earning capacity of their tramways'. But if anything, it was the LCC's competitors that were feeling the pinch. The motor bus was proving to be less profitable and less reliable than expected. And bus company shareholders were becoming restive in the face of falling dividends. In the autumn of 1908, the London General took over the two other largest bus companies in the capital to stave off financial collapse.

It was not just the bus companies that were suffering from tram competition. The railways were similarly hard-pressed. The chairman of the North London Railway, an exclusively suburban line, complained bitterly about rate-aided competition. 'The county council tramcars were equipped apparently regardless of expense; they followed one another in an almost continuous stream, like a moving platform, taking up and putting down passengers at convenient spots, and carrying them for a considerable distance for the sum of a half-penny.' The Great Eastern Railway, a vocal supporter of the Industrial Freedom League, also suffered badly from tram competition on its suburban lines.

However, it was the underground that had the most serious difficulties. In 1908 the Underground Electric Railways Company called in the receiver. Its trains were packed because of the Franco-British exhibition at White City, but the company owed £7 million that it had to repay on 1 June. The company faced a stark choice: call in the receivers or shut the underground. Sir George Gibb, the underground's managing director, was appointed receiver to save the company from going bankrupt.

British Electric Traction was also feeling the pinch, with dividends dwindling from 10 per cent at the beginning of the century to 3 per cent by 1906. And it was paying dividends out of capital rather than earnings. BET's political machinations and its support for the Industrial Freedom League were a huge drain on its resources, according to *Investors' Review*, which pointed to 'a continual outflow of money in what may be called warlike or otherwise unremunerative directions. There is the press agitation to maintain, there are paid lecturers and scribes to find fees and salaries for.'[40] After its defeat in Birmingham, BET now wanted to distance itself from the anti-municipal campaign and improve its relations with councils.

As its backers struggled with their financial woes the Industrial Freedom League was running out of steam. In October 1907, the London Municipal Society held a large meeting of like-minded organisations in Westminster, to fight any expansion of municipal enterprise, or municipal socialism as the union's supporters described it, and higher rates. The meeting decided to set up a new organisation, the Anti-Socialist Union. Just over a year later, the Industrial Freedom League announced that it was merging with the Anti-Socialist Union.

One of the more significant supporters of this new union was its vice-chairman, a young Conservative MP called Wilfred Ashley. As Minister of Transport for much of the 1920s Ashley would play an important part in the future of the tram.

Chapter 8
MUD AND DUST

To passengers on the top deck of the Tooting tram, the *Daily Mail* made droll reading. 'The triumph of the motor omnibus,' proclaimed the paper, had been a 'great revolution in the conduct of traffic'. Lord Northcliffe's papers seized every opportunity to talk up the prospects of the motor bus and how it was about to eclipse the tram. 'The London public…has gained very greatly by the change from horse traction to motor traction. The complaints against the motor omnibus have died away,' claimed the *Mail*. 'As compared with the electric tramway-car it has incontestable advantages for a city such as London.'[41]

The editorial was a paean of praise for the capital's largest bus operator, the London General Omnibus Company. Its annual general meeting in December 1909 was held at the upmarket Holborn Restaurant, on the corner of Holborn and Kingsway, and handy for shareholders who wanted to check out the competition – in the form of the newly opened Kingsway tram subway.

The meeting marked the bus company's golden jubilee. But this milestone was barely a cause for celebration, despite the *Mail*'s partisan spin. Others were less easily impressed. The company had posted heavy losses in recent years. The city editor of *Truth* pointed out that the company's share price was less than a tenth of what it had been ten years before.

The company's chairman, Henry Hicks, used the meeting to launch a trenchant and overtly political attack on the Liberal government's planned petrol tax, which would cost the company £37,500 – £55 for every motor bus.

But shareholders were more concerned about the company's accounts. Why did they fail to make any allowance for depreciation? The irony was inescapable. The municipal reformers had repeatedly accused the London County Council of cooking the books because the council had not allowed for the depreciation of its trams. Hicks condescendingly told shareholders 'there were two kinds of depreciation; there was the necessary depreciation, and there was the desirable depreciation.' He claimed, 'there had been no depreciation in motor buses since the amalgamation in 1908; on the contrary there had been considerable appreciation.'

In other words, after eighteen months of wear and tear on the streets of London, the General's buses were now worth more than they had been. Shareholders weren't convinced. One said, 'no practical man would agree with the chairman's remarks about depreciation on motor omnibuses'. Another shareholder, taking in the news about the new petrol tax, wondered whether it was time for the company to cut its losses and go into liquidation.

So, what was this new petrol tax?

The country's roads were in an appalling state and ill-equipped to cope with modern motor vehicles. On rainy days the wheels of speeding buses bespattered both passers-by and shop windows with mud, an Edwardian euphemism for a mixture of liquid and solid horse excrement. On dry days the problem was dust. Increasing numbers of motor vehicles only highlighted the problem; a speeding car left an acrid cloud of dust in its wake. It was a problem that motorists acknowledged, and the Roads Improvement Association sponsored experiments with tar spraying as a way of dealing with mud and dust.

The mounting clamour about the need to improve road surfaces forced the government to act. In the autumn of 1908, the Chancellor of the Exchequer, David Lloyd George, met a group of MPs who were members of the Royal Automobile Club. He told them that in order to adapt roads for motor traffic, the government would have to tax motorists. The outcome of these talks, as announced in Lloyd George's budget of April 1909, was to set up a 'road fund', which would be financed by 3d on a gallon of petrol and a tax on the horsepower of vehicles, which became known as the road fund licence.

Lloyd George assured the MPs that all the revenue would be spent on roads. 'The whole of the money raised,' said Lloyd George in the budget debate, 'should go to the improvement of the roads.'

The RAC group of MPs were mollified by this assurance. Charles Rose, the chairman of the RAC, who according to the club's official history was a model for Toad in Wind of the Willows and responsible for many a cloud of nauseating dust, even voted for the taxes.

The only real dissent came from William Joynson-Hicks, a Conservative MP who was not only the London General's solicitor but also the son of its chairman, Henry Hicks. The government had granted a 50 per cent rebate of the petrol tax for commercial vehicles but Joynson-Hicks, known to both friends and his more numerous foes as Jix, was not satisfied. He had been briefed by the London General. 'What benefit does…a motor omnibus in London get from this fund?' Jix claimed: 'This tax is going to fall almost entirely upon the commercial undertakings who use petrol vehicles.' It was impossible to raise bus fares, he claimed, because of competition from the LCC's trams, 'which has the purse of the ratepayers behind it'.[42]

Despite this intervention, the government had its way and set up a Road Board to distribute the money raised by the taxes. The board was to be chaired by Sir George Gibb, who ceased to be the receiver of the Underground Railways and also gave up his directorship of the North Eastern Railway (NER). The secretary of the Road Board was to be the car-loving William Rees Jeffreys.

Stanley Spooner, the editor of the *Automotor Journal*, was well tuned in to the undercurrents of the motoring world. 'It has been a more or less open secret for some considerable time past,' he wrote 'that Mr Rees Jeffreys would be appointed to the position,' said Spooner, who praised his mastery of detail and extraordinary capacity for work.

The board members were mostly motorists. They included Rose, from the RAC, and John Macdonald, president of the Royal Scottish Automobile Club. 'The composition of the board', simpered Spooner, is 'eminently satisfactory'.[43]

The motor manufacturers cavilled about Gibb's railway connections but the most prescient objection came from the tramway industry. Tramways should be represented directly on the board 'if only to protect their existing rights and traffic,' said the *Light Railway and Tramway Journal*.

The absence of any tramway voice had an insidious influence on the Road Board's attitudes. In 1911 London's trams (both private and public) carried 765 million passengers, against the 340 million who travelled by London General's buses, so the composition of the board reflected a narrow segment of road users. The London General may have disliked the new taxes, but the Road Board was to prove to be a valuable ally.

William Rees Jeffreys, the leading light in the Roads Improvement Association and from 1910 secretary of the government's Roads Board. (Author's collection)

The real power on the board was concentrated in the hands of the paid officials. Apart from Gibb and Rees Jeffreys, the Road Board initially had a single part-time consulting engineer – who also happened to be vice-chairman of the Roads Improvement Association.

None of these men was a friend of the tram. The NER's services had been hit by competition from electric trams and Gibb, as chairman, had supported the Industrial Freedom League's campaign against rate-aided

Get out of my way: this was one of the postcards that William Rees Jeffreys submitted to the Royal Commission on London Traffic to illustrate how trams held up traffic in Brentford High Street. (Author's collection)

competition. The Roads Improvement Association regularly pilloried trams for obstructing traffic.

The Road Board decided, reasonably enough, that its main priority was to tackle the mud and dust problem, so most grants would tackle what it termed the 'road crust'. Its guidance on how it would distribute its funds specifically excluded giving grants to roads that had been surfaced with 'granite or other surfacing material suitable for heavy traffic'. Tramway operators favoured granite setts to meet their road maintenance obligations because they were easy to lay and long-lasting. So, this was code for excluding any road works that would benefit trams.

In an internal memorandum, Gibb spelt it out clearly.

It is motor traffic which must be principally kept in view in determining questions of distribution. It was the requirements of motor traffic and the damage done to roads by motor traffic which led to the creation of the fund, and the monies are derived from the taxation of motors and motor spirit.[44]

Political frustration: granite setts being laid for the new electric trams at Stockwell. The Road Board refused to give grants to roads paved with granite, the paving favoured by tramways. Effectively the Road Board wouldn't help tramways, but it would improve roads with bus routes. (London Picture Archive)

The Road Board's attitude towards trams became crystal clear towards the end of 1911. After more than a year of handing out grants, the county of London had yet to receive a penny. This was a deliberate policy, according to *The Times*. The Road Board would not do anything to aid the LCC's trams, 'especially as tramways are now in decline…Moreover, tramways are certainly the bane of the motor omnibus and of the ordinary motor and prejudicial to all users of free-wheeled traction'.

The Road Board and the Roads Improvement Association enjoyed close links, to the point where the Road Board often seemed to be an arm of the association embedded in government. The relationship became even closer when Lord Montagu joined the board following the death of Rose. The appointment was 'a wise one', judged the *Daily Telegraph*'s cycling correspondent, 'and is bound to give satisfaction to the Roads Improvement Association the council of which body Lord Montagu has been a member for many years. He has been one of the most regular attenders… and has done much useful work.'

The Roads Improvement Association had begun life in 1886, as a band of cyclists lobbying for better roads. But it had long since outgrown its origins. By 1912 the top four subscribers to the association were the Automobile Association, the RAC, the Society of Motor Manufacturers and Traders and the London General Omnibus company. A substantial slice of its income at the time was spent on a campaign to highlight the 'needless congestion caused by tramways' and particularly those tramways run by the LCC. This campaign was largely financed by unnamed 'special contributors', although it seems clear that the main beneficiary was the London General Omnibus Company.[45]

In January 1912 the Roads Improvement Association petitioned the Board of Trade about the obstruction that LCC trams caused to other traffic, calling for the number of daytime trams to be cut by up to half. Among the signatories of the petition were two Road Board engineers.

The petition stimulated a flurry of interest in the press. For Spooner it was 'a timely protest against the virtual monopoly of the street which the LCC has succeeded in establishing'. Running half-empty trams needlessly obstructed the streets, claimed *Commercial Motor*, a trade magazine devoted to buses and goods vehicles.

The daily papers took up the story. *The Times*, which since 1908 had been part of Lord Northcliffe's empire, stirred the cauldron with an article penned by one of its stable of anonymous contributors. 'The Roads Improvement Association,' was 'the leading association in all road and traffic matters' and the contributor lauded its excellent work for revealing that the LCC was running 'empty tramcars during less busy hours of the day.'

The *Evening News*, another member of Northcliffe's stable, followed this up with a series of six tram-bashing articles. The tram, it said, was out of date and should 'have been thrown on the scrap heap long ago' and it was evident, that 'the motor bus was the coming vehicle'. The articles highlighted declining takings on the trams and had the obligatory attack on municipal trading.

Of course, bus operators stood to pick up extra passengers if council trams were less frequent. It was, said *Municipal Journal*, 'a transparent piece of special pleading'. The motor bus enjoys the privilege of 'the free use of roads' and unlike trams did not have to pay rates on its bus routes. The magazine called on the industry to set up a 'Tramways Defence League'.

The trade magazine *Tramway and Railway World* echoed this call, urging the two tramway associations to form a united front to oppose the efforts of the motor lobby. 'The enemy is thundering at their gates and there is no time to lose.' The message was simple. A divided industry was a weaker one. 'If the tramway industry is to maintain its rights successfully it must stand as one solid unit.' It was a call that fell on deaf ears.

The motor bus may have been the coming vehicle but the bus operators were scarcely prospering. The London General was still in financial difficulties even after the merger with its rivals. Many of the buses it inherited – the ones that were glibly talked up as sweeping the trams off the road – were themselves swept off to the scrap heap.

The first standard London bus, the B-type, hit the streets in October 1910. It was the omnibus equivalent of the Ford Model T. Thanks to mass production, the bus

Fuming: one of the buses that the motoring lobby talked up as sweeping trams off the road pictured in the summer of 1910, with the driver seemingly about to be enveloped in smoke. (Bain News Service/Library of Congress)

cost just £300 – and was cheaper to run than previous motor buses. It was also much more reliable. The company celebrated its arrival by issuing its first bus map under the slogan 'Travel above ground – We carry you all the way', a sideswipe at the lack of trams in the city centre.

Sir Marcus Samuel, the founder of the oil company Shell Transport and Trading, which had a long-standing contract to supply petrol to the London General, forecast that the motor bus was the future and that the majority of trams would be scrapped in ten years' time.

The new bus certainly eased the company's difficulties but it did not solve them. The solution came in the form of yet another takeover, this time by the Underground Electric Railway Company, Gibb's old company. The London General became part of what became known as the Combine, a grouping that included London's tubes, buses and private sector trams.

But the motor bus needed good roads if it was to be successful. London had about 3,000 motor buses in 1912, more than any other city in the world. Paris had fewer than 1,000 of them, Berlin around 200 and there were maybe a dozen in Vienna. 'Continental municipalities were not willing to provide sufficiently good paving for motor omnibuses,' said Henry Gordon, a Progressive councillor on the LCC and civil engineer.

By 1912, discontent about the Road Board's administration was mounting. The board's annual income, which exceeded £1 million, vastly outweighed its spending. Under pressure from the LCC, the Road Board defended its policy. 'The Board do not look with favour on applications for grants,' Rees Jeffreys told the LCC, 'where the congestion is mainly due to local traffic and the existence of tramways.' After exchanges of letters stretching over more than a year, Rees Jeffreys said in a letter to the LCC, that the Road Board's policy was to make good 'the damage being done to the roads…by motor omnibuses and heavy motor vehicles'.[46]

So the board's policy boiled down to this. If heavy buses damaged the tramways or the roads they ran on, then the ratepayer had to cough up. But if buses damaged roads without tramways, the Road Board would pay to keep the buses running. 'The action of the Road Board was largely subversive of the council's policy,' said Gordon. The board seemed to be uncontrolled and the council's protests were 'absolutely futile'.

Some members of the Road Board did not bother to conceal their prejudices. 'The day of the tramway is over,' John Macdonald said in 1913. 'There would be very few laid down in the future – certainly none in large and busy towns.' The tramcar, he forecast, was destined to end up in a museum.

Meanwhile, the Road Board's erratic record was being probed by the Royal Commission on the Civil Service. Both Gibb and Rees Jeffreys gave evidence to the commission. The Road Board, observed one commissioner, had collected more than

£2 million and yet spent less than half that. Gibb told the commission that he had not noticed any criticism of the distribution of the road fund in London and when the commission asked to see the Road Board's minute book Rees Jeffreys brought along a few sheets of paper with a scrappy record of the past year's meetings.

The commission's verdict was damning. 'The oral evidence…was unsatisfactory, and the formal records…were most imperfect. The impression left with us was that the distribution of about one and a quarter million per annum…has hitherto rested in fact with the chairman.'[47]

Undoubtedly the Road Board's policy of improving the surface crust of roads paid off. Complaints about mud and dust virtually vanished – hugely aided by the decline in horse-drawn vehicles – the source of the mud and dust.

However, an equally long-lasting legacy was the Road Board's antipathy to tramways. In the struggle for supremacy between buses and trams the Road Board had tilted the balance against the tram. Although no one could have known it at the time this would prove to be an enduring bias.

Chapter 9

COSYING UP TO THE GENERAL

The outbreak of war in August 1914 brought a new set of problems for the capital's transport operators. For the London General, nearly half of its buses were requisitioned for the war effort, while more than half of its staff were enlisted. Petrol rationing also restricted bus services. The London County Council's operation wasn't so badly affected because it had fewer staff of military age – and an LCC tram wouldn't have been much use in the mud of Flanders.

The London General ran an advertising campaign underlining its war service. In a series of adverts entitled 'Little Notes on "General" History', the company trumpeted how it had supplied more than a thousand horses for the Boer War and in the present war more than '1,250 General motor buses are rendering good service at the front' – illustrating how its buses were indispensable in war and peace.

It all made for good advertising copy, but it wasn't strictly accurate. The popular image, which persists even today, of London General's latest B-type buses carrying troops to the front in Flanders is largely false. Only a small number of whole buses were taken across the channel. It was the chassis that the Army wanted, so it could put commercial vehicle bodies on them and carry stores and other supplies as well as people. Most of the redundant bus bodies were stored in London.

Furthermore, the company wasn't quite as altruistic as it liked to appear. The London General had initiated negotiations with the government on the outbreak of war. The company was 'not unwilling for this commandeering…as they knew they would be fittingly compensated', wrote the MP Wilfred Ashley, who led a short-lived campaign to highlight wartime waste.

Ashley said that by the end of 1915 the government had paid the London General nearly £800,000 and was continuing to pay the company at least £15,000 a year. He wasn't accusing the London General of profiteering, this was simply the result of the government's ludicrously wasteful compensation scheme. Ashley calculated that the compensation was so generous that more than half of this money had been squandered. 'We seem to have gratuitously gone out of our way to make the company a present of £450,000,' Ashley observed.[48]

The cash injection was certainly welcome and the bus company's finances seem to have been relatively healthy during the war. Precise figures are difficult to come by because coincidentally the Combine – London's bus-to-tube conglomerate – adopted a new accounting system, pooling the income of its various subsidiaries, which as the *Financial Times* noted, 'carefully conceals the achievements of the separate concerns.'

During the war the London General developed close links with the government, and in particular the Ministry of Munitions. Engineers from the bus company, including Frank Searle, the man who developed the B-type bus, were embedded in the ministry, part of the team that developed the first tanks. In 1916 Albert Stanley, the head of the Combine, was drafted in to take charge of the ministry's mechanical transport section. These links gave the General access to the government, a privilege that wasn't available to the operators of municipal trams. And Stanley was not shy of using his position to benefit his company.

One opportunity to enhance the London General's position came with demands to improve transport for munitions workers. The war effort saw an enormous increase in the number of people working at munitions factories. The workers needed both lodgings and transport to get them to work. The problem was particularly acute around Woolwich, where the Royal Arsenal supplied virtually all the Army's

The London General's B-type bus, introduced in 1910, was pictured towards the end of its life in 1924. Its success made the General the go-to company when the government wanted engineers to prosecute the war effort. (Collection John Scott-Morgan)

ammunition. At the start of the war, nearly 11,000 people were employed at the Royal Arsenal. By May 1917 the workforce had reached 75,000, of which around 28,000 were women, known as 'canary girls' because their skin went yellow after prolonged handling of TNT.

All these workers had to live somewhere. Much of the land around Woolwich was still fairly rural and the government met the demand for lodgings with a mixture of new housing estates and temporary huts. The local buses and trams struggled to carry the crowds of workers to the factory and home again after their 12-hour shifts. An official inquiry conducted in 1916 found that fatigue was common among workers because of the time spent travelling in crowded buses and trams.

Despite wartime censorship, the discontent surfaced in newspapers with threats of a work-to-rule and it was said that workers were leaving their jobs after a week or two because of housing problems.

In February 1916 the LCC announced plans to double its tracks in Woolwich so that it could run more trams. In July the Ministry of Munitions announced that the London General was to start two new bus services to ease the problem. The LCC was suspicious. James Gilbert, a London Liberal MP and LCC councillor, who took a keen interest in the capital's transport problem, wanted to know if the ministry was paying for these buses. His question was met with an outright denial. 'No arrangement has been made…as regards any guaranteed payment for the two new omnibus services.'[49]

There was only one problem with this answer. It was entirely false. The ministry had already begun to pay the London General for its bus services, in a secret deal that was negotiated with the ministry by Stanley's trusted lieutenant at the Combine, Frank Pick. It would take two years before the ministry admitted to this secret subsidy.

The government also helped the London General in other ways. The outbreak of war had hastened the end of the Road Board. The Treasury had taken over the receipts from fuel tax and the road fund licence in 1915 leaving the Road Board in limbo, although the board – with Treasury approval – was still able to make grants from its accumulated funds.

Between 1915 and March 1917 the Road Board made seven grants and loans for improving roads in London to take heavy vehicles – which would have helped both the London General's buses and lorries making deliveries to the arsenal. All of these roads, without exception, were in Woolwich.

However, the full scale of the subsidy to the London General only began to emerge much later. After months of probing by the indefatigable Gilbert, the government finally conceded that the London General was being subsidised.

Many of the subsidised services were completely unsuited to the needs of munitions workers. There was no attempt to provide extra buses for the change of shifts. The services included the number 15, which ran from Ladbroke Grove in West London to East Ham, on the north side of the Thames. Woolwich Arsenal was on the south bank. On a clear day, passengers on the top deck of a number 15 might just be able to glimpse the chimney tops of the Royal Arsenal on the far bank of the Thames. Another subsidised service did a tour of the Kent countryside.

The London General was the sole beneficiary of this largesse. No other tram or bus operators, including Thomas Tilling, which ran several bus services in the Woolwich area, received a subsidy for running their services. In all, 13,500 workers at Woolwich used the buses. By November 1918 the subsidy had cost the taxpayer £98,000, a figure that did not include the Road Board's smaller grants. The final bill was expected to be higher.[50]

The subsidy vexed the capital's municipal tram operators. The LCC had spent more than £10,000 doubling its tracks in the Woolwich area so that they could put on more trams – although the Ministry of Munitions agreed to pay a quarter of the cost. The LCC had also put on extra trams at its own expense to carry munitions workers and help the war effort.

The municipal operators wrote to Winston Churchill, the Minister of Munitions to complain. The trams were more deserving of help. During rush hours trams passing in front of the Arsenal could carry six times as many passengers as the buses. They were palmed off with a junior minister, who was made to endure an uncomfortable meeting.

The municipal operators felt that this clandestine compact was intended to give the London General a competitive edge when normal service resumed. The subsidy finally finished at the end of November – 19 days after the armistice.

The minister floundered, hinting that the ministry had a moral obligation to see that the General did not lose out because of its efforts to support the war. He never said as much but he implied it was quid pro quo for the General's help at the front. But this was largely a smokescreen. More to the point was the cosy relationship that the General had developed with the Ministry of Munitions.

Chapter 10
ALBERT STANLEY'S WARTIME MANOEUVRES

In December 1916 Herbert Asquith's largely Liberal coalition government collapsed after the Conservatives withdrew their support following the ill-fated Gallipoli campaign. It was replaced by a more Conservative-leaning coalition. Asquith – Squiffy as he was irreverently but accurately known because of his fondness for fine wine – was replaced as prime minister by David Lloyd George, who had been an energetic and effective Minister of Munitions.

Behind the scenes, the man who pulled the strings that caused the change of government was the press baron Lord Northcliffe, the former Alfred Harmsworth. Northcliffe was hugely influential. He controlled roughly 40 per cent of the morning papers at the time and his empire included heavy-weight titles, like *The Times*, the *Daily Mirror*, the *Sunday Times*, the *Evening News*, and his favoured attack dog the *Daily Mail*.

Northcliffe helped to shape the new government and encouraged Lloyd George to strengthen his government by bringing in people from outside the world of politics, people with business expertise. He secured a place in the cabinet for Albert Stanley, who became President of the Board of Trade.[51]

Stanley resigned from his positions at the Combine to take up his post in government. He had a wide-ranging portfolio at the Board of Trade. Not only was he the minister for merchant shipping, gas and water but he was also responsible for electricity, railways and tramways – industries that the Combine had a direct interest in. And these commercial interests were uppermost in his mind. Concealing his intentions behind the smokescreen of war, Stanley concocted a scheme for the Combine to take control of the London County Council tramways.

At the beginning of November 1917, Stanley met the two tramway associations to tell them about his plan. Even before the outbreak of war, the government had foreseen the need to eliminate wasteful competition on the railways and it set up a committee to coordinate the railways. Following this precedent, Stanley now wanted to coordinate the nation's tramways.

Within days of this meeting, rumours began to circulate that Stanley was going to set up a new body to take control of all transport in London, that is the Combine's buses, trams and trains as well as the trams run by the LCC and other municipalities. Stanley launched a classic public relations exercise, drip-feeding titbits of information to sympathetic newspapers to soften up public opinion for a controversial measure.

'Considerable interest has been aroused by the statement that the government contemplate transferring the control of the London tramway system from the London County Council to a body to be set up by the Board of Trade,' reported the *Daily Telegraph*. The newspaper dispatched a reporter to the Board of Trade to tease out the truth behind this rumour.

The plan, as the reporter discovered, was more far-reaching. A new body 'will unify the interests of nearly all the tramway systems of the country and ought to be extremely beneficial both as regards traffic and finances'. The official assured the *Telegraph* that there were no plans to take control of buses.[52]

The next day the *Sunday Times* learnt more about the plan from a 'semi-official source'. The source claimed this was not a government initiative and that it was 'large provincial tramway owners' who had asked the Board of Trade to help them cope with the demands of the Ministry of Munitions to carry munitions workers.

The official announcement came the next week. Stanley announced that he was setting up a new committee to ration supplies of scarce materials for tramways and Stanley's close colleague, James Devonshire, was to chair the committee.

Suspicions about the real purpose of this new committee were quick to surface. Devonshire was managing director of the London United, Metropolitan Electric and South Metropolitan Electric Tramways. All three companies were part of the Combine. If the committee rationed supplies to tramways, would Devonshire favour companies at the expense of the municipal sector? 'If…the railway precedent is followed, municipal tramways on certain routes may be suspended without the local authorities which own them having a voice in the matter,' warned *Municipal Journal*.[53]

Devonshire had a fraught relationship with the LCC going back to the days when he ran a horse tram company in north London. 'To put the matter quite plainly,' commented *Municipal Journal*, 'the nomination of Mr Devonshire…is not acceptable to municipal tramways undertakings.'

Ever alert to attacks on London's municipal trams, James Gilbert tabled a parliamentary question to probe the committee's purpose and question Devonshire's suitability. 'Is it not a fact,' Gilbert asked Stanley, 'that one of the large tramway companies with which Mr. Devonshire is connected is now in the hands of the Official Receiver?' Is the idea behind this committee, he asked, to help insolvent companies which are short of rolling stock and tramway material?

It was a well-directed shaft. Devonshire was the managing director of the London United Tramways Company – and the company's previous managing director was none other than Albert Stanley. The London United was teetering on the edge of

The London County Council's well-maintained tramways made them an attractive take-over target for Albert Stanley's Combine. (Bain News Service/Library of Congress)

bankruptcy. The company had issued £16 million of bonds, known as debentures. In June 1917 it had been forced to call in the receiver because it was unable to pay the interest due on these bonds.

The previous year, the company was so short of rails for track repairs that it had been forced to rip up rails on another part of its system and recycle them. Its failure to keep its track in good repair was the cause of frequent complaints. The wretched state of the track reflected years of past neglect and a failure to set aside enough money for depreciation.

The company's 'failure to provide properly for maintenance in the past is now seriously affecting its earning capacity,' said *Truth*. It was a damning commentary on the stewardship of Devonshire and Stanley.

The LCC, on the other hand, had enough material in stock to be able to double its tracks in Woolwich to aid munitions workers. And far from needing a receiver to sort out its finances, the LCC had made a modest surplus despite the war.

So, control of the capital's efficient municipal trams was to be put in the hands of managers who had brought the London United Tramways to the verge of bankruptcy. Or as one local councillor told the *Acton Gazette* that November, 'since the watchword of the government was efficiency, to appoint the managing director of the most ramshackle tramway anywhere around London…was a strange action.'

The local papers certainly thought that Devonshire would use his position to aid his ailing tramway by requisitioning rails from the municipal sector. The company's main route from Shepherd's Bush to Uxbridge was threatened with closure because of the state of the track. Stanley's Board of Trade wrote to the LCC warning that 'it might be necessary in some cases' to transfer rails from the LCC to the London United.

Herbert Morrison, the energetic secretary of the London Labour Party, was highly critical of Stanley's committee. Morrison could spot a political sleight-of-hand when he saw one. Portraying the Combine as a monster trying to strangle the life out of the LCC, Morrison said Londoners should be 'alive to the necessity, not only of defending municipal tramways, but of assuming the offensive against the London traffic combine'.

The committee's purpose became a little clearer when the Board of Trade announced its terms of reference in February 1918. Apart from ensuring a fair division of scarce supplies – or enabling private companies to raid municipal stores – the committee's remit had become considerably broader. It could recommend closing tramways to improve the supply of scarce materials.

Devonshire toured the country to sell the plan to tram operators. But he wasn't the most tactful of salesmen. In Liverpool he accused tramways with stockpiles of rails of being 'hoarders' and he warned that some undertakings might be 'partly or wholly discontinued in order that material might be transferred to undertakings of greater importance'.

At a meeting in London, Stanley's scheme met with a chilly reception. James Gilbert pointed out that the original intention of the committee had been to ensure the fair distribution of scarce materials – not for the council to close down 'any part or section of their tramways'. There was cross-party unity at the LCC. The Conservative chairman of the council's highways committee said he shared Gilbert's anxiety.

By the spring of 1918 the German U-boat blockade was taking its toll. Ships were being sunk faster than they could be built. The government introduced drastic restrictions to husband scarce resources. In May, the Board of Trade issued an edict rationing tram services. All tramways, private and municipal, south of a line from the Wash to Bristol had to cut their electricity consumption by 15 per cent.

Even then, Stanley still found ways to bolster the Combine's position. The ever-watchful Gilbert spotted that Ilford had been forced to cut its council trams while the company running buses in the area was going to increase its services.[54] Gilbert challenged Stanley about it. Stanley admitted he knew about the tram cuts, but professed ignorance about the buses. He was, after all, a busy man and couldn't be expected to know that the London General was to run buses over the route that Ilford was being forced to cut. He was shamed into promising to talk to the bus company.

Harried by Gilbert in parliament and vehemently opposed by municipal operators, Stanley's attempt at a power grab was dead in the water. There was, however, one final twist to the story. By the end of the war the talk in the corridors of power was of nationalising the railways.

Would a similar recipe work for the nation's tramways? If so, Devonshire's tramways committee was in a good position to be the nucleus of any future organisation. Seemingly in preparation for an enhanced role after the war, the tramways committee appointed its first full-time engineer, on Devonshire's casting vote, the week after Armistice Day. He was the chief engineer of the London United and Metropolitan Electric Tramways companies.

In the end, Stanley's attempt to seize control of the LCC's trams fizzled out. But he still nurtured the ambition, setting the stage for conflicts to come.

Chapter 11

THE LONDON COUNTY COUNCIL SPIES AN OPPORTUNITY

In February 1919 Albert Stanley was taken ill. A deadly third wave of Spanish 'flu was sweeping the country and nearly half the members of the cabinet were on the sick list. Stanley's indisposition meant that he missed a series of cabinet meetings, including one on 19 February, when ministers discussed setting up a new super ministry, a Ministry of Ways and Communications.

David Lloyd George's coalition government had won the post-war general election by a landslide. But the real winners were the Conservatives who won 379 seats. Lloyd George's party, the Liberals, were heavy losers, split between those who supported the coalition and those who did not. It was a watershed moment in British politics and the Liberal Party went into steep decline.

The new cabinet reflected the balance of power in the House of Commons. Most of the ministers were Conservatives, with only a handful of Liberals, like Winston Churchill, remaining. Lloyd George continued his strategy of creating a business government, seeking out captains of industry and turning them into ministers. The new ministry would include transport by air, sea and land, including railways, tramways and electricity supply, responsibilities that had previously been part of the Board of Trade. Eric Geddes was earmarked to become the new super minister.

Geddes was a railwayman, a product of the NER's pioneering management training scheme. He had an impressive war record. When Lloyd George became secretary of state for war, he called on Geddes to 'come and put transport right in France'. The army had been relying on a fleet of 70,000 motor lorries. But the narrow wheels broke up the roads and lorries, weighed down by heavy loads of munitions, got bogged down in the Flanders mud. So, Geddes laid a network of light railways to ensure that the guns at the front didn't run out of shells.

The new super ministry would take over the Road Board, which would be abolished and it would be responsible for the railways. One of the lessons learned from the war was that unfettered competition was wasteful, notably on the railways. So the bill setting up the ministry also included a scheme to nationalise the railways.

The bill horrified the motoring classes and in particular the former secretary of the Road Board, William Rees Jeffreys, who increasingly espoused a conspiracy theory that blamed the railways for the failure of the Road Board. An awkward character with boundless self-regard who was often at odds with his fellow road lobbyists, Rees Jeffreys had retired from the Road Board at the end of the war and was now a free agent, but one who was still well-informed on events inside government.

The emergence of the road lobby as a major political force can be traced back to the events of January 1919. Rees Jeffreys, before he left the Road Board, set up a series of meetings with key figures in the motoring world. They culminated with a meeting on 15 January when the AA and the Society of Motor Manufacturers and Traders agreed to stump up £1,000 each to finance a new group, the Motor Legislation Committee. William Joynson-Hicks, the Conservative MP and lawyer for the London General, chaired the committee and Rees Jeffreys was its vice-chairman. Its first task was to oppose the bill for a super ministry because, the committee said, a railway-dominated ministry would be disastrous for road transport.[55]

The plan for a super ministry meant taking away responsibilities from the Board of Trade. No minister likes to preside over a shrinking empire and Stanley was no exception. Motorists tried to capitalise on this disgruntlement and lobbied Stanley to oppose the plans for a railway-dominated ministry. Writing on behalf of the RAC, Rees Jeffreys sent a memorandum to Stanley arguing that it was essential to keep roads separate from railways.

Rees Jeffreys, who mixed socially with Frank Pick, Stanley's right-hand man at the Combine, knew he was pushing an open door. Laid low by 'flu, Stanley submitted a memorandum to the February cabinet meeting, in which he ingeniously argued that councils would object strongly to 'anything that had the appearance of being controlled by railway interests'.[56]

The road lobby mounted a sophisticated campaign against the plan for a super ministry. The Motor Legislation Committee set up its own group in parliament, which was also chaired by Joynson-Hicks and which gained the support of 280 MPs.

As the campaign moved up a gear, the committee commissioned a series of articles for local newspapers about the iniquities of the new ministry from John Foster Fraser, a travel author and the first man to circumnavigate the world on a bicycle. These days Fraser would be termed a celebrity influencer, someone who could mould public opinion. Fraser called for the resurrection of the Road Board.

Shortly before the bill had its crucial second reading debate in the House of Commons, Geddes wrote to Lloyd George, who was in Paris for the peace talks, with his assessment of the bill's prospects. The road lobby, he said, was 'noisy but I think not very formidable'.[57] How wrong he was.

The arithmetic in the Commons was stacked against Geddes. The Motor Legislation Committee's supporters were overwhelmingly Conservative and had the numbers to defeat the government. The bill was badly mauled during its passage through parliament. Railway nationalisation was dropped and even the name of the bill was changed, to become the Transport Bill. Despite these tribulations a new ministry was set up – called the Ministry of Transport – and Geddes became the minister.

During the debates on the Transport Bill, Geddes, who had been impressed by the contribution of light railways during the war, praised the modern, electrified, municipal tramways. They were, he said, one part of the transport industry that was healthy; 'undertakings that earn 7 per cent on their capital'. Tramways, said Geddes, were an 'increasingly important method of transport along our roads and I hope eventually through the country.'[58]

With a sympathetic minister in Whitehall, one who believed trams had a bright future, the London County Council saw an opportunity to push its tramlines into the very centre of London.

All aboard: a railway strike in 1919 coupled with the postwar shortages of buses increased pressure on the trams, which at times struggled to cope, seemingly leaving mostly women passengers behind. (Author's collection)

While the transport bill was receiving a battering in parliament there was serious trouble on the streets. There were post-war shortages of buses, trams and trains and passengers shoved and fought to secure a seat. In the evening rush hour, an average of 30 to 60 people reportedly fainted on tube trains from Westminster to Barking. And fares were going up. Irate passengers were paying more for less.

To the leader writer of the *Daily Mail* – which could normally be counted on to be friendly to free enterprise – the main culprit was the Combine. 'It is for private enterprise to prove that the business of public traffic is still not too big for it to tackle with success…The existing discomfort and danger of our overcrowded tubes cannot continue. Public patience is nearly exhausted.'

On the evening of 19 May a cross-party group of London MPs met the local government minister. Leading the deputation were the Liberal MP James Gilbert and the Conservative William Kennedy Jones, a newspaperman turned politician, who had been Lord Northcliffe's second-in-command for more than two decades. The minister agreed that a select committee should investigate the problem.

The select committee was to be chaired by Kennedy Jones, 'K.J.' as he was known to his friends. An irascible man, Kennedy Jones was Northcliffe's hatchet man and one of the most hated journalists on Fleet Street. Even after becoming an MP, he remained close to his former boss.

The committee worked swiftly, publishing their report at the end of July. Kennedy Jones was less than impressed by the Combine's evidence, which was given by Frank Pick. The Combine's antagonism to the LCC and its plans 'would not be entertained by any executive authority which aimed at making London transport effective and efficient'. The committee's core recommendation was to end the chaos by setting up a 'supreme traffic authority', with members from local councils, who were likely to be pro-tram, but no members from the Combine.[59]

The report also slammed the veto – parliament's notorious standing order 22 – which effectively prevented MPs from discussing plans for tramways in central London. As a result of the veto, trams had to be reversed at termini on the edge of the centre – a potent cause of congestion.

Would the politicians at Westminster now be more sympathetic to seeing trams on the streets of central London? It wasn't the first time that the LCC had submitted plans to parliament to extend its tram rails into the city centre, but they had previously been dismissed out of hand. Finally it seemed that central London tramways might get a fair hearing.

In October 1919 the LCC unveiled an ambitious plan to build a series of new tramways. Roughly half of the schemes – costing around £4 million – were earmarked for its forthcoming parliamentary bill, the rest were a wish list for future bills. The core of the plan was to eliminate the dead ends around central London.

Reversing trams at these dead ends cut their operational efficiency and hindered passengers who were forced to change onto buses, or to take a tube. At the dead end at Victoria as many as 84 trams an hour had to reverse at busy times. The plan would remove half a dozen of these dead ends. (See map in colour section, plate 2.)

The campaign to derail the LCC's plan began before the council had even approved it. Letters appeared in the *Daily Mail* calling for trams to be scrapped altogether. The paper appealed to its readers' xenophobia and denounced the tram as Teutonic. 'Trams are essentially un-English. They are very German and rather American,' wrote a *Mail* journalist under the heading 'obsolete trams'.

On the eve of the council meeting, an editorial in *The Times* called on the LCC to drop its plans. Trams, claimed the paper, were 'survivals from the past' and city

A tram leaving the terminus at Victoria. In LCC days this busy terminus handled seven tram routes. In peak hours it took less than a minute to reverse a tram. (John Meredith/Online Transport Archive)

tramways were doomed. The bus operators were ecstatic. It was 'tangible evidence' of our effective bus propaganda, proclaimed *Commercial Motor*.[60] More prosaically it was tangible evidence that Lord Northcliffe owned *The Times*.

The *Daily Mail* stepped up its assault with a broadside blaming trams for the council's precarious finances. The antiquated tramway 'is in the process of being superseded by…the motor omnibus'. A bus was safer because 'it picks its passengers up at the side of the street and puts them down there; the tramway car deposits them in the middle of a stream of traffic.'

On 4 November 1919 the LCC narrowly approved the plans, but not before several councillors had lauded the virtues of buses. Isidore Salmon, a Conservative councillor for Hammersmith and managing director of J. Lyons, the nation's favourite purveyor of cakes and biscuits, and owner of the Lyons Corner House chain of tearooms, said buses were more flexible than trams. 'In fifteen or twenty years' time the trams…would be a liability,' he said.

'Tramcars will be an obsolete form of traction in England,' claimed William Bull, the MP for Hammersmith in an article in the *Evening News*. 'The tramways are doomed and London will be the first place in which they are abandoned.'[61] Bull had close ties with the Combine. His intervention was significant because he was the shop steward of London's Conservative MPs. The LCC was in for a stiff fight if it was to persuade MPs to back its plans.

Given the boroughs' hostility to trams in central London, the schemes would inevitably attract the veto. But the LCC was prepared. In November the council met Geddes. No other municipal tramway was affected by the veto, Geddes was told, who was sympathetic. The upshot of this meeting was that the LCC and Geddes came to an understanding: they would work together to sidestep the veto.

Geddes's first move was to set up a new Advisory Committee on London Traffic, once again chaired by Kennedy Jones. In his formal letter to Kennedy Jones, Geddes stressed the need for 'immediate and effective action' to tackle traffic congestion.

The London boroughs, alarmed at the prospect of losing their veto, called an emergency meeting. They voiced strong disapproval 'of any interference with the rights of local authorities' and they urged the government to do nothing. 'It looks as if the end of the veto is in sight,' commented *Municipal Journal*. 'The London borough councils must console themselves with the fact that they have been able to retain the privilege for so long.'[62]

Not all parts of the government wanted trams in central London. The plan's most controversial feature was a new tramway along the eastern edge of Hyde Park. Shortly after the LCC met Geddes, the Office of Works, which was in charge of the Royal Parks, briefed newspapers that it was not going to allow trams in its park. The Office of Works refused to allow the LCC to post notices in Hyde Park publicising its plans – a formal legal requirement. It was a storm in a teacup, as the Office of Works itself conceded. 'Our refusal…merely indicates that we oppose the bill,' an official told the *Daily Herald*. In effect, it was a ploy to whip up public hostility to running trams in central London.

The intervention certainly had the desired effect. The *Automotor Journal* accused the LCC of lacking imagination and 'a sense of decency' for wanting to run 'their infernal double-decked atrocities' in Hyde Park.

The controversy breathed new life into the West End Tramways Opposition Association, which had been moribund since the battle for Westminster Bridge. The decline in equine transport meant the argument that trams would frighten the horses no longer carried much weight, but the association could still play on the fears of its class base by warning that trams would cut property values. The association opposed the LCC's plans on the grounds that trams were obsolete.

In all, more than 80 petitions were lodged against the LCC's bill. They included one from the Motor Legislation Committee and another from the main motoring organisations – the AA and the RAC.

There were also petitions from frontagers, that is people and businesses with premises along a prospective route. These were often put-up jobs. 'In many cases frontagers' petitions have been really organised on behalf of the omnibus companies,' according to one King's Counsel with extensive experience of tramway bills.

How trams would destroy the tranquillity of Hyde Park. A realistic *Daily Mirror* mock-up, illustrating not just the impact of trams on the park but how the Northcliffe press had honed its propaganda skills during the First World War. (British Library Collection)

Certainly the London General loomed large in the behind-the-scenes efforts to stifle the tram plans, lending practical and financial support to third-party petitioners. Its board agreed that 'all necessary steps would be taken in due course to protect the company's interest'. It backed this policy by agreeing to finance the London and Provincial Omnibus Owners' Association to the tune of ten shillings per bus. In 1920 the General owned 2,675 buses on average, so the ten-bob-a-bus pledge was worth more than £1,300. The Combine also paid 250 guineas to a parliamentary agent for what was described as 'certain very confidential work which at the moment it was not desirable to further specify'. The agent was Dixon H. Davies, who had been prominent in the old Industrial Freedom League.[63]

Further competition from the LCC's trams was a touchy subject for the Combine. The Combine was in the midst of a financial crisis and was in secret talks with the government about a state takeover. Officials from the Combine and the Ministry of Transport were in daily discussions, according to a *Daily Mail* exclusive. Albert Stanley, who had been created Lord Ashfield in the New Year's honours following his resignation from the Board of Trade, said that the Combine was facing a loss of £2.6 million.[64]

The story had broken over the weekend. The normally publicity-hungry Lord Ashfield was unavailable. The ministry and the Combine had been caught on the hop and their responses were hurried, embarrassed and changing. By Monday's papers, the ministry conceded it was 'making preparations'.

The negotiations were difficult. A major stumbling block was that the ministry had no legal power to take over the buses. And the London General, hit by rising petrol prices, was responsible for 70 per cent of the Combine's losses. Its problems were compounded because it was now running more buses to compete with the LCC's trams. In January alone the General's buses clocked up a loss of £90,000.

The General had a lot to lose if the LCC's tram plans went ahead. The company's buses reached the parts London's trams couldn't reach. And the central routes, where buses ruled the road, were among the London General's best earners. Haemorrhaging cash, the company could ill afford to lose this monopoly.

In March 1920, in the run-up to the parliamentary debate, a senior, but unnamed, London General official gave an exclusive interview to a London evening paper. 'With many of our fleet at the front, the tramways did well during the war, but I think the County Council are now coming to the conclusion that the conveyance which is restricted to the use of metals in the middle of the road is obsolete,' claimed the official, arguing that buses met the public's demand for travel between North and South London.

In the meantime, the Advisory Committee on London Traffic report was published. The second Kennedy Jones report was not significantly different from the select committee's report. It called for a central authority to control London's transport and an end to the veto.

The future of trams in central London was finally sealed in the House of Commons on the evening of 22 April 1920. The subject of the debate was an arcane technicality: the suspension of standing order 22. James Gilbert, the Liberal MP, complained that the standing order prevented MPs from giving the LCC's plans a fair hearing, or indeed any hearing. He also revealed that a cabal of eight London MPs planned to thwart the suspension. Gilbert didn't identify the MPs. But he didn't need to. Bull was plainly a key organiser and Frederick Banbury, a veteran of the battle of Westminster Bridge, was a prominent heckler of pro-tram speakers.

The turning point in the debate came when Herbert Nield got up to speak. Nield was the Conservative MP for Ealing, a constituency served by the buses, trams and tubes of the Combine. Nield had a letter from Kennedy Jones, who couldn't attend the debate because of a constituency engagement.

Kennedy Jones executed what in Fleet Street is known as a 'reverse ferret'. He had chaired two committees. Both had denounced the veto. Now he torpedoed the move to suspend the veto. In his letter, he said the veto 'must remain as it is until the whole subject can be dealt with under the auspices of one single traffic authority'.

What prompted Kennedy Jones's change of heart is unclear. However, the prospect of trams running through central London horrified his fellow London Conservative MPs and ran directly counter to the editorial line of Northcliffe papers, like the *Daily Mail*. Given his political allegiances and his continuing closeness to Northcliffe, he was plainly susceptible to a bit of arm-twisting.

From this point on the LCC's hopes visibly evaporated. The government's support suddenly seemed half-hearted. Geddes was nowhere to be seen. 'Where is he?' heckled one MP. In his place Geddes sent a junior minister, who tried unsuccessfully to bolster the LCC's case. But the absence of Geddes was more telling than anything the junior minister said. The vote was lost overwhelmingly by almost two to one. Among those voting to keep the standing order were Bull and Joynson-Hicks.

The debate marked the end of the LCC's attempts to extend its trams into central London. The wealthy denizens of Park Lane would never have to put up with council trams disfiguring the eastern edge of Hyde Park. It would be another forty years before Park Lane was turned into a dual carriageway and the eastern edge of the park was covered with a layer of tarmac.

Chapter 12

PIRACY ON THE HIGH STREETS

On Saturday 5 August 1922, the first day of a chilly August bank holiday weekend, Londoners were treated to a novel sensation. A spanking new Leyland bus painted in a mouth-watering chocolate colour began taking passengers on trips around London, undercutting the ticket price of a London General omnibus. It was the opening salvo in what would become a struggle to challenge the Combine's monopoly.

It took a few days for Fleet Street to notice the outbreak of the bus war. But on the following Tuesday a reporter from the *Daily Herald* caught up with the chocolate bus in Parliament Square. The *Herald's* reporter found Arthur Partridge – the part-owner and conductor – standing on the pavement next to the bus attracting crowds like a showman barking at a fairground. Parked immediately behind Partridge's bus was a red one belonging to the London General.

'This way,' shouted Partridge. 'Never mind the others! We've got no American money behind us. Come inside.' The *Herald's* reporter duly climbed on board. The bus set off for Westminster Bridge, followed closely by the General's bus. The reporter interviewed Partridge in the lulls between collecting fares and was regaled with tales of the General's bully-boy tactics. For the General was all for the principle of free enterprise – except where it affected the company's monopoly.[65]

The next day the reporter again caught up with the Chocolate Express, as the bus was soon dubbed. This time the bus had two General shadows, one running just in front, one immediately behind. The sight of a General sandwich with a chocolate filling gave rise to a mixture of amusement and indignation among passers-by.

For most Londoners, the contest was comic relief from the daily drudgery of the post-war metropolis. 'There's a new sport for Londoners,' proclaimed the *Daily Herald*, which followed the story closely to make the most of its scoop. 'It's called chasing the Chocolate Bus. Everybody's playing at it, from the humour-loving cockney to the dear old lady who lives Belgravia way.'

The spectacle continued for the rest of the week. People cheered and waved as the Chocolate Express made its way down the Strand. The owners played up to their

The Chocolate Express was the first pirate bus. One of the company's buses pictured in Trafalgar Square in 1929. (©TfL from the London Transport Museum collection)

new-found fame and on Friday they hoisted their battle-standard on the bus – a Jolly Roger flag. 'We have nailed our colours to the mast,' the crew told reporters.

The contest brought out the British fondness for the underdog and the sympathy for war veterans – for the bus's owners were all ex-servicemen. 'Some people openly say that it is a disgrace to try and chase a little 'un out of business like this,' reported the *Daily Herald*. A British Legion branch passed a resolution praising the 'public-spirited enterprise of our three fellow ex-servicemen'.

Partridge matched the profile of the pirate perfectly. Before the war he and his two associates had been motor cab drivers. During the war they served in the army. After the war they clubbed together, sold their taxis, and bought a bus. It was a family affair. When reporters visited the garage in Battersea, they found Partridge under the bus oiling the mechanical parts while his son polished the brass.

Meanwhile, the General changed tactics. It doubled the number of buses on the Victoria to Liverpool Street run, the route normally taken by the Chocolate Express. At this stage, public opinion was firmly on the side of the underdog and there were reports of passengers slashing the seats of the General's buses.

From this small beginning, the number of pirates proliferated. By February 1923 there were a dozen pirate operators in London; by April the number had grown to seventeen, with Admirals and a Primrose as well as the original Chocolate Express. Brightly painted buses began to appear all over the capital. By the end of 1924 there were close to 500 pirate buses on the streets of London.

In many ways the pirates were repeating the success of jitneys in the United States. Sometime in 1914, an enterprising motorist started stopping at queues for streetcars in Los Angeles and offering to take prospective passengers for a jitney – an old name for a nickel. The idea spread like wildfire. The jitneys creamed off the profitable traffic leaving the streetcars to run at unprofitable times of day. The balance sheets of the streetcar companies soon suffered.

The pirates' initial target was the London General. But bigger interests were lurking in the background. The London bus market was huge and it was largely tied up. The London General bought its buses from AEC – the Associated Equipment

Bus jam: pirate buses and a flood of competing London General vehicles jostle for passengers while clogging up Trafalgar Square in the summer of 1925. (Jeoffry Spence Collection/Railway & Canal Historical Society)

Company – which was part of the Combine. The Chocolate Express ran buses made by Leyland, as did several other pirates. Other bus manufacturers, such as Daimler and Dennis, saw the pirates as a way to gain a toehold in the lucrative London market.

The General's chief tactic in its war with the pirates was to flood the streets with buses, in a bid to use their superior financial muscle to push the pirates out of business. The extra buses clogged the streets, producing a crop of headlines about 'traffic chaos'. Pirate buses were overwhelmingly a London problem. Outside London councils could refuse to license buses if they were likely to cause congestion.

Opposition to the independents – as the pirates preferred to be called – from the established operators was only to be expected. But the pirates also drew criticism from trade unions. The *Daily Herald*, the Labour Party's paper, had initially supported the Chocolate Express. But the reluctance of the buccaneering bus operators to recognise trade unions led Ernest Bevin, the transport workers' leader and a future foreign secretary, to back the Combine in its struggles against the pirates. It was 'sheer nonsense', said Bevin, to talk of the benefits of competition. The Combine was efficient, served the public well and treated its workers fairly, he said. 'It is rare

The Central company was one of more than 200 pirate operators to run buses in London. Its first bus took to the road in March 1923. The company was absorbed by the London General in 1928. (Jeoffry Spence Collection/Railway & Canal Historical Society)

nowadays,' commented the *Sunday Times*, 'that one hears from a Labour leader a single word of business sense.'[66]

The General continued its aggressive tactics to the point where its drivers were fined for dangerous driving after physically forcing pirates off the road. That was embarrassing for the company because Herbert Blain, its operating manager, who acquiesced in the tactics, had taken the lead in founding the London Safety First Council – a body set up to improve road safety. There can be no doubt that Blain and the Combine's top managers knew what they were doing.

Meanwhile, the pirates increasingly turned their attention to the Combine's tramways. It was an uncharacteristically crestfallen Lord Ashfield who presented the financial results for 1923. So long as the Combine's trams had operated 'in close harmony' with the General's buses they had been profitable. But unbridled competition from the pirates had brought 'deplorable results', he told shareholders, and 'the situation had grown worse and worse'.

The Metropolitan Electric Tramways, the Combine's North London operation, had paid a dividend of 11½ per cent in 1922. There would be no dividend in 1923. The picture was even bleaker for the Combine's other operations. The London United was again paying nothing and even the South Metropolitan, which also had a highly profitable electric lighting business, was cutting its dividend.

Trams, said Ashfield, 'had a place in a complete and coordinated system of transport'. But tramways had to make a profit if they were to keep passengers, staff and shareholders happy.

In October 1922 the Conservatives stopped supporting Lloyd George's coalition, precipitating a general election, which the Conservatives won. The new Minister of Transport was only a part-time appointment, so most of the donkey work was left to a junior minister – Wilfred Ashley.

The pirates might have hoped that the new government minister would be sympathetic, for Ashley was now chairman of the Anti-Socialist Union. The union had been founded as a 'strictly non-party' and essentially free-enterprise group to fight the evils of socialism. The supporters of this allegedly non-party group were almost exclusively Conservative, with a fair sprinkling of backers from the old Industrial Freedom League, such as Sydney Morse, British Electric Traction's solicitor. The vice-president was William Bull, the convenor of the London Conservative MPs.

Ashley had a dilemma. Did he back the small independent operators, as several London MPs who were fervent supporters of the Anti-Socialist Union wanted him to do? Or did he back big business, in the shape of Ashfield's Combine?

As a former minister himself Ashfield was on friendly terms with many members of the government, going on regular golfing breaks with a band of Conservative colleagues known as 'the Brigands'. He was one of the guests who Ashley invited down to his Hampshire estate of Broadlands for a spot of partridge shooting. And Ashfield was not shy about twisting the arms of his contacts.[67]

In the summer of 1923 Ashley came off the fence and decided to back the Combine. The government would cut the chaos on London's streets. Its London Traffic Bill would regulate bus competition. Despite being only a junior minister, it was Ashley who presented the legislation to the cabinet and gained approval for it.

At the end of 1923 Stanley Baldwin held an unnecessary general election to cement his position as prime minister. He badly misjudged the public mood and the Conservatives lost 86 seats, opening the way for the first Labour government, a minority administration, kept in power with Liberal support.

At first, Labour hesitated about whether to take up Ashley's London Traffic Bill. In opposition, the Labour party had attacked the legislation as a backdoor way of 'bolstering up the Combine' and Herbert Morrison warned that Ashfield's real motive was to get his hands on the LCC's trams.

The new government was immediately confronted with an industrial dispute that threatened to cripple the capital. In an attempt to restore the profitability of his tramways back to pre-pirate days, Ashfield imposed swingeing wage cuts on the workforce. The Transport and General Workers' Union responded with a pay claim. The union campaign was effectively organised by Bevin, who before becoming a full-time union official had been a conductor on Bristol's horse trams.

The tram workers, supported by the General's bus workers, went on strike. With the strike threatening to spread to the tubes and bring the capital to a halt, an air of crisis pervaded the Cabinet meeting on 27 March 1924. Not long after the meeting began, Ramsay Macdonald, the prime minister, was handed a note from Bevin offering a meeting. Shortly after noon, with the Cabinet meeting still in progress, Macdonald slipped out to have a quiet word with Bevin and three of his colleagues. The two men reached an understanding, and later that day the government announced that it would take up the London Traffic Bill.[68]

The deal was that the government would re-introduce the London Traffic Bill and rein in unbridled competition. As a result, the Combine's finances would improve, the companies would be able to make a pay offer and so end the dispute. The strike was called off.

Under the bill, ministers could limit the number of buses on certain 'restricted streets' within a radius of 25 miles of Charing Cross. The legislation also established the London and Home Counties Traffic Advisory Committee, to advise the minister.

All three main political parties supported the principle behind the bill. Perhaps the main feature of the debate on the bill was to provide the anti-tram faction with a platform to air their views. A former Lord Mayor of London claimed that trams 'were the great curse of London traffic and ought to be scrapped through an area of five miles from the City.' Another backbencher said 'all trams should have been scrapped long ago'. Despite these hiccoughs, the bill sailed through parliament.

By the time the act was fully in force the political roundabout had turned once again. In the general election of October 1924, the Labour government was thrown out of office and Stanley Baldwin's Conservatives came back to power. A new government meant a new Minister of Transport: Wilfred Ashley, one who would stay in the post until almost the end of the decade, although the status of the ministry had been downgraded. Ashley was now a fully-fledged minister, but he was not in the cabinet.

Described by a civil servant as 'a thorough-paced old English gentleman', Ashley was an unimaginative Tory. He was 'courteous and tactful' with conventional views, according to his biographer. Thought to be a model for Lord Darlington in Kazuo Ishiguro's novel *The Remains of the Day*, Ashley was far happier shooting on his estate at Broadlands than dealing with the intricacies of bus regulation.

Not long after taking office, Ashley announced a list of 166 streets in central London where the number of buses would be limited, putting a brake on any attempt by the pirates to expand their operations. In 1925 the ministry expanded the list of restricted streets on the advice of the traffic advisory committee, which was chaired by Henry Maybury, the ministry's senior road engineer, who had previously been the Road Board's engineer.

Maybury was the ministry's all-purpose technical expert. A bespectacled thick-set man of decidedly Conservative politics – he flirted with the idea of becoming a Conservative MP – Maybury was both clubbable and persuasive. Once he had made a decision he stuck to it – something his detractors termed obstinacy.[69]

Ashley came to rely heavily on Maybury. In an exclusive interview with the *Daily Telegraph*, Maybury, who had been sent out to defend the scheme, said that buses would be limited on nearly 700 streets in central London 'including the more congested thoroughfares and those along which there is a tramway service'.

However, such was the scale of objections to the plan that the advisory committee felt it necessary to hold a public inquiry. The pirates clubbed together to set up their own pressure group, the Association of London Omnibus Proprietors, to give them a single voice and a cloak of respectability – because the main trade association, the London and Provincial Omnibus Owners' Association was dominated by the London General.

In February 1926 Maybury's advisory committee recommended an even tougher clampdown on bus competition, because of the soaring losses on the Combine's trams. The committee said that trams were essential. However, 'so serious is the situation that unless some of the undertakings are afforded relief they will be forced to retire.'

The test bed for this new policy was the Uxbridge Road, in west London, where the London United Tramways – part of the Combine – ran trams from Shepherd's Bush west to Uxbridge. Losses on this route were on such a scale that the company was thinking of axing the western half of the route.[70]

The government planned to slash the number of buses on the route by up to half. The pirates were furious at this new turn of the screw and their trade association threatened 'mass protest meetings, road marches, petitions to members of Parliament, deputations and house-to-house canvassing'.

'This is not a question merely of the independent omnibus versus the tramways or the L.G.O.C. A great principle is involved,' said the association's secretary Vernon Burton. 'Namely whether the public have the right to choose their own method of travelling…The public have shown in an overwhelming fashion that they prefer motor omnibuses: are they to be compelled to ride by tram?'

His members, said Burton, would suffer severe hardship. And angling for sympathy he came up with the perfect sob story. 'One of the first to be affected would be a man who spent three years on the Somme and was awarded the D.S.O. for conspicuous bravery.' He had invested the gratuity that the government had paid him for his war service in his bus company and now the government was going to take away three-quarters of his mileage, which would ruin him.

Although the ministry claimed that pirates threatened the LCC's trams, this was largely window dressing. It was the Combine's trams that were most under threat. The London United Tramways had clocked up a loss of £29,000 in the previous year. At the company's annual meeting in 1926, Ashfield warned that if the ministry did not stick to its guns and cut the number of competing buses, the company would go bankrupt. 'It is the immoderate and wasteful employment of omnibuses in competition with tramways which is the evil to be remedied,' said Ashfield. 'There is a place for tramways in the scheme of London transport as a whole and that place is not a small one.'

The pirates ran an energetic campaign and organised a series of petitions. The splendidly scare-mongering text of one petition claimed that the cuts would put ex-servicemen on the dole and mean that the public would be crowded onto the few remaining vehicles. Eventually four huge petitions with more than 900,000 signatures were presented to parliament. They were delivered by one of the pirate omnibuses and it took eleven messengers to carry them. 'The opposition was stage-managed with considerable effect,' as the tramway press acknowledged.[71]

Behind the scenes, Ashley was being put under intense pressure by fellow free-market enthusiasts, causing him some angst. In a private meeting with Ashley, Isidore Salmon, who had become the Conservative MP for Harrow in 1924, said he had received up to 100 postcards from constituents protesting about the loss of cheap buses on the Uxbridge Road. He pressed the minister to relax the restrictions.[72]

In a talk to the prestigious Royal Institution, Maybury stoutly defended the policy, denouncing the dangers of unbridled competition. 'Competition has been detrimental to the railways while it has been nearly disastrous to the tramways.' The poor financial results on the trams were entirely due to wasteful bus competition.

'If one were called upon to visualise such a disaster as the cessation of the splendid services given by the London County Council tramways the financial effect upon every London ratepayer…would be colossal,' said Maybury. He hit out at 'badly informed' critics who claimed that the restrictions were an attempt to protect an out-of-date form of transport. 'Unfortunately for these critics,' said Maybury, the 'facts were…absolutely against them.'[73]

Lord Montagu was one of these badly informed critics. The stand-off between Maybury and Montagu had something of the character of a prize fight. In one corner was Lord 'Scrap the Trams' Montagu, who until 1919 had been a member of the Road Board. In the other corner was Henry 'Save the Combine' Maybury, the government's transport expert. Despite their former association at the Road Board, Maybury harboured a keen dislike of Montagu.

A fortnight later in a letter to *The Times,* Montagu claimed, 'To bolster up a system which has become obsolete, or is rapidly becoming obsolescent by the legal suppression of its rival…is not only very unwise but in the long run can never succeed.' Montagu continued his crusade the next month at the annual meeting of the Roads Improvement Association. 'It is a lamentable spectacle,' he told the meeting, for the ministry 'to keep an obsolete system of transport like tramways on the road, rather than abolish the trams and convey the population by motor omnibuses.'[74]

In the House of Lords, Montagu launched a last-ditch protest. It was pure political posturing. Montagu did not expect to thwart the policy, but he hoped to put down a marker for the future. 'Tramways are a losing form of traction almost all over the world,' Montagu told the peers, listing two dozen places that had scrapped their trams because they clogged the streets. The list was considerably inflated, some of these places were still running trams thirty years later. 'Scientifically,' he claimed, 'the triumph of the motor omnibus over the tram is certain.'

Montagu was backed by the Earl of Crawford, a former junior transport minister, who echoed a chant that was gaining ground in motoring circles. 'In all parts of the country strong and progressive municipalities have realised that the tramways system is not only obsolescent but obsolete.'

Chapter 13

THE ANTI-TRAM CRUSADE

The roaring Twenties was a decade of upheaval, the age of flappers and jazz, the Charleston, a craze for pogo sticks and steadily rising hemlines. Women had the vote, or at least those over the age of 30. A house-building boom designed to create homes fit for heroes returning from the war spawned uncontrolled suburban sprawl. The electric tram had been the epitome of the Edwardian era. Could it find a place in the modern age?

The roaring Twenties was also the decade when the dark art of corporate propaganda came of age. The motor industry and the oil companies quickly adopted the modern means of persuasion. They confronted an inward-looking tram industry that was ill-equipped to fight its corner.

Modern propaganda techniques were honed during the First World War. After entering the war in 1917, the US set up the Committee for Public Information – or public misinformation as it was often called – to prop up public support for the war against Germany. David Lloyd George co-opted the tabloid expertise of two press barons. Lord Beaverbrook, the owner of the *Daily Express*, took charge of the Ministry of Information, while Lord Northcliffe, of the *Daily Mail*, handled propaganda in enemy countries. There was transatlantic cooperation and Northcliffe held talks with American propagandists.

Propaganda, as one political scientist acknowledged, 'has a large element of fake in it'. Northcliffe's chief tactic was to drop leaflets behind enemy lines. The mixture of fact and fable in these leaflets sapped the enemy's morale, to the point where the Kaiser blamed British propaganda for Germany's defeat. Indeed, the word propaganda only acquired its pejorative overtone from its use during the war, when, as one Foreign Office official observed, it had been 'debauched' by Northcliffe.[75]

After the war, propagandists switched their attention to peacetime concerns. 'We are governed, our minds are moulded…our ideas suggested largely by men we have never heard of,' wrote Edward Bernays in his classic work *Propaganda*. Bernays, a nephew of Sigmund Freud, worked on the US Committee for Public Information and is considered by some to be the father of modern public relations. Campaign organisers were 'invisible governors', he wrote, 'who understand the mental processes and social patterns of the masses. It is they who pull the wires that control the public mind.'[76]

An early warning of the coming battle was sounded in 1920 by William Freir, the editor of the trade magazine *Electric Railway and Tramway Journal*. 'There appears to be a persistent and growing disposition to decry tramways in London and elsewhere as being obstructive and even…obsolete,' he wrote. In an allusion to motoring press barons like Northcliffe, he claimed the articles are 'largely inspired, doubtless, by the owners of motor cars…for there is nothing so greatly detested by your autocratic motorists as the tram lines, which are devoted to the carriage of his humbler and much more numerous fellow creatures'.

Presciently, Freir warned of the damaging effect of this propaganda. 'The public, often misled by newspapers…is only too apt to accept at their face value assertions which belittle the tramways.' Ratepayers, he said, will come to believe their 'money is invested in something that is inefficient and out of date.'

In the wake of the war the country's tramways were struggling to catch up with arrears of track maintenance. For the motor industry this was an unmissable opportunity. In March 1921 a writer in *Commercial Motor*, the house journal of the bus and lorry industry, called for an aggressive propaganda campaign to rid the streets of trams. 'The time to hit the tramway people particularly is when they are staggering. They will never become owners to any great extent of motor buses while they can cling to their rails.'

Motor manufacturers scarcely needed prompting. A few months later, identical letters appeared in the trade press, calling on ratepayers to rise up and tell councils to scrap their trams.

'The object of this letter is to point out to ratepayers that now is the time to approach their representatives on various councils with a view to stopping all further expenditure on tramways,' wrote Basil Nixon, a director of the Lancashire bus manufacturers Leyland Motors. Councils should start running buses, he said, which will ultimately replace trams. Nixon, a rising star at Leyland, would later become the company's managing director. The letter's obvious subtext was 'scrap trams and buy buses' – and preferably Leyland buses.

Claims that trams were obsolete surfaced increasingly frequently as the decade progressed. 'The motor bus,' reported the *Yorkshire Post*, 'has shown itself to be altogether superior to the tram.' The article highlighted the tendentious claim that 'the field of the motor bus is a growing one while that of the tram is declining'.

To the proverbial passenger on the Clapham omnibus, the idea that trams were obsolete could only raise a wry grimace. Being drenched on the top deck of one of the London General's open-top buses during an unexpected downpour made trams seem very attractive. With their covered tops, the London County Council's trams running alongside Clapham Common, if not the epitome of modernity, had the practical advantage of being dry come shower or storm, while their bright lights and smooth running made it easy for commuters to read their newspapers.

Buses were superior to trams was the incessant claim of the anti-tram lobby throughout the twenties. But was an open-top bus, with its bone-shaking solid rubber tyres, really superior to the smooth ride of a covered-top tram? (Collection John Scott-Morgan)

Some towns, like Keighley and Taunton, did scrap their trams in the first part of the decade, adding just enough of a factual veneer to sustain the falsehood that trams were obsolete. But these closures were more in the nature of a minor retrenchment.

The broader picture was that the industry continued to grow for much of the 1920s with the number of trams reaching a peak in 1928. Many major municipal tramways continued to extend their networks.[77]

One small but contentious example was the extension of the LCC's trams north over Southwark Bridge into the sacred ground of the City of London. For years the City had steadfastly opposed any incursion of trams into the Square Mile, relying on the veto to obstruct the LCC. However, in 1924 the City suddenly agreed to allow trams to cross the bridge What had changed?

The answer was that the increase in Labour MPs following the general election of December 1923 meant the City could no longer rely on parliament upholding the veto. 'Labour is in the House of Commons and the City knew that a county council proposal to take the trams across the bridge would be carried whether the City consented or not,' said *Municipal Journal*. 'The mere advent of a Labour government has caused the City to realise that Londoners cannot forever be flouted.'

Faced with the first Labour government and the threat that a fresh crop of MPs would not uphold the veto, the City of London grudgingly allowed the London County Council to extend its tramlines over Southwark Bridge in 1924. (Derek Giles/The Bus Archive)

Kicking and screaming, the City of London had been dragged into the twentieth century. Recognising the realpolitik, the City voted to allow trams across the bridge, but not before a lively council debate in which speaker after speaker denigrated the trams. The tramcar was 'absolutely obsolete', said one, and he backed his claim by producing a letter from the chief engineer of the London General, which was naturally keen to have the plan thrown out.

The London tram strike of 1924 produced a fresh flurry of claims that trams were obsolete. Lord Northcliffe had died in 1922, but his papers – now mostly controlled by his relatives – continued the anti-tram crusade. Thomas Marlowe, who had edited the *Daily Mail* since its first issue in 1896, ensured the continuity of the paper's editorial policy. If tramways, 'were subjected to the full competition of modern motor vehicles,' ran a *Mail* editorial, 'they would…be scrapped at an early date.'[78] Later that week the paper carried no fewer than ten letters – mostly signed with pseudonyms – calling for trams to be scrapped.

The war, observed Hamilton Fyfe, a senior Fleet Street editor who had worked closely with Northcliffe, had taught newspaper controllers that 'there was no limit to public credulity…Touch their imaginations, make them angry or afraid, and no lie is too silly to impose on them.'[79]

The letters columns were a prolific source of fake news. Even when correspondents didn't hide behind pseudonyms, published names and addresses were often fictitious.[80] Newspapers had to take correspondents on trust, editors did not have time to check them out. In the new age of propaganda, falsehood trumped fact every time.

Over the next ten days, a flood of letters on the same theme appeared in papers in Bristol, Leamington, Plymouth and Portsmouth. The link was clear. One Warwickshire writer quoted extensively from letters that had appeared in the *Daily Mail*, before decrying those 'useless obsolete tramways', while in Plymouth, a writer using the pen name 'Ratepayer' called attention to letters in the *Daily Mail* claiming that London trams are running at a loss and are considered to be a nuisance.

The *Daily Mirror*, now owned by Northcliffe's brother Harold Harmsworth, weighed in. 'Why not scrap the trams altogether,' asked a columnist. 'The tramway system in big cities is obsolete, too unwieldy to take its place in modern fast-moving traffic…the superiority of the omnibus as a means of quick and easy transit is a thing unquestioned.'

The *Sunday Pictorial*, the *Mirror's* stablemate took up the theme. 'So far as London is concerned trams are an obsolete form of transport,' wrote Lovat Fraser, who had been a close colleague of Northcliffe. Trams, he claimed, 'added seriously to the congestion and dangers of our streets'.

Motoring correspondents enlarged on the theme. One syndicated column claimed that the tram strike presented 'an excellent opportunity for disinterested propaganda' and that 'that obsolete and expensive anachronism the tramway… should have been consigned to the junk pile years ago'.

There is some circumstantial evidence that motoring interests were aiding and abetting this campaign. The ponderously named Standing Joint Committee of Mechanical Road Transport Associations, a coalition of motor industry groups, had set up a propaganda committee in 1923, with a lavish budget of £1,000. The London and Provincial Omnibus Owners' Association put up a quarter of the budget and its representative on the propaganda committee was Emile Garcke, who orchestrated BET's prewar anti-municipal campaign.[81]

In America, the most thoroughly investigated propaganda campaign was that mounted by the National Electric Light Association – with the active support of the streetcar industry – to oppose municipal ownership of electricity supplies. It was 'probably the greatest peace-time propaganda campaign ever', concluded the Federal Trade Commission, which spent six years uncovering a trail of dirty tricks. 'A favourite method of attack,' pointed out the commission, was not to argue a case but to label advocates of municipal ownership as 'bolsheviks, reds, or parlour pinks'.

On this side of the Atlantic the comparable line of attack was to simply label trams as obsolete and to sidestep arguments about congestion, road safety or finances. The point of press publicity, explained a contemporary public relations manual, was to inject a subliminal message, such as 'obsolete tramways', into the public consciousness. 'Few people remember what they read in the papers from day to day in detail…but as they glance through an amusing or instructive item and see a certain name or phrase that name or phrase will be familiar the next time it is seen.'[82]

In 1925 the tram industry finally woke up to the damage that this flood of anti-tram propaganda was inflicting on its industry. 'Every effort is being made to prejudice the public mind,' concluded the Municipal Tramways Association, adding that it was 'suggestive of an inspired campaign'.

It was an editorial in the *Daily Mail* celebrating Chesterfield's decision to replace its trams with trolleybuses that finally roused the Municipal Tramways Association from its slumbers. 'The fact of the matter is, as Chesterfield knows, tramways are out of date,' said the paper, trumpeting the success of its long-running campaign.

Chesterfield replaced its trams with trolleybuses at the end of 1924. The news was seized on by the tram's opponents as the death knell of the tram. (Roy Marshall/The Bus Archive)

'Twenty years ago, the *Daily Mail* saved London from a vast and costly eruption of tramways…we then said that the motor omnibus would sooner or later do the work. It is doing it and the public is well satisfied.'

The association deputed Jabez Beckett, its general secretary, to counter the propaganda onslaught. He wrote to the *Daily Mail* disputing its thesis that trams were doomed and pointing out that one of the Combine's tramways in London had just renewed its lease from the council for another thirty years. 'There can be no more effective reply to those who declare that the days of tramcars are over.'

The *Mail* refused to publish Beckett's letter. It was scarcely surprising. With its anti-tram crusade in full swing, no newspaper would be keen to publish anything that undermined the editorial line. But it did not have to look far for an excuse to reject the letter. What was called for was a pithy and prompt response. Beckett's riposte was worthy, and oh-so wordy. Longer than the original editorial and about four times the length of most letters in the *Mail* – it was also two weeks late.

Before joining the association in 1919, Beckett had been the highly respected treasurer of Accrington Corporation. He had worked for the council for thirty-five years, an industrious public servant, who organised soup kitchens for the poor and who oversaw the council's buyout of the town's private tramways.

When parliament launched a probe into municipal accounting practices – a result of the anti-municipal trading campaign – Beckett gave evidence on behalf of the country's borough treasurers. He effectively defended the accuracy of council accounts, pointing out that company accounts habitually concealed inconvenient facts. 'Few printed accounts of companies disclose the truth, the whole truth and nothing but the truth,' he told the committee.

With his neatly clipped moustache, Beckett was a model of municipal respectability, an ideal man to appear before a parliamentary inquiry or to conduct pay negotiations. But in the jazz age, the MTA desperately needed someone with a flair for public relations, someone alive to the gossip in the corridors of power, a spin doctor who would defend trams in political circles and the press.

The MTA was based in London, with offices just a stone's throw from the Kingsway tram tunnel. Beckett celebrated his new job by leaving Accrington and moving – but not to London; he moved to Lytham St Annes in Lancashire. It was a five-hour commute by train to the association's offices in London. Beckett was semi-detached, not someone with his finger on the political pulse.

It would be unfair solely to blame Beckett for the industry's public relations failings. The MTA council, its ruling body, was a collection of tramway managers. They knew how to run trams, but they didn't have a clue about how to run a propaganda war.

The anti-tram crusade cruelly exposed Beckett's shortcomings. A month after the *Mail* rejected his letter Beckett, on one of his visits to the metropolis, turned up at the newspaper's offices. He wanted to know if the letters column was closed to the MTA. An editor was despatched to deal with the disgruntled Beckett. He placated him by promising to consider a short letter for publication.

The visit doubtless made for some ribald exchanges that evening in the Harrow, the off-Fleet Street watering hole favoured by *Mail* hacks, not the least because Beckett's discomfiture showed that the paper's crusade was hitting its target.

Beckett's second letter to the *Mail* was closely argued, with seven bullet points detailing the case against scrapping trams. The letter was returned to him the same day, with a note from the editor saying it was 'too long for him to publish'. He had a point. It was as long as the original article.[83]

If the *Mail* wouldn't publish his letter, commented Beckett, 'other means are available'. The other means were to publish the letters in the MTA's house magazine. So instead of putting the case for the tram before the *Daily Mail*'s readership, which numbered millions, the letters were destined to be read by a few dozen tramway managers. The MTA's shortcomings didn't go unnoticed.

'I am glad to see that the official circular of the Municipal Tramways Association has at length been roused to say something in general defence of tramways. It is a belated effort, and if I may say so, is even now put forward in the wrong place,' wrote Freir. It was 'preaching to the converted'. Trams, he said, should be defended in the public newspapers that attack them.

The news in 1925 that the LCC's trams had lost more than £½million allowed the Harmsworth press to ratchet up the anti-tram campaign. The loss was debatable but the *Daily Mail*, with scant regard for the facts, claimed the results proved the tramways were 'hopelessly insolvent'. Under the headline 'those bankrupt tramways' the paper wanted 'to get rid of this costly encumbrance to street traffic.' The *Daily Mirror* was more direct: 'scrap those trams'.

The *Morning Post*, a heavyweight Conservative paper, joined in. It was time to 'cut your losses', said the editorial. 'Trams cumber the road, blocking the traffic, they are increasingly expensive and they are steadily piling up an immense load of debt,' said the paper. 'The truth is that trams are obsolete.'

The editorial drew a robust rebuttal from the LCC. 'You evidently share the widespread impression that the trams fail to cover their running costs,' wrote the chair of the finance committee. 'The revenue from the trams has always been sufficient to pay the running costs and, in addition, except on a very few occasions there has been enough surplus to pay not only interest on the debt, but a substantial amount towards the reduction of that debt.'

A lot of the confusion on debt arose from the fact that there were different rules for company and council finances, a consequence of the campaign against municipal trading. Councils could borrow money: but they had to pay back the capital and pay interest on it. Company accounts were a lot more elastic. Companies were expected to pay dividends to shareholders, but they weren't expected to pay back their capital. The result was that company and council accounts were difficult to compare and municipal accounts often looked a lot worse than they were.

A more dispassionate view of the LCC's tramways came from *The Times*. The paper hadn't historically been friendly towards trams. But following the death of Lord Northcliffe in 1922 his estate had been forced to sell *The Times* to pay death duties. Under new ownership, the paper was now free to criticise its former stablemates. The LCC's tribulations, observed a *Times* columnist, had encouraged the opponents to raise the cry of 'scrap the trams'. It was 'easy to say that motor omnibuses are better than tramcars because they are more mobile'. But 2,300 buses would be needed to replace 1,500 trams, dramatically increasing congestion. It was an inconvenient fact that 'glib critics find it convenient to ignore'.

The *Mail* excelled itself in July 1925. 'Sunderland tramway services ceased to exist yesterday, motor omnibuses having been substituted for tramway cars…Other towns which have decided that tramways are obsolete and have replaced them with other methods of transport include Walsall [and] Leeds.' The same article appeared word for word in the *Mail*'s stablemate the *Evening News*. It was the product of 'inexcusable ignorance or calculated lying', commented the MTA.[84]

Certainly, the news that Sunderland's trams had closed must have bemused passengers on the Sunderland Corporation trams that morning, or at least those who had seen the *Daily Mail*. What had closed over the weekend was the Sunderland District Electric Tramways, a private company that owned tramways to the south of the town. Just in case anyone had missed the news, the *Daily Mail* repeated the story at the end of the month. The claim was just as fictitious then as it had been a fortnight before. The trams would run for many years in both Leeds and Sunderland.

Leeds was an attractive target for the propagandists. The city had one of the largest tram networks outside London and had flirted with the idea of replacing its trams. But the council was now buying 200 new ones. This time the *Daily Mail* grudgingly published a short paragraph about Leeds buying new trams. But it did not admit that its previous stories were wrong.

This was very much the *Mail*'s crusade. Lord Beaverbrook's *Daily Express*, the other mass circulation mid-market daily paper, largely stayed aloof from the bus versus tram controversy. Its reporting was far less slanted – with the exception of a handful of hostile editorials, which may easily have been the product of a leader writer riding a personal hobby horse.

It was all very reminiscent of newspaper propaganda during the First World War. The new journalism – as it was known – that emerged after the war often saw the publication of stories that had only a fleeting acquaintance with the facts. Criticism of these methods was widespread. The Conservative prime minister Stanley Baldwin complained of 'direct falsehood, misrepresentation, half-truths, alteration of the speaker's meaning…[and] suppression' in newspaper articles.[85]

There was no shortage of fake news, which soon became amplified and distorted in the echo chamber of the country's letters columns. When the London United Tramways scrapped a minor tram route in South West London, a correspondent in the *Scotsman*, writing under the pen name of 'a Londoner' claimed that London 'is scrapping its trams in favour of the small motor bus which can run in and out of traffic anywhere and draw up at the pavement'. The same distortion turned up in at least one other paper.

As the decade wore on, so Fleet Street's finest ratcheted up the pressure on the tram. 'There is no future for tramcars and the sooner they are scrapped the better,' claimed Eustace Wright, a motoring journalist, who had been sent by the *Sunday Pictorial* to cover the MTA's annual conference. A bus, he said, is 'able to move about the street, dodge obstacles and get on with the job'. The bus also pays its way. 'What clinches the argument,' wrote Wright with a fine rhetorical flourish, is that 'even where trams are more comfortable…where they are just as fast…and where they are cheaper…the public prefers buses.' Wright would go on to become a propaganda organiser for Big Oil.

The article exposed the MTA's ramshackle machine. Freir had warned the MTA that it needed a press clippings service so it could launch a prompt counterattack. 'In my opinion all the daily papers should be perused carefully,' he wrote. 'I regard this as being really important, seeing that at present all sorts of virulent and veiled attacks are launched against tramways and there being no response the judgment of the public goes by default against them.'[86]

Plainly, the *Sunday Pictorial* was not required reading in Lytham St Anne's. It was ten days before the MTA reacted. 'Copies of that paper reached me from a number of members,' said Beckett as a way of explaining the delay. When he finally replied, his letter was impossibly long, late and had four embarrassing poetic couplets of bewildering relevance. It was unpublishable.[87]

In the absence of a vigorous response to the propaganda war, the constant drip feed of stories about scrapping obsolete trams began to shape the national conversation. Councillors across the country began to question why more money was being poured into propping up an obsolete technology. Fake news was shaping transport policy.

Chapter 14

'AN ENEMY OF THE PUBLIC INTEREST'

Readers of the *Devon and Exeter Gazette* on Monday 4 May 1925 may easily have turned to the letters page in the hope of learning more about the controversial plans for a cooperative bacon factory in Crediton, or the wanton shooting of heron on the River Dart. But lovers of local news were to be disappointed. The only letter in the correspondence column was about buses and trams.

Headed 'The Great Tram Myth', the writer said the tram was no longer the best thing in passenger transport and that 'it would be in the public interest to scrap the tram car for something more mobile and driven by the cheapest motive power in the world, petrol'. The only people who would object to scrapping the trams were 'those local authorities who have secured for the wheeled thunderstorm within their streets an exclusive field of operation'.

The letter was signed E.H. Davenport, a correspondent who gave an address in the Inner Temple, London's legal quarter. He rounded off his rant by urging the Ministry of Transport to ban trams, especially from congested districts. One of the more telling features of the letter was that while it expounded on the superiority of buses over trams, it signally failed to mention Exeter's trams, which would have been of more immediate interest to the *Gazette's* readership.

The *Devon and Exeter Gazette* had a strict policy on letters, in common with other papers, designed to foster lively correspondence about issues of both local and national interest. Correspondents not only had to provide their name and address, 'as evidence of good faith' but 'if publication is desired in the *Gazette* the letter must be addressed exclusively to ourselves'.

It was a praiseworthy aspiration, but difficult to enforce. The letters editor was a busy journalist, with a daily column to fill as well as other editorial duties. A neatly typed, double-spaced letter, with a ready-made headline, only needed a cursory once-over before being sent to the typesetters. It was so much easier than dealing with handwritten scrawl about pig farming, heron shooting or the vicar's fete.

The letters editor was unlikely to have ever seen the *Hull Daily Mail* of the same day, which ran exactly the same letter in its correspondence column under exactly the same headline. Davenport clearly believed that dozens of newspapers would be

Wheeled thunderstorms: the Embankment trams were within easy earshot of Davenport's flat in the Temple. (John Meredith/Online Transport Archive)

interested in his views on the superiority of buses and the letter appeared in many other provincial papers as well as in a national paper, the *Morning Post*, mostly under the same 'great tram myth' headline.

Two weeks later another letter with precisely the same headline appeared in the *Devon and Exeter Gazette*, this time written by Herbert Warren, who also wrote from a London address and like Davenport had no obvious connection with Exeter. Warren happily agreed that petrol was 'the cheapest motive power in the world' but worried that because a tram carried more passengers than a bus, scrapping trams would increase the number of buses on the road causing more traffic jams.

Davenport was ready with his reply. The London General Omnibus Company, he claimed, was going to put a double-deck bus on the road that could carry more people. It would also have a covered top. He continued with a side-swipe at the

London County Council. 'An anticipated deficiency of nearly £200,000 in the LCC tramways…emphasises my point, that the bus system, especially with petrol at the present low prices, is the most paying proposition.'

There was much more to these letters than met the eye; an identical exchange of letters appeared in other provincial papers. The exchange betrays an orchestrated campaign. How did Davenport know that Warren had written a letter challenging him? Davenport had no known connection with Exeter. Nor, it can safely be said, was the breakfast table in his flat in King's Bench Walk regularly graced by the *Devon and Exeter Gazette* or the dozens of newspapers he favoured with his thoughts on 'the wheeled thunderstorm'.

The answer is that this was a professional letter-writing campaign employing a press clippings agency that monitored the papers looking for key phrases, such as the 'great tram myth'. Every day, the agency would send relevant clippings to the organisers so they could keep tabs on the campaign's progress and so that letter writers would know which papers to reply to.

By the mid-1920s the number of anti-tram letters in the press was running at about two to three times the number at the beginning of the decade, reaching a peak in 1925-26. Some letters were undoubtedly genuine, grumbles about trams being full, not turning up on time or uncomfortable wooden seats. But many were part of an organised campaign.

Despite the subterfuge, it was perfectly obvious to people in the industry that the letter writing was orchestrated. 'An organised scheme of propaganda is being pursued,' wrote one local authority electrical engineer. One distinctive feature of the campaign was the number of letters appearing in the press – 'mostly over a nom de plume'. He pinned the blame for the campaign on 'the great oil companies and motor car manufacturing interests' who wanted to replace trams with buses.[88]

The same themes and the same words cropped up time and again. Trams were obsolete, outdated, old-fashioned and anachronisms. Buses were more mobile. Tramways were bankrupt, a drain on the rates and they should be scrapped. Many of the correspondents in the provincial press, like Davenport and Warren, were plainly not local. Some writers employed the disclaimer 'as a visitor to your town' to explain away the lack of local knowledge. Many letters, even in the provincial press, were no more than attacks on the LCC's trams, with readers invited to deduce that the alleged failings of the LCC also applied to their local trams.

In December 1925 the campaign re-emerged. The *Daily News* carried a letter pillorying the tram as 'an obsolete means of transport' and as an obstacle to other traffic. 'Let the motor bus and the motor car have a clear road,' was the letter's concluding rhetorical flourish. It was signed 'J.O. Armstrong', who gave an address near Tufnell Park tube station in north London. Precisely the same letter appeared in the same day's *Daily Mirror*, and more than a dozen provincial papers.

The ploy was rumbled by one keen-eyed Portsmouth councillor who spotted that Armstrong's letter in the local evening paper was identical to one in his morning paper, the *Daily News*. 'I shall be glad,' he wrote to the *Portsmouth Evening News*, 'if you will publish this letter so that the public can judge how a lot of agitation against the trams is aroused by interested parties, who do not wish any tramway system to succeed.'[89] The letter writer can now be identified as James Armstrong, a jobbing journalist and former car salesman, who was one of a number of scribblers recruited by Davenport for the campaign.

Davenport himself returned to the attack in 1926, this time writing from his country address of Nonsuch Close in Gerrard's Cross and pegging the letter to the topical restrictions on buses in the Uxbridge Road, which were beginning to bite. He began the blitz on 18 March with a letter in the *Daily Mirror*. 'London taxpayers, who have read with something like despair that our omnibus services are to be restricted in order that the trams may live, will not be slow to appreciate the significance of the new motor buses with the covered top deck.' The new covered top omnibuses, he claimed, seem to be 'the most economic solution'. He rounded off the attack with a clarion call to 'scrap the tramcar' because of its hideous clanging noise.

The same letter appeared in London local papers and a revised version with a new opening paragraph was distributed to the provincial dailies. So, readers in Leeds learnt that the new motor bus could replace trams in 'Leeds and every important town which is at present in the toils of the tramway lines'.

The London General began to put covered tops on buses in late 1925, like this bus pictured outside Crystal Palace. (Ernest Masterman/The Bus Archive)

By simply changing the name of the town the same letter was published in other major provincial titles, including papers in Liverpool, Newcastle, Portsmouth and Sunderland. Dozens of these letters were sent to provincial newspapers. Many were doubtless filed in the wastepaper basket, either because the editor had seen through the subterfuge and spotted an organised campaign or because the letter lacked local interest. Many others were published.

Sometimes the scheme backfired. One journalist on the *Newark Advertiser* picked up Davenport's letter. Instead of publishing a letter lamenting that Newark was 'in the toils of the tramway lines' the letter featured in the paper's diary, with suitably acid asides. 'This Nonsuch gentleman is badly off the lines,' wrote the diarist. Newark never had trams. 'Newark has its fishing lines, clothes lines…and marriage lines', but no tram lines.

The *Sheffield Independent* also derided Davenport's lack of local knowledge. 'In the first place let me inform Mr Davenport that Sheffield knows all about motor buses with covered top decks. They had been running here for months before London thought about them,' wrote the paper's diarist.

> When Mr Davenport suggests Sheffield should scrap its trams and go in for motor buses he is obviously writing without much knowledge of the subject. Sheffield… has a service second to none. It is maintained in first class condition and not only pays its way but makes a handsome contribution to the relief of the rates as well.

The *Derby Daily Telegraph* was equally alert and an editorial in the paper goes some way to disclosing the full extent of this covert campaign. The paper didn't publish Davenport's letter but the editorial reveals how letters editors were being bombarded by the 'libellous poison' of the anti-tram crusaders.

> It would be interesting to know the source from which the campaign to "scrap the trams" derives its inspiration. Anyway, we would warn our readers against being misled by the well-organised and very deliberate propaganda that is going on at the present time and which appears to take its time from some central body in London.

Davenport's letter was only the tip of the iceberg. The *Derby Daily Telegraph* said that it regularly received similar letters for publication, ostensibly dealing with other matters, from 'lordly chambers and well-furnished mansions in London' that contain 'cleverly veiled attacks on the whole system of tramways'. The paper warned that the campaign could have a corrosive effect. 'It is as well not to be too indifferent to the libellous poison that is being so artfully distributed for the consumption of all too credulous readers.'[90]

The *Derby Daily Telegraph* was spot on. This was a sophisticated stage-managed vendetta, designed to discredit trams in the provincial press, that echoed the anti-municipal trams campaign before the First World War. 'Despite the natural tendency to grumble at the handiwork of municipal enterprise,' observed the *Derby Daily Telegraph*, trams were 'popular for the simple reason that they are efficient'. The person behind the 'anti-tram agitation is an enemy of the public interest'.

In the 1920s when radio was still in its infancy the written word had enormous power. The press, said the PR guru Edward Bernays, 'remains the great single medium for reaching the public mind'. Public relations had become a thriving industry as corporations sought to mould public opinion to boost sales of their products.[91]

One of the key battlegrounds for this new industry was the correspondence columns of provincial papers. The provincial press in the 1920s was far more important than it is today. Many people only took their local paper and not a national paper. The combined circulation of the provincial titles was a third greater than that of the London dailies. A well-placed letter could spark a genuine controversy – or simulate a false one.[92]

The anti-tram letters were part of a long tradition of fake news and they were designed to create the impression that trams were loathed. The same technique is widely used today on social media, where influencers and bloggers are paid to peddle half-truths and misinformation to help, for example, tobacco companies to frustrate smoking bans, or oil and gas companies to fend off environmental regulations. Davenport's letter writers and today's social media posters are peas out of the same pod. They create a false impression of widely held grassroots opinions, when in fact they are the product of duplicitous corporate propaganda.

Davenport was just one of dozens – possibly hundreds – of letter writers paid by companies to puff their products and burnish the corporate image. A lot of the correspondents, like today's social media commentators, were untraceable. However, Davenport stands out from the crowd. He not only signed his letters and gave addresses for publication – anonymous letters were less likely to be published – but he later owned up to his part in this deceitful practice.

Davenport was a key organiser of this astroturfing campaign. But these campaigns were not cheap. A press clippings agency had to be employed, typists had to be hired and Davenport and his letter writers had to be paid. So who was bankrolling the anti-tram letters? To answer this question we have to delve into the murky world of petroleum politics.

Chapter 15

THE SECRETS OF THE SECOND-FLOOR FLAT

The nerve centre of the letter-writing campaign was a second-floor flat in King's Bench Walk, an elegant terrace in the secluded gaslit sanctum of the Inner Temple and within earshot of the 'wheeled thunderstorm' of trams on the Embankment. The flat's discreet location, above dozens of barristers' chambers and overlooking the verdant Inner Temple Gardens, concealed a closely guarded secret; the second-floor flat was an MI5 safe house.[93]

Two men shared the flat: Ernest Harold Davenport, a maverick barrister, economist, journalist and prolific letter writer, and Sidney Russell Cooke, a stockbroker and former senior officer in MI5. Cooke and Davenport had been best friends since their schooldays in Cheltenham and they worked closely together and often helped each other out.

A tall handsome man, Cookie, as he was known, was extremely well-connected. He was a close friend of the eminent economist John Maynard Keynes and one of his lovers. He and his wife also rode to hounds with the Duke of York – the future George VI who as a small boy had been so keen to sample the thrill of riding on the top deck of the Tooting tram. Although Cooke had formally retired from the secret service after the war, he stayed in close touch with his old colleagues and still carried out the odd job for them. He also had a family connection – Cooke's sister was married to Oswald 'Jasper' Harker, the deputy director-general of MI5.[94]

Davenport knew about Cooke's clandestine work and his post-war dealings with senior Soviet agents and he cannot have been unaware that MI5 was using his flat. Harker interviewed informants there and received correspondence addressed to him there – including an astonishing telegram from an informant who wanted MI5 to send him a revolver because Soviet agents had tracked him down.

Davenport himself was no stranger to confidential work. He was friendly with Harker and spent much of the First World War handling secret telegrams in the War Office. After the war he became company secretary of an Anglo-American company set up to supply oil to ocean liners. It was a lucrative high-powered position, but Davenport's commercial career came to an abrupt end when he was sacked after leaving confidential papers about an oil deal on the squash court of a transatlantic liner, the *Olympic*.

When the liner docked in Southampton in December 1920, Davenport was jobless, disgraced and deep in debt. It was a desperate time for the young lawyer. His wife had 'a serious breakdown' and was taken into a nursing home. The fees were 'shattering' and he took to freelance journalism as a way of staving off his creditors. His first foray was to contribute articles about oil and politics to *The Times*, as one of that paper's stable of special correspondents.

While Davenport was down on his luck, Cooke's postwar career was thriving. After retiring from MI5 he had a temporary job working for the oil company Shell on a secret assignment before becoming a stockbroker. In late 1921 he moved into Davenport's two-bedroom flat, helping to pay the rent and other expenses. The two men continued to look out for each other and they jointly wrote a financial column for the *Nation*, a left-of-centre magazine that had just been bought by a consortium led by Keynes.

Towards the end of 1923 the two men published a book - *The Oil Trusts and Anglo-American Relations* – condemning Britain's 'oil imperialism'– the government's

Obsolete trams? When the Duke of York, later George VI, was pictured driving a Glasgow tram in September 1924 it was an implicit recognition that trams were still an integral part of city life. (Author's Collection)

takeover of the Anglo-Persian Oil Company before the war to secure oil supplies for the Royal Navy. It was the impoverished Davenport who mostly wrote the book. Cooke, as befitted a semi-retired secret agent, stayed behind the scenes, helping to nudge the project along. Cooke and Davenport argued that the government should sell its stake in Anglo-Persian to a major oil company like Shell. It was 'common knowledge in oil circles' that Shell was behind the book, and presumably helped pay for its publication. The *Daily Telegraph* named the work as its book of the day and it was lauded in the *Manchester Guardian*.[95]

The book was very timely and its favourable reception set Robert Waley Cohen, a senior executive of Shell in the UK, thinking about what more the two propagandists might achieve. The oil company had indeed been trying to buy the government's stake in Anglo-Persian and was on the point of doing the deal when the general election in December 1923 scuppered it. The Labour government stopped the negotiations and aborted the agreement.

Shell could usefully harness Cooke and Davenport's more surreptitious skills and Waley Cohen asked the pair to come to see him. The upshot of this interview was that Davenport agreed to do some freelance work for Waley Cohen. Davenport makes an oblique reference to this agreement in his autobiography: 'Later on I was to write some pamphlets on oil economics for this remarkable man.' The meeting is likely to have taken place early in 1924.[96]

It was true that Davenport helped Waley Cohen write one paper on oil economics. However, the phrase 'some pamphlets' falls a long way short of describing the full extent of his other work for Shell. Davenport started churning out black propaganda – publicity campaigns where the source is concealed to avoid damaging accusations of vested interest. The anti-tram astroturfing was a core part of a broader campaign to further the interests of the oil industry and the evidence, although mostly circumstantial, clearly points to Shell as the financial muscle behind the black propaganda.

At the time, Shell was deeply concerned about cheap oil imports, and particularly those from the Soviet Union. A gallon of Bolshevik petrol could be as little as three-quarters the price of Shell's. In the summer of 1924 Shell got wind of a move to step up the sales of Soviet petrol, with the registration of a company called Russian Oil Products, which aimed to improve its distribution of petrol. Shell's response was swift. Henri Deterding, the managing director of Royal Dutch Shell and Waley Cohen's boss, liked to be known as the 'petrol Napoleon' and like his idol he had a taste for speedy counterattacks.

Davenport was selected to lead the counterattack. He launched an anti-Soviet petrol campaign with a letter to the *Daily Express*, warning of the dangers of dirty 'pirate' petrol. He then sent the same letter to many other papers, including the major provincials and the *Daily Telegraph*. 'One unnecessary repair bill wipes out

Ernest Davenport wrote his 'great tram myth' letters at a desk in a second-floor flat in King's Bench Walk overlooking the Inner Temple Gardens. (Mick Hamer)

the whole saving of buying cheap petrol,' he claimed. The pirate petrol campaign became a model for Davenport's subsequent campaigns.

In 1925 Davenport was diverted to start fresh astroturfing campaigns, notably his 'scrap the trams' letters, the third campaign he ran for Shell. The anti-Soviet petrol campaign was taken up by the Association of British Creditors of Russia, part of a broader 'orchestrated press campaign' that Deterding initiated with the object of swinging public opinion behind a boycott of Bolshevik petrol.[97]

After the Russian Revolution, the Soviet government had confiscated foreign assets, including the country's oil wells. Aggrieved investors set up the association to publicise the theft of their assets. By the mid-1920s it had become a front for Shell, according to Louis Fischer, an American journalist who interviewed the association's leaders.

The association turned out a barrage of pamphlets and letters to the papers arguing for a ban on the sale of 'stolen petrol'. The campaign was supported by several MPs, including Nicholas Grattan Doyle, a Conservative MP who wrote letters and pushed the case in the House of Commons. Grattan Doyle became one of Davenport's stable of letter-writers.

Towards the end of the year, Shell finally showed its hand. Deterding himself wrote to selected London papers, including *The Times*. 'I have seen in several papers a letter by Sir N. Grattan Doyle,' he wrote disingenuously, complaining that Russia was selling stolen petrol. Of course he would have seen it – it was part of Shell's campaign to scupper imports of Soviet petrol and he would have seen the press cuttings.

After the general election of 1924 Stanley Baldwin's Conservatives again took over the reins of government. The incoming home secretary was William Joynson-Hicks, a leading light in a reactionary Conservative faction nicknamed 'the diehards'. Jix, described by the cartoonist David Low as 'the most intolerant, narrow-minded and dictatorial of anti-democrats' had long-standing links with motoring interests and he was legal adviser to the London General.[98]

Known disparagingly as Mussolini minor, Jix was vehemently opposed to communism. And the issue of Russian oil imports was near the top of his in-tray. The security services were already grooming oil companies to supply them with industrial intelligence and Shell's petrol-distributing arm regularly passed on information about the activities of Russian Oil Products. So Jix asked Shell to suggest ways to cut off this source of income for the Soviet Union. Shell was cementing itself an influential place in political circles.[99]

Russian Oil Products hit back with an advertising campaign in the *Daily Herald* extolling its lower prices and urging motorists to ask for R.O.P. petrol 'in the lilac cans'. The choice of the *Daily Herald* for this campaign was a double-edged sword. The paper was undoubtedly sympathetic – other papers refused the adverts – but MI5 was already tailing the paper's foreign editor, who was a Soviet agent.

The anti-Red petrol campaign, backed by sympathetic papers like the *Daily Mail,* reached a peak in early 1927. The *Daily Mail* revealed, to a chorus of outrage, that the April edition of the London telephone directory, which was printed by His Majesty's Stationery Office, contained an advert for Russian Oil Products.

The pressure to do something about the Reds was becoming irresistible. The campaign was extremely well-focused. The cabinet was split. Jix was agitating for a ban on Soviet trade. But Austen Chamberlain, the foreign secretary, didn't want to see a permanent breach with the Soviet Union. The campaign aimed to strengthen Jix's hand in his tussle with Chamberlain. Then Jix got the pretext he wanted.

In 1927, Harker interviewed an informant in an MI5 safe house – Davenport's second-floor flat in King's Bench Walk. Harker learnt that secret military documents had been copied in the City of London offices occupied by Arcos, the Soviet trade co-operative and Russian Oil Products. MI5 told the Home Secretary. Jix was outraged. 'Raid Arcos,' he yelled. 'Do you want it in writing?'[100]

William Horwood, the Metropolitan Commissioner of Police, duly obtained a search warrant. Only then did Jix tell the prime minister and the foreign secretary what he was about to do. They felt they had been bounced into approving the raid.

The next day, 200 police and Special Branch officers swooped on the offices in Moorgate occupied by Arcos and Russian Oil Products. The raid proved to be a damp squib and despite turning the place upside down Special Branch failed to find any secret military documents. Accredited staff had diplomatic immunity under the British-Soviet treaty of 1921, but the police rode roughshod over these claims. Unsurprisingly the result of the raid was a major rupture in Anglo-Russian relations, which seems to have been Jix's intention.

In the House of Commons, David Lloyd George challenged an embarrassed Chamberlain, who was forced to toe the government's line, about the necessity for the raid. Lloyd-George told MPs that Chamberlain's hand had been forced by his 'hot-headed colleague' – Jix – and that the home secretary seemed to be dictating foreign policy. Lloyd George implicitly questioned the motive for the raid.

What was the motive? The answer emerged slowly and the trail led back to Shell. The Soviet government had been negotiating a new trade deal with Britain, which would increase imports of Russian oil. It was not something Deterding could countenance and he had put pressure on the government to break with Russia.[101]

While most of Fleet Street grappled with the international fall-out from the raid, the *Daily Mail* distributed 13,000 posters to garages up and down the country as part of a campaign to boycott Russian petrol. Hundreds of petrol station forecourts were festooned with banners proclaiming 'No Soviet Petrol Sold Here'.

Towards the end of July, Deterding gave the *Daily Mail* an exclusive. 'My reasons for refusing to handle Soviet petrol,' claimed Deterding, 'are precisely those which have prompted the *Daily Mail* to take the wonderful stand that it has.' It was a declaration oozing with high principle and conveniently ignoring the fact that earlier in the decade Shell had been importing Russian oil.

Both the campaign against Red petrol and the one that vilified trams were backed by broader press coverage. Shell was able to enlist the efforts of a coterie of motoring journalists who often wrote syndicated columns for the provincial press. A select group of these journalists had already appeared in Shell's advertising – and doubtless been paid handsomely for it. Those hacks who had taken the Shell shilling duly

'No Soviet Petrol Sold Here': a Morris owner fills up with Shell petrol, while the garage proudly displays a *Daily Mail* poster urging motorists to boycott Bolshevik petrol. (Jarman Collection, National Motor Museum)

produced a backdrop of supportive propaganda in the editorial columns, casting doubt on the quality of Soviet petrol and for the anti-tram campaign labelling trams as obsolete.[102]

While the nation's oil supplies were a subject of keen interest to the secret services, it would be preposterous to think that a number 31 tram trundling along London's Embankment past Scotland House, the home of Special Branch, could be a threat to national security and of the remotest interest to MI5.

So what role did the security services play in the anti-tram propaganda? Certainly the secret services had a keen interest in propaganda and Cooke's connections put him in a great position to pass on handy hints and malleable press contacts to his flatmate. Cooke's best man when he got married in 1922 was Sir Campbell Stuart. Stuart was Lord Northcliffe's right-hand man, and instrumental in organising the black propaganda campaign in enemy countries during the war. At the time of Cooke's marriage he was managing editor of the *Daily Mail*.

Most of the key actors in the Red petrol saga, Davenport, Cooke, Horwood and Jix as well as the *Daily Mail* and Shell, also played a prominent part in the anti-tram crusade. Doubtless this is partly a reflection of the establishment's views, its sympathies were more closely aligned with motorists than passengers on a tram. But perhaps the most plausible explanation for the known facts is that the people behind these campaigns were keen to recruit people with links to the Secret Service, to profit from their contacts and their expertise in subterfuge.

There is clear evidence of the way this worked in another one of Cooke and Davenport's covert campaigns. This one was for Montagu Norman, the governor of the Bank of England.

By 1926 Norman was concerned about the scale of Australia's borrowing and he wanted a clandestine press attack on its inflationary fiscal policy. So Norman cast around for someone with the right experience to organise black propaganda.

Norman had a taste for this type of wheeze. 'Norman behaved so much like a secret service man,' wrote Davenport, who had no shortage of opportunity to observe MI5 officers close up. As a former MI5 officer and familiar face on the floor of the Stock Exchange, Cooke was a rising star in the City of London and an ideal source of advice. Only a few months earlier he had been made a partner in stockbrokers Rowe and Pitman, a firm with close links to the security services and a reputation as a haven for spies.

Cooke told Norman he knew just the man for the job – his flatmate Davenport – who had also been taken on by Rowe Pitman. One day in the summer of 1926 the two men met Norman in the governor's parlour at the Bank of England. Norman cut to the chase. Could they write a critical pamphlet, he asked Davenport, to expose the policy 'without leaving a trace of [me] having inspired the attack?' Davenport said he could, after all, he was doing the same for Waley Cohen.

After publishing a booklet condemning Australia's financial policy, Cooke and Davenport drew on their stable of letter writers for a supporting astroturfing campaign, sending a flurry of letters to the provincial press. This was a very establishment operation. Among Davenport's hired scribblers was the man who organised government publicity for the Wembley exhibition of 1924, the MP Grattan Doyle and a certain 'K. Hall', who wrote from the same address in Tufnell Park as James Armstrong, the anti-tram letter writer. This was a simple piece of subterfuge. Hall was the maiden name of Armstrong's wife Kate.

The Australian campaign worked well and the identity of its paymaster remained secret. 'The governor was delighted,' Davenport later wrote.[103]

Davenport ran more than a dozen astroturfing campaigns for Shell during the 1920s. There is a glimpse of the machine behind Davenport's blizzard of letters in the notes of press coverage circulated by Shell's public relations department to company directors. The subjects dovetail neatly with those of Davenport's letters. The targets ranged from replacing coal in ships' bunkers with oil to closing railway branch lines and replacing them with buses, which would spell 'the doom of the slow train' – not to mention the boost it would give to the profits of the oil companies.[104]

It was a lucrative decade for Davenport. The combination of letter-writing, journalism and his stockbroking work paid off and to his 'great relief' Davenport could at last settle all those heavy and pressing medical bills.

On 3 July 1930, Violet Fancy, the flat's housekeeper, arrived shortly after 8 am to find Cooke in his pyjamas lying on the sitting-room floor in a pool of blood. His body was still warm and a double-barrelled sporting gun was lying a yard or two away. Davenport, described as Cooke's closest friend, told the press it was 'a mystery'.

The inquest concluded that Cooke had accidentally shot himself while cleaning his gun. The verdict was a common euphemism at inquests to avoid the stigma attached to suicide and Cooke's family were represented at the hearing by one of the country's leading lawyers – to ensure a socially acceptable verdict. But not everyone subscribed to this sanitised version of events. The wound was at an unusual angle and Cooke, an experienced sportsman, had allegedly been cleaning a loaded gun with the safety catch off. His employer, Hugo Pitman, who was not given to conspiracy theories, later claimed he had been assassinated by a Soviet agent.[105]

After Cooke's death, Davenport moved out of the flat in King's Bench Walk that he had rented since 1916 and began calling himself Nicholas. As Nicholas Davenport, he worked in public relations for the government during the Second World War and became an adviser on finance to Harold Wilson's Labour government of 1964. He died in 1979. His entry in the Dictionary of National Biography glosses over his activities in the 1920s.

Chapter 16
DANGEROUS ANACHRONISMS

Just before Christmas 1924, Cyril Price, a 17-year-old engineering apprentice who had been trying to catch a bus in Hackney, was squashed between two buses. He died of his injuries. At the inquest the coroner pinned the blame on trams and called for them to be scrapped.

It was common practice among bus drivers to drive along tramlines – it made for a smoother ride. In this case the rear wheels of one of the buses became trapped in a tramline and the driver couldn't take any avoiding action – or, it seems, stop. 'I would like to emphasise very strongly my own views of the dangers of these tramway lines,' said the coroner, Leslie McCarthy. 'They are responsible for a large number of deaths in London, especially in congested parts, and I hope to see trams abolished before many years.'

McCarthy was a very well-connected medic. His views not only made the London papers but a news agency took up the story and distributed it to the provincial press so that virtually identical paragraphs turned up in dozens of newspapers around the country. The poor apprentice ceased to be a significant part of the story and was sometimes dropped altogether. The main thrust of the articles was 'coroner says scrap trams'.

The Municipal Tramways Association wrote a lengthy letter of protest to the coroner, saying he had no evidence to back his claims. McCarthy didn't reply. Establishment figures like coroners, senior police officers and judges were normally drivers – McCarthy listed motoring as a recreation in *Who's Who* – and this coloured their view of trams.

McCarthy was far from the only outspoken coroner who gained their view of trams from behind the steering wheel of a motor car. Another London coroner complained that the 'enormous lumbering size' of trams obstructed the vision of drivers and in two separate inquests he found that deaths were caused by the 'bulk' of trams. A coroner in West Bromwich was similarly antagonistic, lambasting these 'lumbering things' not just because they deposited their passengers in the middle of the road but because 'they occupy the greater portion of the most important part of the road'.

Tram stops were a potent source of conflict between motorists and tram passengers. Tramlines normally ran down the middle of the road – a consequence of the nineteenth-century legislation designed to provide kerb space for horse-drawn carts to drop off milk, beer or coal on the pavement without disrupting other traffic. As a result, passengers had to leave the relative safety of the pavement and walk into the road to catch a tram, and similarly dodge traffic when they got off. According to the London County Council, more than 400 passengers a year in the early 1920s were knocked down by drivers overtaking its trams at tram stops.

It was not just good manners for drivers to stop to allow passengers to get on and off trams, they also risked being prosecuted for careless driving or even manslaughter. One case was the tragedy of 22-year-old Mary Blakemore. She was getting on a tram in Manchester to go out to a party when a car travelling at between 35 and 45 miles per hour hit her, carrying her on the car's bonnet for some 55 yards. The driver, who was on his way home from playing rugby, was charged with manslaughter. He was acquitted after the judge summed up for the defence, telling the jury that trams were obsolete. 'There they are stuck in the middle of the road and the fact that they cannot draw up to the footpath for people to get on is the most fertile source of accidents.'[106]

During the 1920s the National Safety First Association was the main organisation campaigning to improve road safety. The association had a compromising genesis. It evolved from the London Safety First Council which had been set up by the London General Omnibus Company in the First World War. Some commentators at least thought its activities were designed to distract attention from the worryingly high number of bus accidents.

Motoring interests were prominent backers of the association and its early work often seemed to be influenced by the need to avoid alienating its paymasters. So the association highlighted the need to educate pedestrians to avoid accidents. It was victim blaming.

In March 1925 John Moore, the chief constable of Huddersfield, told the National Safety First Association conference that trams were more dangerous than any other vehicles. Moore, an enthusiastic motorist, was a major influence on the association's road safety publicity. He gathered statistics from a dozen cities that purportedly showed trams were involved in six times as many accidents as motor buses. It was grist to the mill of Fleet Street, which was already running stories about the dangers of trams with headlines like 'the murder gang'.

The statistics didn't bear close inspection. Moore's figures were debatable, his deductions phoney. Buses were involved in more accidents and their accidents were far more likely to be fatal. Scotland Yard's figures showed that buses in London were responsible for nearly eight times more road deaths than trams – thirty-eight as opposed to five. But it wasn't in Fleet Street's nature to let the facts get in the way of a story.

Above: For most of its working life this London United tram ran out of the terminus at Hammersmith and beyond Chiswick to deepest west London. It is now in the National Tramway Museum at Crich. (Mick Hamer)

Below left: Allegorical figures representing Electricity and Locomotion still adorn the former power station in Chiswick, which once supplied current to the trams of London United Tramways. (Stephanie Pain)

Below right: In the early years of the twentieth century British Electric Traction's magnetic logo was a familiar sight on trams in more than seventy-five towns. (Jim Dignan)

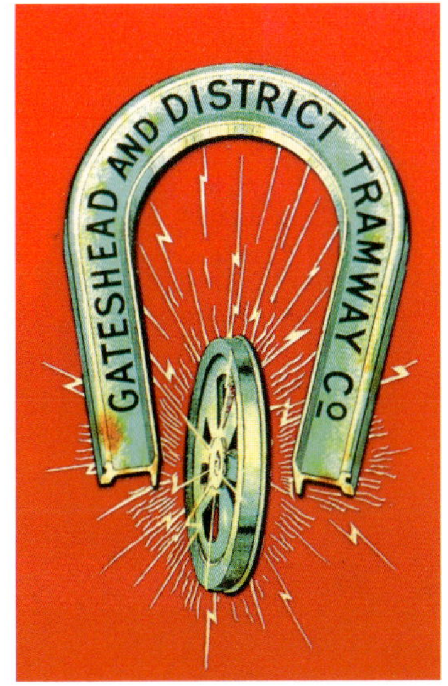

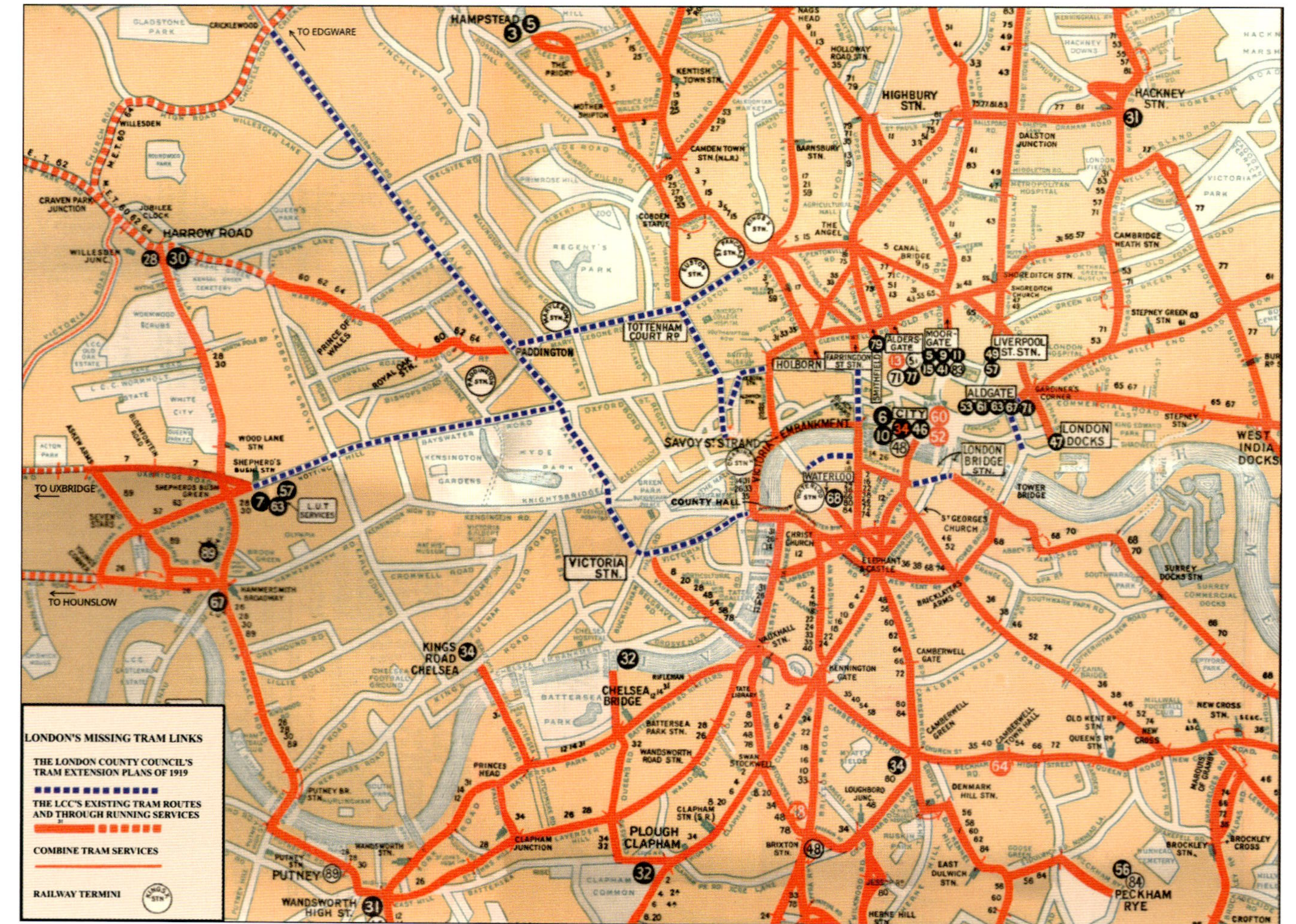

London's missing tram links. In 1919 the London County Council produced a plan to expand its tramways into the very heart of London's West End. The dotted blue lines were schemes of 'special urgency' – the council had a far longer wish list. But MPs threw out the plan. (Based on an LCC tram map in the author's collection)

Above left: The London General boasted that its buses would take you all the way, emphasising the lack of tramways in central London. The LCC's riposte was that trams protected passengers from the weather, come rain or come shine. (F.H. Spear/©TfL from the London Transport Museum collection)

Above right: In the mid-1920s the LCC upgraded its trams with upholstered seating. By 1926 the LCC could boast of a comfortable ride compared with an old boneshaker of a bus. (RB Studios/©TfL from the London Transport Museum collection)

Right: The Chocolate Express was the pioneer of London's pirate buses. This immaculately restored vehicle is now in the London Transport Museum. (Mike Sutcliffe)

Above left: This LCC advertising campaign somewhat optimistically aimed at improving the behaviour of drivers. Motorists were meant to stop to allow passengers on and off a tram – but they often didn't, sometimes with fatal results. (J.S. Anderson/London Picture Archive)

Above right: When the enlarged Kingsway subway re-opened in 1931 tram passengers could travel from Westminster to Holborn in just seven minutes. Today, the same journey takes twenty-five minutes by bus and fourteen minutes by car. Such is progress. (R.F. Fordred/London Picture Archive)

Left: The end of the line: a tram sets off for Victoria from the terminus at the Blackwall Tunnel in 1951. (C. Carter ©TfL from the London Transport Museum collection)

Graveyard: One of London's last trams passes the churchyard of Eltham Parish Church. (©TfL from the London Transport Museum collection)

Right: A Feltham tramcar at the Elephant and Castle in 1951. (C. Carter ©TfL from the London Transport Museum collection)

Below: The Feltham trams were sold to Leeds where the second-hand cars continued running until the Leeds tramways closed in 1959. (M.J. Lea/LRTA (London Area) Collection/Online Transport Archive)

Left: In June 1932 the LCC's new modern tram, nicknamed Bluebird, took to the streets of London. It was intended to be the first of a new fleet of trams, but the plans didn't survive the takeover by London Transport. It is now in the National Tramway Museum at Crich. (Gareth Prior)

Left: In the early 1950s Leeds planned to modernise its tramways and introduced this modern tram based on the latest American research. But the city decided that buses were a cheaper alternative. (F.W. Hunt/LRTA (London Area) Collection/Online Transport Archive)

Below: Trams returned to the streets of Croydon in 2000, after a gap of nearly half a century. (Gareth Prior)

Right: Blackpool's electric trams first ran along the front in 1885. The system has been modernised over the years and its latest trams date from 2018. (Alstom)

Right: The old and the new in Blackpool. The double-deck trams are nearly ninety years older than the modern single-deck tram. (Gareth Prior)

Below: A modern tram in Sheffield, passing the brutalist architecture of the Park Hill housing estate. (Ed Douglas)

Above: Look no wires: overhead wires often prompted aesthetic objections to trams and trolleybuses. The historic centre of Nice, in France, has trams without any overhead wires. The trams are powered by batteries that are kept topped up when the tram stops at a station. (Alstom)

Left: The ramp leading to the Kingsway subway. It is now a listed building and was restored as part of the construction of Crossrail. (Mick Hamer)

Below: A rare survivor: Brighton Corporation built this tram shelter at the end of the line that ran along Dyke Road. The trams stopped running in 1939. Today it is a shelter for bus passengers. (Author's collection)

Moore blamed the victims for the accidents. Tram passengers, he claimed, 'are some peculiarly constituted people to whom any motorist is an anathema. These people, I'm afraid exist in fairly large numbers, and they actually go out of their way to annoy drivers…They deliberately spread themselves across the roadway holding up the motorist as long as possible.' Moore said they should 'facilitate the passage of traffic' by huddling close to the tram or scurrying swiftly to the kerb when getting off.[107]

One remedy was to provide refuges to protect passengers from speeding vehicles. But few tram stops had any protection. Pro-motoring groups like the Roads Improvement Association were long-standing opponents of refuges because they held up traffic.

An alternative was to ban motorists from overtaking. In many cities around the world, including the Scottish cities of Edinburgh and Glasgow, it was illegal to overtake a stationary tram at a tram stop. The death of a man in East London, who was run over by a bus while trying to catch a tram, prompted a coroner to urge the Ministry of Transport to extend the ban to England. The ministry refused.

Island refuges for passengers at tram stops, like this one in Streatham, were few and far between. Passengers normally had to dodge the traffic when boarding or leaving a tram. (John Meredith/Online Transport Archive)

The Motor Legislation Committee regularly thwarted attempts by councils to have a 'stop law' enshrined in their private bills. When Newcastle tried to prohibit overtaking stationary trams, the Motor Legislation Committee organised a campaign in parliament and the ban was thrown out at the instigation of Lord Montagu of the Roads Improvement Association.

The Metropolitan Police were certainly no fans of trams and often opposed attempts to improve conditions for drivers and passengers, such as shelters at tram stops on the Embankment. Towards the end of 1927, Sir William Horwood, the Metropolitan Commissioner of Police, gave the after-dinner speech at the annual staff gathering of the London General Omnibus Company at the plush Hotel Cecil. It was a convivial occasion and Horwood felt among friends. He seized the opportunity to launch an attack on trams.

'Relations between the company and the Metropolitan Police had never been better,' he told his audience, which included the General's managing director, Frank Pick. 'I hope the day is not far distant when we shall see the end of those

A London County Council tram passes Scotland House, part of Scotland Yard, the office of the tram-loathing Metropolitan Commissioner of Police, William Horwood. (Author's collection)

anachronisms of the street which we now see running on lines. I refer to tramcars. I can assure you when I see roads blocked by one of those ancient vehicles it makes my blood boil,' he said. His remarks were met by sympathetic laughter.[108]

His post-prandial remarks were soon bouncing around the bars of Fleet Street. Horwood has done much to 'promote good feeling between motorists and the force,' chortled the motoring journalist Eustace Wright, happy to tighten the thumbscrews in the *Sunday Pictorial*. 'Makes his blood boil! How sympathetically that trenchant statement echoes within the breast of any of us who have to travel daily along a tram-ridden route.'

Horwood's speech sparked a protest from the municipals. Jabez Beckett, the Municipal Tramways Association's long-winded letter writer, fired off a typically tortuous letter to Horwood's boss, the Home Secretary William Joynson-Hicks, complaining about his bias.

Jix could hardly be expected to be sympathetic. Quite apart from his long-standing links with motoring interests, the diehard home secretary was implacably opposed to socialism in all its forms and loathed municipal enterprise.

Horwood and Jix had worked together closely. With Horwood's support, Jix pursued an obsessive vendetta against late-night drinking clubs in the West End of London. The two men also organised the controversial raid on the offices of Arcos, the Soviet Trade Mission, and the petrol distributor Russian Oil Products.

Not surprisingly, Jix gave the municipals' complaint short shrift. The home secretary's reply was brief and to the point. 'Chance remarks made on an informal occasion,' he wrote, 'do not represent the attitude of the police or the Home Office and there was no question of the police being prejudiced against trams.'[109]

The *Daily Mail* pounced on the opportunity of broadcasting the idea that trams were anachronisms. Horwood, it claimed, was just having a laugh and Jix would undoubtedly have a guffaw when he read the 'confused buzz of fury' from the MTA. Beckett wrote a letter of complaint to the *Daily Mail*, but it vanished without a trace, while the commercial vehicle trade magazine, *Motor Transport*, gleefully rubbed salt into the wound by repeating the *Mail*'s piece word for word.

Other papers joined the feeding frenzy. Horwood's straight talk on trams, wrote Valentine Williams in the *Sunday Graphic*, had mightily incensed bumbledom, in the shape of the municipal association. 'The trouble with the tram is that in its essential characteristics it has never changed,' wrote Williams. 'The bus moves: the tram is static. Its vintage is 1900 or thereabouts; but the vintage of the bulk of the vehicles it obstructs is a quarter of a century later.'

Tardy as ever, two weeks later Beckett wrote to the *Sunday Graphic* asking for a right of reply. The editor said it was too late for that. Instead, he told Beckett, he would take a short letter 'hitting with as much vigour as you desire'. How long, asked Beckett. Two hundred words came the reply. Beckett refused, saying he couldn't deal with a 1600-word article in just 200 words.[110]

The article temporarily jolted the association out of its torpor. Who was Valentine Williams? It might, after, all be a good idea to know who your enemy was. Beckett was asked to make enquiries. The enquiries seem to have been perfunctory. 'I have not yet found anyone who knows Mr Williams,' he reported.

It was a reflection of just how out of touch the association was with the cut and thrust of political life. In the murky world of pressure politics, the municipals were like lambs to the slaughter. Anyone who asked around the watering holes of Fleet Street would soon have discovered that until recently Williams had been a star reporter on the *Daily Mail*. He even featured prominently in the newspaper's official history, which had been published in 1921, price 1 shilling. It might have been a wise investment for the MTA as the *Mail* was such an implacable enemy of the tram.[111]

George Valentine Williams, his full name, was certainly well-connected. Since leaving the *Mail* he had written several spy thrillers. He was also good friends with his fellow motoring enthusiast Mansfield Smith-Cumming, the head of MI6, and a frequent visitor to Smith-Cumming's offices in Whitehall. In the Second World War, Williams himself joined MI6.

Chapter 17

A LICENSING FREE-FOR-ALL

In the 1920s, Drighlington was a village on the road to Wakefield about four miles south of the Yorkshire woollen town of Bradford. Drighlington was where the Bradford corporation trams stopped. With a population of little more than 4,000, this frontier outpost was to become a flashpoint in the battle between motor buses and electric trams and in the struggle between the forces of municipal enterprise and the private sector.

In the summer of 1924, a local bus company applied to Bradford for a licence to run motor buses from Wakefield into the centre of Bradford. Local authorities had wide-ranging responsibilities for licensing, everything from buses and dogs to public houses. The council's watch committee, which had a semi-judicial function and was supposedly independent, could grant licences – or refuse them. But bus companies believed – often with good reason – that where councils ran their own trams, local councillors couldn't be blind to private buses creaming off the trams' profits.

Bradford refused to license the company's buses, on the grounds that the council's trams provided a good service. So the bus company appealed to the Minister of Transport. This type of appeal was a recent innovation. Before the Roads Act of 1920, the only recourse for an aggrieved bus operator was to go to the quarter sessions, the local courts. However, the Roads Act gave operators a right of appeal.

The appeal process quickly became popular with bus companies. In the first three years of operation, the number of appeals averaged sixty-nine a year. Under the old procedure, appeals were so rare that the ministry didn't know when the last one was.[112]

It wasn't hard to see why the new process was so popular. If a bus company appealed to the courts, it had to prove that the council had made a legal error. The burden of proof was on the company. Under the new process, an inspector from the ministry would hear the case all over again. The burden of proof was upended; the council had to prove its decision was reasonable.

The ministry held an inquiry into Bradford's refusal to grant the bus licences in November. The bus company was supported by Bradford's shopkeepers, who entertained wonderfully exaggerated visions of packed buses pouring endless customers into their shops, and the happy sound of continually ringing cash registers.

Drighlington: the end of the line for Bradford's number 16 trams – and the focus of a long legal battle that limited the power of councils to fend off bus competition. (Omnibus Society/Bus Archive)

'Trams had no more right to monopolise and block the streets than anything else,' the local Chamber of Trade told the inquiry. 'The bus was a modern thing, and… would eventually oust the tram.'

The ministry's inspector backed the bus company and told Bradford to think again. Bradford dug its heels in and stuck to its decision. This stand-off was a first and other towns with municipal trams awaited the outcome with keen interest.

Underlying the dispute was a change in urban geography coupled with a marked improvement in the reliability of motor buses. The post-war house-building programme generated suburban sprawl, with housing estates springing up beyond borough boundaries. But the tramlines often still stopped at the city limits. With more reliable buses, longer-distance routes, such as the run from Wakefield to Bradford, became practical and profitable.

Meanwhile the ministry stepped up the pressure on Bradford. Henry Maybury, the chief roads engineer and Wilfred Ashley's right-hand man at the ministry, told a press conference that where long-distance buses linked up settlements 'passengers would suffer considerable inconvenience' if they were forced to change to trams. The arrangements for the event exposed a party-political agenda. Although it was an official government press conference, about twenty newspapers received their invitations from Conservative Party headquarters. In the press handout, Maybury said Bradford's motive, was 'the protection of their trams'.[113]

The Municipal Tramways Association believed that private operators were deliberately using the long-distance bus as a Trojan Horse to undermine municipal trams. The association convened a council of war to discuss the crisis. The councillor chairing Cardiff's tramways committee told a packed meeting that the ministry was using the appeals process to push private ownership. 'In five out of seven of these appeals…the ministry had decided against the corporation.'

The Lord Mayor of Bradford accused the ministry of double standards, pursuing one policy in London and another in the provinces. While it was true that the ministry was protecting London's trams this was not a contradiction that Ashley would recognise. For him, the issue was ownership, not technology. In London the ministry protected the trams that were most at risk from bus competition – those that belonged to the private-sector Combine. Outside London, the minister put the interests of private buses over municipal trams.

The upshot of the meeting was for the MTA to send a deputation to the minister. The MTA had two demands. It wanted a return to the old appeals system – effectively to help councils protect their trams from bus competition. Its second demand was to make it easier for councils to run buses, so that they could counter competition from private companies. Restrictions on municipal trading meant that councils had to persuade parliament to pass a private bill before they could put a single bus on the road. It was an expensive and time-consuming process. All a private company needed was a bus.

The London and Provincial Omnibus Owners' Association countered the MTA's initiative by convening a meeting with MPs. Almost all the major bus companies were members of the association, including the London General and British Electric Traction, which was now more interested in buses than trams.

BET's Richard Howley told the MPs that municipalities banked on trams and companies banked on buses and now buses had proved successful councils wanted part of the action. The skilful management of private companies should not be subject to 'rate-aided competition'.[114] A group of five MPs conveyed the message to Ashley.

Two days later the slanging match spilled over into the House of Commons, when northern MPs, briefed by the MTA, took Ashley to task over the ministry's bias. In some cases, said one MP, the ministry's inspector was more like 'a witness on the part of omnibus proprietors'.

The debate provided a platform for Frederick Macquisten, the Conservative MP for Argyllshire and one of the standard bearers for pirate buses in parliament, to give vent to his views, deriding municipal tramway operators as 'bumbles' running an obsolescent system, 'which if left to the due course of science and nature is bound to die a natural, economic death'.

Ashley did not hide his private-sector proclivities. He dropped a heavy hint that the ministry's inspectors would continue to favour private buses over municipal trams. 'I am not going to allow private enterprise to be entirely elbowed out of those districts,' he said.[115]

Bradford's dispute wound its way through two public inquiries before ending up in the high court. The ministry easily won its case. The three judges unanimously ruled against the council and refused to grant a stay of execution. Bradford capitulated and issued licences both for the Drighlington buses and for other services that had been stuck in the pipeline pending the result of the test case.

It was a turning point. The trams to Drighlington limped on for another eight years. But the decision had wider ramifications. 'Will Bradford scrap its trams,' asked *Commercial Motor* in the wake of the court decision. The answer was that the city would now look very hard at any major spending to replace worn-out tram lines.

The MTA went back to Ashley asking him to support an Omnibuses Bill, which would give councils the right to run buses without the need for a private bill. At the end of 1925, Ashley told the MTA that the bill was 'a fair proposition' and he pledged the ministry's informal backing. His civil servants would help the MTA draft the bill.

The bill was carefully crafted to minimise opposition from the obvious sources. It banned councils from building buses – to avoid the otherwise inevitable barrage of protests about rate-aided competition from motor manufacturers. It also didn't apply to London, so there was no question of council buses taking on the London General.

Nevertheless, the legislation was strenuously opposed by the private sector. The Conference of Tramway and Light Railway Companies, an exclusively private sector group that normally dealt with pay negotiations, circulated a manifesto liberally sprinkled with capitals urging MPs to reject the bill.

There is a timeless quality in the rant about the evils of municipal trading that would not have been out of place in BET's propaganda blitz a quarter of a century earlier.

The following are five reasons why you should VOTE AGAINST THE BILL
The bill provides for an Extension of Municipal Trading
The bill is a direct attack on Private Enterprise
The bill alters existing public legislation by:
removing Parliamentary control on expenditure of Ratepayers' money
removing Ratepayers' Control…
The bill will result in unfair rate-aided competition by local authorities against established statutory undertakings
The bill seeks to establish the principle of trading by local authorities beyond their areas to an unlimited extent.[116]

The omnibus owners were resolutely opposed to more municipal buses. With the bill's crucial second reading looming, in March 1926 the London and Provincial Omnibus Owners' Association asked the omnipresent Howley – a key figure in BET's political lobbying – to organise a meeting of MPs to oppose the bill.

Howley and Frank Pick, of the London General, were the two main speakers. They said that it wasn't reasonable or fair to allow local authorities to run buses when private companies met the needs of the travelling public. Rate-aided competition would run private buses off the road.

Although drafted with the aid of the civil service, the Omnibuses Bill was a private member's bill, proposed by a Conservative MP, and down for debate on a Friday. Fridays were traditionally a day when attendance was sparse, with MPs going off early to far-flung constituencies for the weekend. 'You are particularly requested to attend on Friday 12 March,' ran a circular from the bus owners to sympathetic MPs, 'to vote against the Omnibuses Bill, which proposes to facilitate a serious extension of municipal trading and thus by rate-aided competition to menace omnibus services provided by private competition.'[117] Five Conservative MPs signed the round robin including William Bull, who six years before had been instrumental in defeating the London County Council's plans to run trams through central London.

The discontent on the backbenches provoked a wobble in Westminster. Ashley was summoned to attend a Cabinet meeting, held two days before the vital vote. Ashley defended the bill, arguing that it would put councils 'on the same footing as private companies or individuals wishing to start an omnibus service.' The Cabinet minutes record several objections by more senior ministers. Ashley was forbidden to support the bill and told to 'adopt a strictly non-committal attitude'. The cabinet minutes do not disclose the source of the objections. But the prime suspect, given his links to the London General, must be the Home Secretary William Joynson-Hicks.[118]

Several Conservative MPs seized the opportunity presented by the debate to denounce the evils of municipal trading. Others saw the main issue as being bus versus tram. 'This proposal is a mere plan to save tramway systems, and it will plunge the ratepayers deeper and deeper in the mire,' claimed Macquisten. The bill was narrowly defeated, by five votes.

The municipals' new-found interest in buses did not pass unnoticed, however, and the motor industry started to eye up the huge municipal market for public transport. Could the industry persuade councils to junk their trams and buy buses? A month after the vote, the motor industry launched a charm offensive, aiming to seduce tramway managers with their gleaming new buses. Alfred Hacking, the secretary of the Society of Motor Manufacturers and Traders, wrote to Beckett, his counterpart at the MTA, inviting its members to the biennial Commercial Motor Show, which was to be held at Olympia at the end of the year.

Soft power: Leyland's Leviathan was a great draw at the Commercial Motor Show at Olympia in 1925, imbuing in local councillors the subliminal message that buses were better. (Roy Marshall/Bus Archive)

Hacking candidly admitted that the approach was unusual, but as councils were now so interested in buses they would be welcome to attend the motor show's lavish luncheon and swap transport tales with their opposite numbers from the London and Provincial Motor Omnibus Owners' Association.[119]

The tramways association took the bait, not only attending the motor show but also helping to stage a conference about the future of transport alongside their new-found friends from the omnibus owners' association. And as if to seal the deal, the association changed its name to the Municipal Tramways and Transport Association, to underline the point that it was no longer a trams-only body.

The motor show was a great success and council leaders were beguiled by the bright new buses. Equally impressive was the conference, which featured speakers representing municipal tramways and bus manufacturers. Edinburgh's tram manager Stuart Pilcher, a rising star in the industry, enthused about the potential of pneumatic tyres, while Wolverhampton's Owen Silvers waxed lyrical about replacing trams with trolleybuses.

As the decade unfolded a growing cosiness developed between the motor industry and the tram operators. In 1927 the motor manufacturers invited the municipal tramways to organise its own conference alongside the long-established commercial motor show. 'Our industry welcomes the motor bus,' said the municipals' president in his opening speech. 'Today, we who operate tramways are one of the motor industry's best customers. Believe me...we are not wedded to tramways.' The love-in continued. Pilcher who would soon move from Edinburgh to Manchester, effusively praised the initiative. 'We have had several opportunities of meeting the Society of Motor Manufacturers and Traders and I think the cooperation between that association and ourselves has been very beneficial.'[120]

Despite the bus's progress, council-run trams were still in a healthy state. The number of municipal trams on the streets increased steadily during the 1920s, reaching a peak of 12,000 in 1928. But the private sector was in trouble. In 1920 there were more than 3,000 privately owned trams. By 1929 the private sector had shrunk by a third. Almost all of this decline was outside London, where trams were protected by the restrictions on bus competition. In the provinces privately owned trams were rapidly becoming an endangered species.

Improvements in bus technology were only partly responsible for the parlous state of private tramways. Equally important were the financial burdens imposed half a century earlier by the 1870 Tramways Act – the need to maintain the road surface between the tram rails and for 18 inches outside the rails. This burden was increasingly onerous for the private sector. The growth in the number of heavy lorries and buses caused enormous damage to roads that had only been built to cater for a horse and cart. On tram routes the companies were expected to pay towards the reconstruction of roads to take heavier traffic. Not surprisingly many of them decided to throw in the towel.

In June 1925 the company tramways mounted a deputation to the minister of transport. An accompanying memorandum highlighted the unfair obligation. The eighteen-inch rule, said the Tramways and Light Railways Association, might have made sense when trams were horse-drawn 'and the wear of the paving by the horses' feet formed some justification for making...[tramways] responsible for the upkeep of paving.' But with the advent of the electric tram 'the passage of the tramcar causes no wear to the paving but only to the rails'.

It was, wrote Jabez Beckett, the MTA's secretary, 'an interesting memorandum... representing the views of company interests and an organisation which includes members that operate motor omnibuses on a grand scale.'

The Tramways and Light Railways Association consulted its parliamentary advisers about changing this archaic law. They said a bill would only succeed if the industry presented a united front. But attempts to agree on a joint approach failed.[121]

Relations between the two main tramway organisations had become more than usually strained during the conflict over the Omnibuses Bill in 1926 and the MTA dragged its feet. The fundamental problem was that income from tramways – and especially private-sector tramways – helped to subsidise the cost of road maintenance and that kept down the rates.

At the beginning of 1927, the municipals tried a different tack, asking the Minister for help from the road fund to pay for maintaining roads with tramlines. The idea wasn't a new one. The Tramways and Light Railways Association had even asked the Roads Improvement Association if it would support the idea. Unsurprisingly it wouldn't. Helping trams was never on William Rees Jeffreys' agenda.

It seemed there was at last common ground among the tramways associations. But far from supporting the councils' initiative, the Tramways and Light Railways Association scuppered it, writing to the Ministry urging it to take no further action without first consulting the private sector.[122] When the times called for a united front, companies and councils were at each others' throats.

Chapter 18

MODERN TRAMS FOR MODERN TIMES

'When you bury a tram,' ran the advertising copy, 'mark the spot with a Titan.' In 1928, Leyland's Titan was the last word in motor buses. With pneumatic tyres and a covered top deck, the Titan was a vast improvement on the bone-shakers that were commonplace at the beginning of the decade. Perfect, said the Lancashire bus maker, to replace all those outdated and obsolete trams which were only fit for the graveyard.

While Leyland ran knocking adverts, the motor manufacturers stepped up their charm offensive, adopting a softly, softly approach. The Titan's pneumatic tyres brought two important advantages: it was cheaper and it was quicker. In his 1928 budget, the chancellor, Winston Churchill, cut road tax by 20 per cent for buses with pneumatic tyres – in response to lobbying from the motor industry – because vehicles with solid tyres caused more road damage. And in the same year the Minister of Transport, Wilfred Ashley, under pressure from motor manufacturers and the Commercial Motor Users' Association, increased the speed limit for buses with pneumatic tyres from 12 to 20 miles per hour.

Softened up by the charm offensive and goaded by Leyland's aggressive advertising, councils the length and breadth of the country bought the Titan. Even the Scottish tram stronghold of Glasgow bought 100 of them.

Grave concern: Leyland's knocking advert aimed to convince local councils that trams were obsolete. (Municipal Journal/British Library Collection)

For decades the motor lobby had over-optimistically forecast that modern motor buses would replace obsolete trams. Was the Titan finally about to do it?

In the late 1920s about 4.6 billion tram tickets were sold every year – equivalent to 100 tram journeys for every man, woman and child in the country. It was only towards the end of the decade that more people started to travel by bus. So, the obliteration of the tram was far from a foregone conclusion.

If trams were to compete successfully, they needed to outdo their pneumatic-tyred rivals. They needed to be just as speedy. They needed to be just as comfortable. They needed to be quiet. They needed to be cheaper. They needed to be just as convenient. They needed to keep their edge as a crowd-mover. That much was obvious to forward-thinking managers.

The modern tram needn't fear the bus, ran the editorial in one tramway journal, before warning that there were very few modern trams – which it blamed on the industry's lethargy. It was not just trams that were obsolete. So too were the managers. 'The 1910 mind of the average tramway manager,' was the reason 'trams had fallen into disrepute' said one of them.[123]

The key figure in the move to modernise the tram was Chris Spencer, the general manager of the Combine's London United Tramways. He had moved from Bradford Corporation's trams to the Combine in 1919.

As someone who straddled the private and public sectors, Spencer was one of the most respected figures in the industry. He had been president of both tramway associations and had a well-honed understanding of the ways of both councillors and capitalists. 'Both in his managerial capacity and during his years in the leadership of the two tramways associations, he displayed always the same qualities – quiet efficiency, profound commonsense and a firm belief in the efficiency and safety of tramways as a principal means of moving large masses of the population,' said an admiring colleague. Spencer was also keenly aware of the importance of research and had several patents to his name, including one that allowed trams to automatically adapt to a different track gauge, so that Bradford's trams, which had a track gauge of 4 feet, could also run through to Leeds, which used the standard gauge of 4 feet 8½ inches.

A year after Spencer joined the Combine, Lord Ashfield sent his most senior executives – including Spencer and Frank Pick – on a six-week study tour of the United States. Ashfield thought that Britain's managers were too insular and had a lot to learn from other countries.

Spencer was particularly struck by some American innovations. In New York, trams had doors and the driver couldn't start the tram until the doors were closed. In America air brakes were common. Some trams in Britain still relied on handbrakes.

On his return to Britain, Spencer set about spreading the word. 'The [tram]car which most of us are using today bears a remarkable resemblance to its prototype,

After returning from a study tour in America Chris Spencer, the general manager of London United Tramways, launched a new single-deck tram in 1922. Spencer is in the trilby hat on the right of a group of chilly employees, with a dusting of January snow covering the ground. (Topical Press/©TfL from the London Transport Museum collection)

The single-deckers, operated by just a driver, featured another Spencer innovation, a moving indicator that informed passengers where they were and was intended to compensate for the lack of a conductor. (TopicalPress/©TfL from the London Transport Museum collection)

the horse car,' he told the Tramways and Light Railways Association. In subsequent years he returned to the theme. 'If the tramway industry had had the benefit of the almost Herculean efforts of the automobile engineer during the last ten years, we should have been running today a much more up-to-date type of vehicle.'

It was an obvious point. Bus design had advanced by leaps and bounds, producing models like the Titan, while tram design lagged. Behind the scenes the government had promoted motor industry research during the war. After the war the Department of Scientific and Industrial Research continued its support, helping to establish a motor industry research association. The motor manufacturers set the research priorities; the government helped to foot the bill. There was no similar arrangement for the tram industry.

Spencer's magisterial analysis had the desired effect. The private-sector association approached the municipal association to discuss collaboration. The associations set up a joint committee to develop a modern tram for modern times. And Spencer was to chair the committee. It was a rare outbreak of cooperation, as Spencer noted wistfully in the *Tramways and Light Railways Association Journal*. 'It is a pity, in my view, that these two associations do not work even more closely together.'[124]

The committee produced its report in 1926. Spencer told the annual conference of the Tramways and Light Railways Association, held that year in Torquay, that tramways were 'paying the penalty for neglecting research in the past…whilst the motor bus, our great rival, has been taking gigantic strides.'

One key issue for research was to cut the unsprung weight of trams. Vehicles – from cars to trains – have a mixture of unsprung and sprung weight. The high proportion of unsprung weight in trams was a particularly bad design flaw, with tramrails embedded in an unyielding concrete base. The constant hammering of steel wheels on rail joints shortened the life of the track, motors and gears and created an ear-shattering din, particularly at junctions.

Increasing the proportion of sprung weight would dampen these repeated blows, lengthen the life expectancy of track and trams, and cut noise. 'I do not think there should be much more noise with a steel wheel running on a steel rail than a rubber tyre on a macadam road,' Spencer said.

Spencer also wanted to improve the lot of drivers. Trams did not normally have windscreens because, historically, the driver had needed to hold the horses' reins. It was an absurd anachronism in the days of electric trams, and the Transport and General Workers' Union had pressed operators for years to improve the protection of drivers. But the police, and particularly the Metropolitan Police, were reluctant to allow windscreens on buses and trams, arguing bizarrely that they would obscure the view for drivers. The rule was only finally relaxed in 1929.

The comfort of passengers was just as important. Bus passengers already enjoyed upholstered seating and tramways began to replace the wooden slatted seats with cushioned ones. The London County Council had the biggest programme. The improvement was such that the refurbished trams were nicknamed Pullmans, after the legendary luxury of pullman carriages on the railways.

The pursuit of speed was close to a national obsession in the 1920s. 'The public demand more speed and we must give it to them,' said Glasgow's general manager. But buses often broke the speed limit, on an astonishing scale, with published timetables compelling drivers to break the law. If buses obeyed the law, he said, 'they would have no chance against the tramcar'.[125]

The maximum speed of trams was controlled by the Ministry of Transport and each local system had to apply to increase the speed limit. Speeds did increase, but progress was patchy. However, more important than the maximum speed for passengers who wanted a quick journey was the average speed of the vehicle. And this depended on the tram's rate of acceleration and how rapidly it could brake.

By the time of the Torquay conference, Spencer was putting his ideas into practice. Despite an uncertain start with two experimental trams, the Combine pressed ahead with plans for a fleet of modern trams. In May 1929 the Metropolitan Electric Tramways ordered two prototypes from the Union Construction Company,

A prototype Feltham tram at Golders Green in June 1929. Lord Ashfield was so impressed by the smooth ride and nippy performance of this tram that the Combine ordered a hundred Felthams. (Topical Press/©TfL from the London Transport Museum collection)

a Combine subsidiary with a factory that had been built on a disused aerodrome at Feltham, in southwest London.

In October 1929, Ashfield and other top brass in the Combine went for a test ride on the new tram. They were impressed. On 7 November Frank Pick, the new managing director of London United Tramways, produced a lengthy report about the company's plans, which included relaying worn-out track for the new trams as well as replacing trams on less well-used routes with trolleybuses. Two months later, Ashfield proposed buying forty-six of the new trams at a cost of about £3,000 each for the London United and a further forty for the Metropolitan Electric. In April 1930 the chairman's meeting decided to up the order to 100 trams.[126]

The first of the new Felthams, as the trams came to be called after the London suburb where they were built, incorporated many of the improvements that Spencer had been agitating for. They were speedy and they were comfortable. They could accelerate from 0 to 20 miles per hour in just 10 seconds. They had air brakes – as well as a backup magnetic brake in case the air brakes failed. The driver had a seat and a hinged windscreen. The upholstered seats were as comfortable as those on the tube trains that the Union Construction Company was building.

The tram was a revelation to all who travelled in it. Spencer treated colleagues from the Tramways and Light Railways Association to a test ride so they could compare the Feltham, a trolleybus and a modern London General bus. Ned Edwardes, the manager of the South Lancashire Transport Company, was on the jaunt. He was scarcely an impartial observer, because he was in the throes of scrapping his obsolete trams and replacing them with trolleybuses. But he was bowled over by the new tram.

The party drove to the test ride in a London General bus:

Then we got on to a modern trackless vehicle, which was noiseless and perfectly comfortable; then we got on to a really modern tramcar, the only modern tramcar I have ever been on in my life. I was told the track was 20 years old… but the tramcar went along in such a way that you could not hear any noise at all. It was very fast, the acceleration was absolutely marvellous and we went several miles on what was one of the most comfortable roads I have ever been on in my life.

Everyone on the trip, said Edwardes, thought the modern bus 'was by far the worst of the lot in comfort and noise'.[127]

Chapter 19

'HANDS OFF THE PEOPLE'S TRAMS'

In January 1928 London's plague of pirate buses fizzled out when the Combine bought out fifty-two out of fifty-seven buccaneering bus companies, paying £2,500 a bus. With tougher curbs on the number of buses allowed on the capital's major roads, the pirates had been cajoled into selling up. Now that the pirate threat had evaporated, the Combine could turn its attention to another menace – that of its most troubling rival, the London County Council's trams.

The Underground had a long-term plan to extend the Piccadilly Line northwards. Initially it ran into stiff opposition from the London and North Eastern Railway but by 1925 the railway had dropped its opposition. So Wilfred Ashley asked the

The last days of the pirates: a 'British' pirate photographed in Victoria Street in June 1933. The General had bought up most of the pirates in 1928, but still kept the old branding even on General buses. A month later all these buses, both General and pirate, became part of London Transport. (Collection John Scott-Morgan)

London and Home Counties Traffic Advisory Committee to hold a public inquiry to consider extending the tube.

The main issue for the inquiry, which was chaired by Henry Maybury, was the chaotic congestion at Finsbury Park, the northern terminus of the Piccadilly Line. Frank Pick told the inquiry that the Underground would only extend the Piccadilly line if they could 'raise money at a reasonable rate of interest'. The Underground was already mortgaged up to the hilt.[128]

Pick was the rising star in the Combine and worked closely with Lord Ashfield. He was 'a stickler for detail', recalled an admiring Herbert Morrison, the London Labour Party leader. 'Both of these men had great individual ability. Together they made a formidable pair.'[129]

Slowly but surely Pick set out his stall. The Underground could only raise the money if competition from street traffic was restricted, by which he meant cutting back council trams.

Pick's plan was to have common management for all forms of transport and a common fund which would gather in all the fares. Maybury's committee was much taken by the idea. 'The proposals…appear to the committee to present a possible solution of the whole problem of London passenger transport.'

In fact, Pick's proposals were little more than an extension of the Combine's own arrangements. The Combine had a common management. It also had a common fund. Pick wanted to expand the arrangement to include the LCC's trams and the independent Metropolitan Railway.

In its report, the Traffic Advisory Committee endorsed Pick's arguments. 'So long as the present competitive methods are pursued, the railway companies…are not in a position to raise the capital necessary for substantial schemes of extension or improvement.' The report, known in government circles as the 'blue report', was signed by sixteen out of the nineteen members of the committee, including the Combine's representative – Pick.

Such was the importance of the report that it was said – somewhat implausibly – that the prime minister, Stanley Baldwin, took the slim 12-page document for his holiday reading when he went to take the waters at Aix-les-Bains during parliament's summer recess.

What is much more certain is that Ashley took the still-confidential report to his estate at Broadlands, from where in August there was a flurry of press reports publicising the key proposals. In a memo to fellow ministers, Ashley said the great advantage of Pick's pooling plan was to avoid the threat of nationalisation. The cabinet supported him.

Ashley was in the middle of his own political fire-fight. He was a relatively junior minister and many of his initiatives needed the acquiescence of the Home Secretary, William Joynson-Hicks.[130] On top of that, the Chancellor of the Exchequer, Winston

Churchill, with one eye on the overflowing coffers of the road fund, had announced that the Ministry of Transport was going to be scrapped. Ashley was being lined up for a place in the House of Lords. So, the timing of the report – and the issues it raised – strengthened Ashley's hand in his struggle to keep the ministry.

The committee's report was widely welcomed by those on the right of the political spectrum. It was the only scheme, said the president of the London Municipal Society, the London Conservative organisation, 'that is going to help to solve the perpetually increasing and perplexing question of London's traffic'. Herbert Blain, a former manager of the London General, founder of the Safety First Association and now the Conservative Party's national agent, said some arrangement between competing operators was essential.

By the end of 1927 the threat to the Ministry of Transport had receded. Ralph Blumfeld, the editor of the *Daily Express* who was taking a winter break in Monte Carlo when he heard the news, wrote to Ashley to say how pleased he was that he was staying as minister and not going to be kicked upstairs.[131]

With the cabinet's backing, Ashley asked Maybury and his committee to talk to interested parties, notably the Combine and key Conservative councillors on the LCC. For much of 1928, the ministry-brokered negotiations continued behind closed doors. By October the Combine and the LCC had agreed that each of them would promote private bills in parallel.

When the twin-bill plan became public at the end of the month it was immediately attacked by Labour and Liberal politicians. It was, said Morrison, a 'great plot against London' and 'an insult to the intelligence of the public'. Ashfield had long wanted to get his hands on the LCC's trams and the hidden agenda behind the bills was for the Combine to take them over. 'Those who carried out negotiations with Lord Ashfield were…utterly incompetent for the delicate task of negotiation with some of the acutest capitalist minds in the country,' said Morrison.[132]

Ashley and Morrison were the key protagonists in this ideological struggle. Ashley was happy to see the private sector take over London's municipal trams. Morrison on the other hand wanted to see London's transport run for the benefit of the public and owned by the public. Trams were just pawns in this political power play.

Morrison led the campaign against the great tram grab, warning that if the Combine got its hands on the municipal trams, it would scrap them. Ashfield moved quickly to counter the spectre of scrapping the trams. 'It is not intended to scrap any one means of transport, for buses, railways and tramways have each and all their important uses,' he told the *Daily Mirror*.

The LCC held two all-night debates in December to discuss the bills. The council's bill was 'a monstrosity', said Morrison, 'which the council ought to be ashamed of'. The Liberal councillor and MP Percy Harris accused Ashfield of wanting

The Combine tram grab, as seen by the London Labour Party. The threat to the people's trams prompted many voters to switch their support to Labour, helping the party to win the general election of 1929. (British Library collection)

a monopoly of public transport. But the Conservative councillors approved the bills.

With a general election on the horizon, the Combine's tram grab was political gold dust for the Labour Party. The future of the trams was an issue that resonated with London voters, who felt threatened by higher fares and poorer services. The London Labour Party launched its London Traffic Campaign with the slogan 'hands off the people's trams', warning in its first circular of the 'threat to a great municipal property'.

In January 1929 the London Labour Party stepped up its campaign with a 24-page broadside titled *The London Traffic Fraud, being the True Story of the London Traffic Monopoly Bills.* Written by Morrison and featuring a foreword by Ramsay Macdonald, the former – and future – prime minister, the penny pamphlet was a penetrating exposé of the Combine's takeover bid.

As always, the devil was in the detail. The common management boiled down to a 20-member directorate, headed by Ashfield. The LCC would have two places on this directorate. The common fund was similarly one-sided. The LCC would hand over its fares directly to the common fund. But the Combine's receipts would only be handed over after unspecified deductions had been skimmed off. 'The scheme of the Tory LCC is a fraud, a delusion and a snare. It secures the permanent subordination of municipal interests to private interests,' wrote Morrison.

'Lord Ashfield was not always as strongly against competition as he is now,' Morrison acidly observed. 'His omnibuses for years conducted an aggressive and reckless competition with the municipal tramways.' Ashfield's aim, said Morrison was 'to coerce municipal tramways…into subordination'.

Morrison cleverly wove into the pamphlet a long section about the press campaign to scrap the trams. He never said as much in so many words, but he implied that once the Combine had its hands on the LCC's trams it would scrap

Herbert Morrison, the fiery leader of the London Labour Party, who went on to become Minister of Transport. (Bain News Service/Library of Congress)

them. Londoners liked their trams. A recent referendum in East Ham, where the main issue was replacing trams with trolleybuses, had been comprehensively defeated by more than three to one, although other factors undoubtedly influenced the scale of this vote.[133]

This part of Morrison's attack wasn't entirely fair. At the time, Ashfield was still backing the programme to build modern Feltham trams and not to scrap them.

The Labour Party was on stronger ground in its campaign leaflet warning of a fares hike: *Speak up! Or your Fares will cost more!* The Combine was out to make money for its shareholders and that meant axing cheap fares. 'Unless you like high fares – Vote always for the Labour candidates.' The shaft struck home. Ashfield had form on fares. He had previously tried – and failed – to persuade the LCC to abandon cheap off-peak fares to make the Combine's buses more profitable.

A by-election in Battersea South gave added piquancy to the protests. The by-election had been caused by the elevation of the motor racing MP Francis Curzon to the peerage following the death of his father Earl Howe. The constituency had one of the densest networks of tramways in the country and the Co-operative Society, which was affiliated to the Labour Party, plastered 'Save Your Trams' posters all over the constituency. It was the crucial issue, said William Bennett, the Labour candidate.

The parties wheeled out the big guns for the crucial pre-poll public meetings. Ramsay Macdonald spoke on behalf of Bennett, while Churchill supported the Conservative candidate. According to a lengthy report of his speech in *The Times*, Churchill didn't mention trams.

Labour won the by-election, overturning a comfortable government majority. The Conservative candidate blamed his loss on 'cross-currents…such as the LCC question'. The future of the trams was 'one of the foremost issues in the South Battersea by-election', said a London Labour MP. With one eye on the coming general election, Ramsay Macdonald spoke of Battersea being a test case, while the government-supporting *Times* criticised Labour for unfairly using local issues, such as the trams, to sway voters.[134]

The Battersea South result was a tangible success for the 'save our trams' campaign, allowing the normally neglected voice of tram passengers to be heard on the other side of the river in Westminster. Seeking to capitalise on the political momentum, the Labour Party held a bumper protest meeting to kill the bills. Morrison was among the high-profile speakers.

But behind this display of unity, the Labour movement was divided. Early on, Morrison secured the support of the national Labour Party, and the Transport and General Workers' Union, the union representing tram workers. He also tried to gain the backing of the Trades Union Congress. Walter Citrine, the TUC's well-respected general secretary, was cautious. He asked his staff to find out the exact position as to how far the unions were supporting the policy of the London Traffic Campaign.

The TGWU, came the reply, backed this movement, but no other union had signified its support. Shortly after this note, the electrical workers, including the powerful Electrical Trades Union, came out in support of the campaign. But the silence of other unions was deafening. The three most notable absentees were the railway unions, the National Union of Railwaymen, ASLEF and the Railway Clerks Association. So the TUC withheld its support for the campaign.[135]

The two bills came up for their crucial votes on the second reading in the House of Commons shortly after the Battersea by-election. William Bennett, the victor of Battersea, spoke up. 'I made this question of the trams and the Combine a leading question in the by-election which has just taken place in Battersea.' However, the Conservatives had the numbers to see off Labour. Henry Jackson, a Conservative MP and a member of the advisory committee, denied that the real purpose of the bills was to scrap trams and said London's transport should be conducted in a business-like manner, which was thinly veiled code for being in the hands of private enterprise.[136]

He was strongly backed by Kenyon Vaughan-Morgan, a Conservative MP who chaired the Western Exits of London Society – a body campaigning for better roads that was closely linked with the Roads Improvement Association.

With the government backing the bills it was inevitable that they would be approved by parliament. Lord Ashfield, warned one MP, was set to become 'the dictator of London traffic'.

While the bills worked their way through parliament, the future of the trams became a key issue in the forthcoming general election. Morrison crisscrossed the capital attacking the bills at a series of meetings. Sensing a lack of public support, the Conservatives hadn't organised a single meeting in support of the bills.

However, before the bills could become law, parliament was dissolved and the country went to the polls at the end of May in what became known as the flapper election – because women between the ages of 21 and 29 were allowed to vote for the first time. Although short of an outright majority, Labour won the largest number of seats. The swing to Labour was particularly pronounced in London and a slew of seats – eighteen in all – switched from Conservative to Labour, all in areas that had municipal trams. Bennett kept Battersea, Morrison regained his old seat in Hackney South and one of the more notable Conservative scalps was the Combine cheerleader Henry Jackson in Wandsworth.

Ramsay Macdonald made Morrison Minister of Transport in his new government. And on 17 July 1929, Morrison killed off the Combine takeover bills, promising to introduce his own legislation.

The trams were safe. Or were they?

Chapter 20

THE ACCIDENTAL RIGGING OF A ROYAL COMMISSION

All politicians are prone to be snagged by the law of unintended consequences. And Wilfred Ashley, as Minister of Transport, was certainly not keen-witted enough to be an exception. For much of the 1920s, Ashley had eschewed his free market principles and intervened to protect London's trams – and in particular those trams run by the Combine. Now, with the Combine about to introduce a fleet of truly modern trams, Ashley embarked on a course of action that brought the British tram to the brink of extinction.

By the end of the decade the seemingly unstoppable rise of motor transport was causing severe growing pains. The number of motors on the road rocketed in the 1920s. In 1919 there were 330,000 of them, by 1928 the number was close to 2 million. The roads were choked with traffic and the number of road deaths more than doubled in a decade. Newspapers began to run regular columns headlined 'the toll of the road' with details of local fatal accidents.

On top of that, the rise of motor transport was causing serious difficulties for the shareholding classes. From Victorian times railway shares had been a blue chip investment, one that provided a regular and reliable income. Now motor transport was gnawing away at the railways' earnings, undermining the companies' finances and causing a sharp drop in dividend income.

Mounting public concern put the government under severe pressure. The Labour Party naturally capitalised on the discontent. In February 1928 Ramsay Macdonald tabled a parliamentary question asking the government to 'institute a full inquiry into the whole question of the need for better regulation and control of transport and of the possibility of its co-ordination'.

Prime minister Stanley Baldwin agreed to set up an inquiry 'without undue delay'. Undue delay was an elastic term. The process of setting up an inquiry didn't get underway until May, when Ashley, with half an eye on dispelling any lingering doubts about the future of his ministry, wrote to Baldwin suggesting that the inquiry should be upgraded to a Royal Commission. Baldwin agreed.

The outstanding decision for the government was the membership of the commission. In public Ashley said he wanted a thorough-going inquiry, one that

Wilfred Ashley, the transport minister who appointed the members of the Royal Commission on Transport in 1928. (Bain News Service/Library of Congress)

would be his crowning achievement as Minister of Transport. He 'felt a deep sense of responsibility in having to select the gentlemen who would hold the inquiry,' he said. But whatever Ashley's protestations this was a heavily political process.[137]

In the ministry's headquarters at Whitehall Gardens, the names of several potential members were bouncing around the corridors. An early frontrunner for the job of chairing the commission was a law lord. He was ruled out, with a pencil-written note adding the damning words 'a Liberal'.

One civil servant suggested Lord Montagu of Beaulieu as a member, adding that he had 'carefully studied the problems of transport and is prominent in all discussions upon such matters'. Henry Maybury, the chief roads engineer, had strong views about some candidates. 'For God's sake,' said Maybury, 'keep Montagu of Beaulieu off: everyone mistrusts him and with good reason.' Montagu was dropped. A senior civil servant noted he 'may be said to be too closely connected with road transport'.

Maybury was endearingly forthright about some of the other suggestions. Ernest Hiley, a former town clerk of Birmingham 'was too fat and lazy'. But he was 'strongly in favour of the Marquess of Northampton, Eton and Balliol' having 'a high opinion of his capacity and industry'.[138] Several Conservative MPs were also in the running, including Henry Jackson, the vocal anti-municipal critic and all-round tram-hater who was touted as an expert on London traffic.

By late June the question of who would chair the commission had finally been settled. He was to be Arthur Griffith-Boscawen, a former Conservative agriculture minister, who lost his seat at the general election of 1922, and then lost a subsequent by-election when the government tried to find him another seat. That ended his political career. Griffith-Boscawen was the fifth or sixth choice for the job.

Meanwhile, Ashley wrote to cabinet ministers to canvass their opinion on the commission's membership. The 'fat and lazy' Hiley, a former Conservative MP, secured his place after being backed by the Minister of Health, Neville Chamberlain, who had family links with Birmingham. Chamberlain also backed Northampton.

Jackson was squeezed out after the Scottish secretary said Scotland should have two representatives. The minister of agriculture suggested William Lobjoit, a man with wide experience as a market gardener and salesman in Covent Garden, while the Board of Trade suggested the Conservative MP Isidore Salmon, who continued to be a vocal supporter of pirate buses on the Uxbridge Road.

Gradually the commission began to take shape. It was to have twelve members. The Earl of Clarendon, who had been chief Conservative whip in the House of Lords as well as chairing the BBC, became a member, while John Jacob Astor, the Conservative MP for Dover and owner of *The Times*, was named vice-chair.

Baldwin had assured MPs that the commission would be politically balanced. The political balance, such as it was, was provided by a Liberal MP, Horace Crawfurd, and two MPs nominated by the Labour whips, Frederick Montague and Walter Smith, an official in the National Union of Boot and Shoe Operatives.

Vetting was an amateur and haphazard process, the main feature of which was to thumb through a two-year-old edition of the Directory of Directors – 'the latest I have' apologised the civil servant who had been given the task – to check for conflicts of interest.[139]

On 17 July Baldwin approved the membership and the commission's terms of reference. The news that Griffith-Boscawen was to chair the commission was leaked to lobby correspondents the next day. The official announcement also named the commission's secretary – Robert Tolerton, who had a reputation in the ministry as a safe pair of hands; he had chaired one of the public inquiries into Bradford's bus licensing.

Griffith-Boscawen's appointment got a decidedly mixed reception. 'I must confess my absolute amazement at the appointment as chairman of Sir Arthur Griffith-Boscawen, a rank political failure, to such an important commission,' said Ernest Bevin, the general secretary of the Transport and General Workers' Union.[140]

Within days of his appointment, Griffith-Boscawen announced the item that was top of the commission's agenda – the summer holiday. 'I am desired by the chairman,' wrote Tolerton to the members, 'to say that having regard to the approach of the holiday season he does not propose to convene the first meeting of the commission until…18th October.'[141]

The next day Montague replied suggesting a list of holiday reading so that his fellow commissioners could 'give some preliminary consideration to the problems… before the commission begins its meetings.' Griffith-Boscawen's reply was a put-down: the ministry's memorandum 'will suffice'.

The tension between Griffith-Boscawen and Montague was one of the features of the commission and their disputes often spilled over into public hearings. The two men came from very different backgrounds. Griffith-Boscawen was a product of Rugby School and Oxford. In 1921 he had married his secretary at the Ministry of Agriculture and the couple lived in some style in a gracious Georgian mansion in Pangbourne, a village on the River Thames. Griffith-Boscawen had a keen interest in amateur dramatics and often staged the village's annual pantomime.

Montague was self-educated, a man who rose from being a newsboy to become an officer in the army and an Islington alderman. He was elected to parliament in 1923. His was a political career that was on the rise, just as Griffith-Boscawen's was in free fall. The two men did, however, share a common theatrical interest. Outside politics Montague was a noted conjurer and the author of a well-received book on conjuring tricks.

Although born only eleven years apart, the two men came from different eras. Montague was a keen cyclist with a modern take on transport, concerned that the risks of the road prevented him from cycling. Griffith-Boscawen was on the other side of the steering wheel. He was a member of the RAC and listed motoring as a recreation in his entry in *Who's Who*. In 1902 he even signed a letter to *The Times* arguing against the national speed limit.

The commission, as originally conceived, was to be politically balanced and its members were to have no conflicts of interest. 'No attempt should be made to constitute the commission on the basis of representation of all the transport interests, but they should be excluded from such representation and left to present their case through the witness box,' was the civil service advice.[142]

In some respects, this line was rigidly adhered to. Being a railway director was incompatible with the impartiality expected of a commission member. But in other respects, the ministry was blind to conflicts of interest. Being associated with the motor lobby was not thought to be a conflict of interest.

The commission, as Herbert Morrison later pointed out, had 'a definite Conservative majority, and an eminently Conservative chairman'. And the unintended consequence of packing the commission with members drawn from the Conservative establishment was they nurtured other prejudices. Most members' sympathies, from the chairman down, were with the motorist.

Griffith-Boscawen was a member of the Standing Joint Committee of the Mechanical Road Transport Associations – a forerunner of the British Road Federation, the pre-eminent road lobby group from the 1930s on into the 1980s. Apart from him, the letterhead of the Mechanical Road Transport Associations has several familiar names. The chair was Edward Shrapnell-Smith, of the Commercial Motor Users' Association. The vice-chair was BET's Richard Howley while the secretary was Frederick Bristow of the Commercial Motor Users' Association. The London and Provincial Omnibus Owners' Association was represented by Richard Tilling and Frank Pick, while another co-opted member was William Joynson-Hicks, the Home Secretary. Griffith-Boscawen seems to have resigned from the committee after taking up his role in the Royal Commission, but as late as December 1928 the letterhead still listed him as a member and he certainly took a close personal interest in the correspondence between this committee and the commission.

Other commission members had axes to grind. William Lobjoit was vice-president of the Commercial Motor Users Association. The commission's two peers were both enthusiastic motorists. Both of them had convictions for speeding – and Northampton was the archetypal road hog. By the summer of 1926 he had clocked up thirteen convictions for speeding and dangerous driving, while Horace Crawfurd, the token Liberal, regularly spoke for motoring interests in the House of Commons and had opposed restricting bus competition with trams.

The original intention was that the Royal Commission's task would take about two years. One of the great advantages of this timescale, from the government's point of view, was that the report would not be published until after the next general election, which had to take place before October 1929. However, proceedings were blown off course before the commission heard a single word of evidence, when Lord Robert Cecil published his own Road Vehicles Regulation Bill. The bill was given its first reading in the Lords, four days before the commission started to hear evidence. Cecil's intervention laid bare the commission's pro-motoring bias.

Cecil came from a traditional Tory background and had a strong social conscience. Horrified by the rising toll of the road he felt that the government's attempts to tackle the problem were utterly inadequate. His bill was full of radical ideas, such as compulsory driving tests, engineering roads to force traffic to slow down and fitting vehicles with speed governors, so that drivers could not exceed the speed limit.

The bill dismayed the motor lobby. Lord Denman, who spoke in the House of Lords for various motoring groups, took aim at the plan for speed governors. 'I think there is a fallacy underlying several of the clauses of this Bill,' said Denman, 'that high speed is the main cause of accidents on the road.'

The peers had little sympathy for this argument. Lord Londonderry, the government's spokesman, tried to defuse the situation by saying that the Royal Commission was 'investigating the whole problem' and promised it would produce an interim report covering Cecil's proposals.

The government had been bounced into making a concession. A contrite Londonderry wrote to Ashley to explain that the mood of the peers gave him no option.

As a result of the debate, Ashley wrote to Griffith-Boscawen asking him to produce an interim report on road safety 'including the proposals contained in Viscount Cecil's bill'. Griffith-Boscawen's private reply – sent to Ashley's home address – revealed his irritation. He complained that the commission had been forced to upset its work programme to take evidence about Cecil's bill. There was a large dose of hyperbole in his gripe. The chief change was for Griffith-Boscawen to alert the AA and the RAC that he would ask them about Cecil's bill.

The motoring organisations scarcely needed any warning. When the commission started to hear evidence, Griffith-Boscawen's questioning was obsequiously leading. 'In this bill,' he asked the AA's long-time secretary Ernest Stenson Cooke, there was a proposal for 'what is described as a mechanical check on speed…I imagine that such checks could all be tampered with very easily?' Stenson Cooke could not help but agree. 'Easily,' he said before reiterating the motorists' mantra that 'speed is not by itself responsible for the majority of accidents'.

The commission's approach to the future of the speed limit was equally one-sided. The exchanges between witnesses and the commission reveal a common interest, a sense that as motorists they were all in this together. 'I do not think I am betraying any confidence when I say there is not one single member of this honourable commission who pays the slightest attention to the speed limit as it stands today and that speed by itself is not a factor of public danger,' said Stenson Cooke.[143]

The cosiness between commission members and their friends in the motor lobby produced some extraordinary exchanges. 'It has been urged by various witnesses that there should be no speed limit for the private car,' Griffith-Boscawen told Edward Shrapnell-Smith from the Commercial Motor Users' Association. 'I myself, I do not mind telling you, have driven in a Rolls-Royce at seventy miles per hour,' he continued. 'I think we all have,' replied Shrapnell-Smith.[144]

The motor lobby misjudged its audience in one respect. Montague didn't drive and he was the only commissioner to seriously challenge motoring witnesses and their allies.

However, Montague got short shrift from the chief constable of Kent, Major Harry Chapman, who wanted to abolish the speed limit. Montague told him speeding motorists spoilt the pleasure of walking along the Dover Road. The chief constable barked:

If you know Kent, you will know there are certain parts of Kent where, very often, you can see perfectly straight for four, five or six hundred yards…I say a man could drive at sixty miles an hour and hurt nobody but himself or the occupants of his car because he could see a rabbit on the road two or three hundred yards away. Do you follow me? It is perfectly safe.[145]

When the Royal Commission published its first report in July, its conclusions were unsurprising. It dismissed the idea of speed governors. 'Not a single witness who referred to this proposal appeared to be willing to support it…no mechanical device of the kind has been invented which cannot be easily tampered with.'

And the report recommended abolishing the speed limit for cars:

> We have given very careful and anxious consideration to the question and have examined the evidence from every point of view. As a result, we have come to the conclusion that provided all wheels are fitted with pneumatic tyres there should be no general speed limit for motor cars…or for motor cycles.

The report was signed by all of the commission, including Montague.

There was never much doubt about which way the commission was going to jump. It was dominated by motoring interests and was going to give short shrift to anything that held up the speedy progress of the car – from pedestrians to trams.

Chapter 21
THE DEATH WARRANT

The verdict of the Royal Commission on Transport was stunning. 'After carefully considering the evidence which we have received from various witnesses,' said the commission, 'our considered view is that tramways, if not an obsolete form of transport, are at all events in a state of obsolescence and cause much unnecessary congestion and considerable unnecessary danger to the public.'

The commission's final report, published in 1931, was a hatchet job on the tram. In the commission's mind, 'the easy and unobstructed flow of traffic and the safety of the public' were the two most important problems for it to solve. 'Tramlines laid in the carriageway…and rail-bound vehicles which cannot pull up at the kerb but have to pick up and set down in the middle of the street, constitute most grievous obstructions to all other forms of traffic.'

The commission concluded that 'the tramway is the direct cause of many accidents'. Tramlines caused motor cars and cycles to skid in wet weather and 'the fact that a tramcar cannot be steered involves a greater liability to collisions than is the case with other vehicles'.[146]

Trams, concluded the commission, should be killed off as soon as possible.

It was an indictment that could easily have been penned by the Fleet-Street friends of the motor lobby. Full of hyperbole, specious in many respects and in others just plain wrong. Why was the Royal Commission so set against trams? The short answer is that the sympathies of most commissioners were those of the motorist. The commissioners loathed trams as much as they hated the speed limit.

The words obsolescent and obsolete had gained political currency in the debate over naval cutbacks. After the war the Royal Navy had been reduced to twenty-three battleships. Many of these vessels were 'obsolescent, although not obsolete,' wrote one naval analyst. Motorists and the press picked up the words from the armchair admirals as a handy weapon to use against trams. 'The tramcar, if not obsolete, is at any rate obsolescent,' claimed the *Yorkshire Post*.

Virtually the same phrase cropped up in a well-reviewed book – *The Problem of Motor Transport* – that was published in the autumn of 1928, just as the commission was starting work. Electric trams, along with horses and railways, said the author Christopher Brunner, were 'in danger of becoming obsolete, or at any rate obsolescent'. Advances in bus design, wrote Brunner, echoing the arguments of

What the papers said: from the *Morning Post* to the *News Chronicle* the message was clear: trams were to be abolished. (Headlines from the British Library collection)

Ernest Davenport's letter-writing campaign two years before, 'have made it possible for the bus to carry as many, or nearly as many passengers as the tram'.[147]

Brunner sent copies of his book to every member of the commission with an offer to help, drawing on his expertise in transport. Who was paying for this largesse? The clue was in the notepaper. Brunner's letter was written on the headed notepaper of Shell-Mex, the petrol retailing arm of Shell.[148]

The 26-year-old Brunner was an economics graduate from the University of Manchester. Shortly after graduating, he wrote to Shell-Mex suggesting that the company should have a statistical department. The company hired him and expanded his brief to make him a full-time propagandist – replacing the freelance efforts of people like Davenport. He would go on to become a leading light in the British Road Federation.

There was little in Brunner's book that was original but it was an easy read and a useful primer for the commissioners. And the message that buses would sweep trams off the roads reinforced the commission's prejudices. Brunner's sentiments would surface in the commission's report, in slightly different words. Because of improvements in buses 'as regards comfort, capacity, design, reliability and economical running' the commission said buses would soon supplant trams. These thoughts led the commission to the dramatic – and arguable – conclusion that 'had the motor omnibuses been invented at the time when tramways were first authorised, not a single mile of tramway would ever have been laid down'.

On 7 October 1928, Arthur Griffith-Boscawen, the commission's chairman, had lunch with Cyril Hurcomb, the Ministry of Transport's most senior civil servant, to agree on the ground rules for the commission's work. The commission's official terms of reference were that it should look at better regulation and control of transport. Griffith-Boscawen told Hurcomb that the commission was interested in bus licensing, particularly the restrictions on buses in London. The ministry saw the London Traffic Act, which enabled buses and trams to work in near-perfect harmony, as a successful example of coordination. The commission had other ideas.

On 16 November, the third day of its hearings, the Earl of Clarendon launched a full-frontal assault on the tram – the first of many. The witness on the receiving end was Henry Maybury, the ministry's technical expert. Why, Clarendon asked, had Maybury's London and Home Counties Traffic Advisory Committee concluded that 'it would be unwise even to consider…the abolition of tramways in London'.

If trams were replaced 'by the more mobile form of transport, namely the motor bus' would not buses be able to meet the needs of the travelling public, Clarendon wanted to know. 'I cannot conceive the time arriving when buses will take the place of all tramways,' replied Maybury. 'I asked that question because there are certain narrow streets in London where the tramways are a distinct inconvenience,' said Clarendon, who saw trams through the goggles of a motorist.

The AA's long-serving secretary Ernest Stenson Cooke was the first motor lobby witness to give evidence at the end of January 1929. His working assumption was that the commission would recommend scrapping trams, and he casually threw in asides like 'with the abandonment of tramways'. One of his main beefs was that tramways occupied the 'majority of the carriageway'.

He was taken to task by Frederick Montague, the commission's one-man awkward squad.

'Would you not say that private cars take up a tremendous amount of room compared with tramways or any other kind of public conveyance?'

'They are very much more mobile,' replied Stenson Cooke.

Montague pointed out that London's theatreland was gripped by gridlock for half an hour every night. The problem was caused not by trams but by a 'great number of motor cars' serving few people. Stenson Cooke was non-plussed. 'What harm are they doing?' was his lame reply. At this point, Griffith-Boscawen moved to protect Stenson Cooke and closed down this damaging line of questioning.

The commissioners' agenda became even clearer when they began to take evidence from the tram operators. There was a noticeable change in the atmosphere, from one of collegiate probing to a more pointed and inquisitorial tone.

The tram associations put up two witnesses, one from the councils and one from the companies. The larger municipal sector was represented by William 'Bill' Chamberlain, the manager of Belfast's tramways, who until June had been at Leeds. It was his turn to be president of the Municipal Tramways and Transport Association, which made him the automatic choice to give evidence. The automatic choice for the company trams was Chris Spencer, head of the Combine's trams and that year's president of the Tramways and Light Railways Association.

Early on, Chamberlain was asked about 'the statement that is so frequently made in the press and elsewhere that the tramway systems are becoming obsolete'. Trams were not becoming obsolete, Chamberlain replied, and many undertakings were extending their networks.

Many of the commission's questions were based on second-hand tittle-tattle, which fared badly when confronted by the facts. In the commission's view, the main test of obsolescence, was whether tram operators were scrapping trams. Griffith-Boscawen wanted to know how many miles of tramways had been scrapped. Chamberlain told him that only a short distance had been scrapped over the past five years and there had been a net increase in municipal mileage of 62 miles. Griffith-Boscawen was taken aback.

Spencer faced similar challenges. He was well prepared for the assault. Getting his retaliation in first, Spencer spelt out his view that trams were not obsolete and provided the conditions were right there was 'no substitute for the tramcar'.

Griffith-Boscawen led the questioning.

'Of course there are, as you know, many people who hold that the motor bus can do everything the tramway does and they even go further and think that the tramways should be abandoned. What is your view about that?'

'I should like to go a little further than merely expressing views,' said Spencer. 'I should like to demonstrate before this commission…the contention that in every case tramcars should be abandoned and buses could take their place is verging on the absurd. I have brought with me some charts…'

At this point, Griffith-Boscawen suddenly discovered an urgent need to eat. 'You can go further into that after lunch,' he said, with the air of someone whose preconceptions were about to be confounded by awkward facts. The after-lunch discussion was short and boiled down to the fact that it would take a hundred buses to replace sixty trams.[149]

The commission had no more luck with the trade unions. The Transport and General Workers' Union represented both bus and tram workers. John Cliff, the union's assistant general secretary, had worked on the trams in Leeds before becoming a full-time trade unionist. Here was a man with a shrewd grasp of transport and its problems. Cliff denied that trams were obsolete and said they had a bright future. 'We do not accept the view that tramways are obsolete or that they have reached the limit of development' and he wanted to see more express trams.

Clarendon tried to drive a wedge between bus and tram workers. The peer wanted to know whether Cliff would want a new housing estate to be served by trams or buses. Wouldn't a more mobile bus service be better, he asked. Cliff disagreed.

All the commission's hearings were held in London. It only once ventured out of the metropolis. On 12 April 1929 the commissioners visited Manchester and Wolverhampton, which had inaugurated Britain's first automatic traffic lights just over a year before. The choice of these places was significant. Manchester's new transport manager, Stuart Pilcher, had become a vocal proponent of replacing trams with buses. While Wolverhampton's manager, Owen Silvers, was an enthusiast for replacing trams with trolleybuses.

Only weeks before the visit Silvers had claimed that his trolleybuses were 25 per cent faster than trams, much to the chagrin of other tram managers. It was 'downright nonsense of the most blatant type', said one of them.[150] The commission was reportedly much impressed by Wolverhampton's trolleybuses.

At the time of the visit the commission had one eye on the looming general election. Who knew what the election would bring? The commission accelerated its work and started drafting a second interim report, on bus licensing.

The law on bus licensing, wrote Griffith-Boscawen, 'is positively archaic'. He had a point. As is often the case, the law regulating technology had been outstripped by technological advances. Bus licensing was in the hands of local authorities, about 1,300 of them, and a single long-distance bus service could easily require licences from half a dozen councils or more.

But far more important for the commission's Conservative members was the use of the licensing system to protect council trams and buses. The commissioners had scant sympathy for municipal enterprise and they seized on the evidence of Richard Howley, a BET director, who represented the Omnibus Owners' Association. Howley claimed there had been several cases where companies had been refused licences to run buses because the councils wanted them to be municipal. He wanted licensing to be taken away from councils and given to new bodies covering large areas of the country. The commission adopted his suggestion.

By June Griffith-Boscawen had written a draft report. It had a whole chapter about tramways, which largely reflected Spencer's evidence. Spencer had told the commission that three-quarters of the money spent on the trams' permanent way went on maintaining the adjacent road surface and short leases discouraged companies from keeping their trams up to date, producing 'the unfortunate result that old-fashioned and, in some cases, ill-maintained tramcars are in service', Spencer said. 'This…accounts to a large extent for what is undoubtedly a popular prejudice at the present time against the tramcar.' The draft report proposed road fund grants to tramways and for 'greater security of tenure' for private tramways.

Griffith-Boscawen's plain intention was to adjust the rules to favour private enterprise. News of the recommendations soon leaked and the trade press reported that the commission was going to ease the road maintenance burden for trams. But at its meeting on 17 July 1929 and for unrecorded reasons, the commission dropped the chapter on tramways from the final version of the report.[151]

In the meantime, following the May general election Herbert Morrison replaced Ashley as Minister of Transport. It is not difficult to imagine the unease in the Royal Commission's offices. Morrison was an enthusiast for public enterprise and the brains behind the 'hands off the people's trams' campaign.

In September, Griffith-Boscawen wrote to Morrison to say that the second report on licensing would be published in October. Morrison's reply was cordial and implied he supported scrapping the speed limit – the main feature of the first report. Morrison was a keen motorist. 'Your first report has certainly received a friendly reception from the press. At this I am not surprised since, apart from the merits of its recommendations, the presentation of it was fresh and vigorous.'[152]

The LCC tried to capitalise on the shifting political sands. It was concerned about the commission's apparent prejudice and wanted to present the case for trams more forcefully. 'There still appears to be a need in certain quarters for education on this matter, and we think it well that the Royal Commission should be fully seized of the important part which the council's tramways play in carrying London's population.'[153]

The council wrote to the ministry – tellingly, not to the commission – asking to give evidence. The ministry passed the letter on to the commission, a tacit hint that the LCC should be given a hearing.

On an overcast afternoon in early October, Charles Matthews, who chaired the LCC's highways committee, crossed the river from County Hall and ventured into the commission's lair, a committee room in the House of Lords. Seated in the comfortable red-leather upholstered chairs, Matthews explained that trams were essential. 'Some people suggest that tramways are an obsolete form of traction which should be superseded by motor omnibuses…The council is convinced of the vital part which tramways necessarily play in…Greater London.'

Top of the LCC's shopping list – and a long-standing grudge – was scrapping the boroughs' veto on building new tramways in central London. But for the veto, said Matthews, the LCC 'would have many more miles of tram lines'. The bid to scrap the veto brought an irate riposte from two inner London boroughs, Westminster and Holborn. The veto had largely 'saved the borough from the disaster of tramways' said Holborn's borough engineer.

The LCC, echoing Spencer's evidence, also wanted help with the cost of road maintenance. Matthews highlighted the invidious rules for road fund grants. The bias against tramways in doling out grants, initiated by the old Road Board, had been continued by the Ministry of Transport. On main roads the ministry gave a grant of 60 per cent, but if the road had a tramway that grant only applied to those parts of the road that weren't maintained by the tramway. It was absurd. Why not, he said, give the same grant to the centre of the road as the shoulders?

It was a singularly lacklustre hearing. Here was one of the most senior Conservative politicians in local government extolling the virtues of municipal trams to a Conservative-dominated commission, which had completely different ideas about both municipal enterprise and trams. The commission politely pulled its punches. The elephant in the room was the word obsolete.

The LCC's reception was part of a broader pattern. The commission spent nine days listening to evidence from the motor lobby but dodged listening to anyone who spoke up for trams, such as an eminent economist who was advising the government on dealing with its post-war debt mountain.[154] It could, however, find time to listen to the meanderings of Earl Howe, the racing driver Francis Curzon, whose elevation to the peerage had precipitated the Battersea by-election. The commission only wanted to hear facts that chimed with their pro-motoring prejudices.

The evidence of the Federation of British Industries, which represented the country's industrial muscle, was more to the commission's liking. It wanted to abolish trams in city centres. There was a curious back story to this demand.

The FBI had set up a special committee to draft its evidence. The representative of the non-ferrous metals trades couldn't attend the crucial meeting, but he wrote asking for the mention of trams to be removed. Tramways were an important user of copper. The committee demurred and slightly watered down its evidence. It told the commission it wanted to take trams 'out of the centre of many towns'.[155]

The FBI's evidence was given by Walter Gaunt, a senior manager of J. Lyons and Co. Surely, he was asked, removing trams from the centre means abolishing the whole tramway system. His response was awaited with particular interest by one of the commissioners – Isidore Salmon, the managing director of J. Lyons and Gaunt's boss. 'Those who I represent,' replied Gaunt, 'want something other than the tram.'

In September John Jacob Astor, who had just become a director of the Great Western Railway, resigned. His resignation allowed Morrison to redress, to a tiny extent, the political balance of the commission. The new commissioner was the Liberal-leaning Robert Donald, who since leaving *Municipal Journal* had edited several major Fleet Street papers – including the *Daily Chronicle* – and who had been such a doughty defender of trams and municipal enterprise in his younger days.

Meanwhile, the commission began work on its final report. Griffith-Boscawen circulated his initial thoughts in November 1929, followed by a sketchy version of the final report. 'We are convinced that gradually tramways must disappear and that it is to the public advantage that they should. Opportunity should be taken when rails [are] worn out to substitute either motor buses or trackless trolley systems.' When the draft was circulated, Clarendon said he was 'very glad you suggest that the tram has reached the evening of its life'.[156]

The commission's stately progress was suddenly thrown off course when Griffith-Boscawen met Morrison just before Christmas and Morrison dropped a bombshell: he wanted to delay the final report for a year, because of his bill to nationalise London's transport. This was the big prize for Morrison: bringing all London's trains, trams and buses into public ownership. Morrison's pretext was that he wanted the commission to have a closer look at how things were done abroad. In reality, the last thing Morrison wanted was for the Royal Commission's report to throw his plan for state control of London transport into disarray.

The commission started some desultory hearings again in May 1930, after a five-month hiatus. The penultimate witness on the penultimate day was Kevin Fenelon, a transport economist from the University of Edinburgh. Transport economists were a rarity back then, and the commission had specially asked Fenelon to give evidence. It was the closest the commission ever came to hearing an impartial and independent witness.

If the commission hoped that Fenelon would add a veneer of academic respectability to their prejudices, they were to be disappointed. 'The bus versus tramway controversy had not yet been definitely settled, but…there is still scope for a modernised tramway,' said Fenelon. A modern tram still had the edge over a bus and he didn't move from this position despite close questioning.

Shortly afterwards, Griffith-Boscawen circulated an updated draft of the final report. At a series of meetings held in the Ministry of Labour in June and July, the fate of the tram was sealed. On 21 July 1930 the commission's secretary circulated the conclusions from these meetings. The 'commission will recommend that no new tramways should be constructed' and that buses or trolleybuses should replace trams. The commission ruled out any help with road maintenance, because a tram licence was only 15 shillings. It also ruled out extending tram leases 'as greater security would only tend to prolong the life of an undertaking'.[157]

By September rumours were circulating that the Royal Commission would recommend scrapping trams. The *Daily Mail* was cock-a-hoop. The tram was 'a source of great danger…and of extreme obstruction', it claimed, 'the disappearance of the tramway is only a question of time'. The *Daily Herald* also reported the rumours, together with a flat denial from one commissioner, William Lobjoit. 'No decision had yet been considered,' he said, conveniently forgetting the meetings he attended in June and July when the commission agreed to recommend killing off trams.[158]

In October 1930 the bus versus tram row erupted in the pages of the left-of-centre magazine *Nation*, which trotted out the familiar complaint that trams were 'noisy and…one of the chief causes of traffic congestion'. The increase in the seating capacity of buses meant trams were no longer needed. The unsigned article would doubtless have met with the approval of Ernest Harold Davenport, the magazine's oil correspondent.

The author was taken to task by John Benn, the grandson of John Williams Benn. This prompted a response from Brunner, who chose to conceal his job with Shell-Mex by writing a letter from his home address in Bloomsbury. 'The congestion caused by trams is common knowledge to every motorist,' said Brunner. 'The present century is the century of the internal combustion engine.'

The commission's final report was eventually published on 8 January 1931. Fleet Street gave it the red-carpet treatment with fulsome coverage and friendly editorials from right, left and centre of the political spectrum. The *Manchester Guardian* summed up the report in five headlines: 'Electrified railways; Faster trains; Wider roads; Better harbours and No more trams.' The *Daily Mirror* applauded the commission's verdict that trams were obsolete. 'We say hear, hear!' The abolition of trams was the centrepiece of coverage in the Conservative *Morning Post*, the Liberal *News Chronicle* and – predictably – the *Daily Mail* and the *Evening News*.

The week after publication, Donald revealed the inside story – or at least part of it. When he joined the commission, said Donald, 'I found that the majority of the members were inclined to the view that tramways should be scrapped. The feeling seemed to be that the death sentence should be passed upon them without the option of delay.' The prejudice against trams, he wrote, ignored 'the utility, economy or convenience of this popular means of transport. It is due partly to opposition to municipal trading…[and partly] to the general belief that the motor bus is a more convenient, comfortable and economical means of transport.'[159]

Donald was unquestionably right about the commissioners. He was probably right to say he persuaded them to replace summary execution with a more lingering death. But the bottom line was that he too signed the death warrant.

Candide, the *Sunday Pictorial*'s irrepressible society-cum-motoring correspondent, had a completely different take on the report – 'a well-considered and constructive effort'. Griffith-Boscawen 'has approached the heavy task set before him with great earnestness. He is himself a motorist. I had several talks with him while

Gunning for the tram: little more than a week before the Royal Commission's damning verdict, Wilfred Ashley held a shooting party on his Broadlands estate. Ashley, the minister who set up the Royal Commission, is on the left, next to him is the Earl of Clarendon, a strident anti-tram voice on the commission and on horseback is William Joynson-Hicks, lately home secretary and advocate for the London General Bus Company. (Illustrated Sporting and Dramatic News/Author's Collection)

the commission was sitting and it was obvious in each that he had a first-hand knowledge of the difficulties of the owner-driver.'[160]

While the report was still at the printers, Griffith-Boscawen was taking part in the annual village pantomime. The production of the Pangbourne players that year was *Cinderella*. Griffith-Boscawen played the part of the wicked baron.

Chapter 22

THE TIPPING POINT

L ondon, the world's largest city and beating heart of the British Empire, was always going to be the crucial battleground in the struggle between buses and trams. London had the world's largest network of trams and for both politicians and the press, the capital was the epicentre of the arguments about the future of the tram.

The first truly modern trams, the Felthams, took to the streets of west London on Monday 5 January 1931. Nine days later the London County Council opened its enlarged Kingsway tram subway. Both events – initiated by the private and public sectors – were powerful and costly statements of faith in the future of the tram. But sandwiched between these two events came the Royal Commission's report condemning trams as obsolete. And although few knew it at the time, the fate of the Felthams had been sealed eight months earlier.

Enlarging the Kingsway subway to take double-deck tramcars had cost £326,000 and it was an effective counterblast to the Royal Commission. The previous week's headlines were, at least temporarily, eclipsed by the reopening of Kingsway. The subway was 'London's new travel boon,' said the *Evening News*. The formal opening 'was a triumphal journey made in a pullman tramcar of white, relieved with gold and blue,' reported the *News Chronicle*, while the *Daily Telegraph* said the subway was 'an indispensable link'.

'Last week we were reading the final report of the Royal Commission on Transport, which pronounced that tramways are "in a state of obsolescence" and recommended no more should be constructed,' said the *Daily Telegraph*. 'The wit of man cannot provide a substitute for those strings of heavily laden tramcars which move every day a large proportion of London's workers to and from their homes.'

The opening was a minor sensation, an attraction on a par with the New Year sales. 'Large crowds gathered on the Embankment to witness the re-opening,' reported *The Times*. About 70,000 passengers used the subway on the first day, more than twice the number using the Kingsway trams in single-deck days. And over the following days small knots of people gathered on the Embankment just to watch the trams go by.

Almost the only sour note came from the *Daily Mirror*'s motoring correspondent, who bemoaned the return of 'Freddie the Flag Wagger, a familiar figure to thousands of London motorists'. Freddie – a made-up name, there were several of them – directed traffic at the exit of the tram tunnel onto the Embankment. Armed with a red flag and dressed in an LCC uniform Freddie held up the traffic so that trams could turn onto the Embankment 'while the rest of London waited', as the *Mirror* put it.

Plans to enlarge the subway to take double-deckers had been approved by the council in 1927. But the LCC still needed parliamentary approval and discontent simmered among motorists. It was a 'tram folly' claimed one motoring magazine, which complained about 'more money to be spent on an obsolete system', while the fervent road lobbyist William Rees Jeffreys ranted about the LCC's tramway bias. 'The L.C.C. is interested in tramways to the exclusion of all other forms of transport, and this fact operates to bias…the principal municipal authority in London,' he said.

The LCC, complained Rees Jeffreys, had appropriated one-third of the Embankment for trams, erecting 'shelters and other obstructions on the roadway with little regard to the needs of non-tramway traffic'.[161] He tried to get the Motor Legislation Committee to thwart the LCC's Kingsway plan and even suggested, unsuccessfully, running a propaganda campaign to secure the election of a less pro-tram council.

Despite this dissent, parliament approved the plans. In February 1930 the subway was closed for reconstruction and the council laid plans for a grand

'Freddie' the flag wagger, was the dismissive soubriquet among well-heeled motorists for several LCC employees, whose job was to stop the roar of London's traffic to allow trams leaving the Kingsway subway to turn onto the Embankment. (Author's collection)

re-opening. The Prince of Wales, who as a small boy had so much fun on the top deck of the first tram to Tooting, had been pencilled in to perform the opening ceremony. In October the LCC sanctioned the spending for a specially decorated car, a tram fit for a future king.

In the event, the building work over-ran slightly and the opening ceremony was postponed for a month. The Prince of Wales – the future Edward VIII – didn't open the subway. The surviving records give no clue as to why he was unavailable. But what is indisputable is that a royal opening ceremony would have been tantamount to endorsing tramways – the technology that the Royal Commission was on the point of declaring obsolescent. The potential for political embarrassment was huge.

In the absence of the Prince of Wales, the LCC's first thought was to have a low-key event instead. The news reached the ears of Charles Matthews, who had defended the LCC's tramways before the Royal Commission. Matthews was on his way to Jamaica to spend the winter in warmer climes for the sake of his health. He telegraphed the LCC urging it to pull out all the stops.[162] In response the council drew up a generous guest list. Matthews would never see the results of his intervention. He died not long after landing in Jamaica.

The LCC put on three tramcars for the event. The white-painted tram, which had the topical number 1931 and which was driven briefly by the chairman of the council, carried the most distinguished guests and appeared in almost all photos of the event. The second tram was for lesser mortals and the third was for the press.

After driving through the subway, the party returned to Holborn Station, where guests could inspect the handsome well-lit new station, which replaced the dingy old picking-up place, and listen to speeches. Ernest Kemp, the vice-chair of the highways committee, seized the opportunity to lambast the tram's critics – and the Royal Commission. Standing on a bench at Holborn Station he told the crowd, 'If a transport business that paid its dividend, redeemed its stock, maintained the road, which it did not altogether use and at the same time showed a clear profit was obsolescent,' he said, the word had lost its meaning. After the speeches were over the guests got back on their respective trams and returned to County Hall for tea.

The guest list gives a clue to the event's political sensitivity. Henry Maybury, who although he had retired from the ministry still chaired London's Traffic Advisory Committee, was there, as was Chris Spencer, the Combine's tramways manager. But the real interest was in the absentees. Who was not there? The most notable absentee was Herbert Morrison, the minister of transport and champion of the people's trams. Nor was there any other politician from the Ministry of Transport. It was one way of avoiding awkward questions about trams being obsolete.

There can be no doubt that the LCC would have welcomed Morrison's attendance. The only minister at the ceremony was Frederick Pethick-Lawrence, a junior treasury minister, barrister and supporter of the suffragettes who had served nine months in

A special white-painted tram carried the VIPs for the reopening of the enlarged Kingsway subway on 14 January 1931. (Author's collection)

prison for the cause. Pethick-Lawrence was a familiar figure on the Kingsway trams, he lived in Lincoln's Inn Fields, a stone's throw from Holborn station and found the tram extremely handy for travelling home from the House of Commons – it was virtually a door-to-door service. Morrison's parliamentary secretary dropped a note to the LCC on his behalf. 'Pethick-Lawrence…tells me he uses the tram subway… very frequently and consequently would much appreciate an invitation to the official opening.' The LCC was only too glad to oblige and gave him a place on the first tram, with the rest of the VIPs.[163]

Spencer's press launch for the new Feltham tram was much more low-profile and overshadowed by a leak of the Royal Commission's report to the *Daily Mail* three days before the launch. It was a particularly effective spoiler. According to the *Mail*, which had seemingly been briefed by the Ministry of Transport, the Royal Commission would recommend that trolleybuses or buses should replace trams in the suburbs of London – precisely those lines earmarked for the Felthams.

The new trams impressed journalists when they first appeared on the Uxbridge Road. The *News Chronicle* found the tramcar exceptionally comfortable. 'It is as

Brightly lit stations replaced the old dingy stopping places in the new Kingsway subway. Holborn station pictured in 1933. Travelling from Holborn to Westminster has never been quicker. (Topical Press/©TfL from the London Transport Museum collection)

comfortable as a motor coach and can reach a speed of 20 miles an hour in ten seconds,' reported the *Daily Herald*. 'It looks like an overgrown "tube" coach.'

But few other Fleet Street editors thought it worth sending a reporter out to the wilds of West London, so it was left to local papers to plug the gap. With its nippy acceleration and powerful air brakes, the new tram's average speed, including stops, was 12mph, more than 2mph faster than the capital's buses and other trams. 'In speed, therefore, as well as comfort, the new tramcar is held to bear comparison with any other form of transport,' wrote the reporter from the *West Middlesex Gazette*.

It was not just the passengers who would enjoy the new tram's comforts. The drivers too had a separate compartment and a seat, just like drivers on tube trains. And a windscreen with safety glass protected the driver from the elements, a long-standing demand of the Transport and General Workers' Union. To hard-pressed commuters struggling to keep their jobs as the great depression began to bite still

The Feltham tram had impressive acceleration: from 0 to 20 miles per hour in just 10 seconds – and from cutting-edge technology to obsolete in just two days. (Topical Press/©TfL from the London Transport Museum collection)

deeper, the luxurious, speedy and quiet new trams were a beacon of hope. They were, as one headline writer put it 'trams de luxe'.

Two days later the Royal Commission published its damning report. In just forty-eight hours the Feltham had morphed from ultra-modern to obsolescent. The irony of the luxury trams being declared obsolescent did not escape reporters. 'The new tram is as comfortable and efficient a vehicle as any bus and it may well bring the tramways a new lease of popularity,' said the reporter from the *Middlesex County Times*. 'I prefer them to the new buses.' In its editorial the paper said the new trams undermined the Royal Commission's conclusion that trams were obsolete and should gradually disappear.

After years of under-investment, the Combine's tramways faced a stark choice. Should they modernise the trams, or should they scrap them? The decision to build 100 Felthams was tangible evidence that the Combine had been leaning towards modernisation. Spencer had a twin-track strategy to replace his ramshackle fleet of trams with a mixture of modern trams and trolleybuses. The Felthams were earmarked for busy routes and trolleybuses would replace trams on quieter ones.

One of London United's spanking new trolleybuses posed alongside a rather ramshackle-looking tram. (Author's collection)

A few months later, in a move that would have been more to the Royal Commission's taste, London United Tramways replaced some of its tramways around Twickenham in southwest London with trolleybuses. In contrast to the low-profile launch of the Feltham, the Combine's public relations team pulled out all the stops. A new trolleybus posed for photographers alongside one of the ageing trams it was destined to replace. After the photo-op company officials and guests took a trolleybus to Fulwell garage, where they enjoyed a celebratory lunch. Frank Pick, the managing director of the Underground group, was on hand to tell guests and reporters that the company intended to replace 17 miles of tramways with trolleybuses by the summer.

It was a sign of the times. Pick already knew no more Felthams would be built: trolleybuses were the future. The Royal Commission's report damning trams coupled with the deliberations of an obscure Treasury committee had scotched any hope of building more Felthams.

As part of its efforts to combat the depression, the government had set up a fund to hand out grants to schemes that eased unemployment and improved public amenity. Many grants went to railway companies, such as one to Southern Railway to improve the docks at Southampton. Lord Ashfield was particularly adept at tapping government funds to support the Combine's finances. In March 1930 he applied to the government for two grants. One was for the long-cherished plan to extend the Piccadilly line. The other was to help pay for a further 250 Felthams.

The purse strings for this fund were in the hands of an obscure Treasury committee, the Development (Public Utility) Advisory Committee. In his bid for a grant, Ashfield said the Combine 'would be prepared to place an order for tramcars involving an expenditure of around £750,000 if financial assistance could be afforded on terms similar to those granted to the [London] railway companies.'[164] Ashfield already privately harboured doubts about the plan. Given the success of the London General's new buses and London United's trolleybus plans, he warned, companies should consider carefully any further spending on trams.

Ashfield's grant application was considered by the Treasury committee on 10 April. The meeting was attended by Alfred Robinson, one of the Ministry of Transport's most senior civil servants, who was there to advise on transport grants. The committee was sympathetic to the tube extension and ended up giving a grant that was worth nearly one-fifth of the cost.

It then considered the bid to build more Felthams. Senior civil servants like Robinson were well aware that the Royal Commission would recommend phasing out trams. The committee's conclusion was a tipping point. 'It was decided to write to Lord Ashfield informing him that the committee would not be disposed to recommend assistance on the suggested scheme for providing new tramcars for the Metropolitan Electric Tramways Limited and the London United Tramways Limited.'[165] The plan for more Feltham trams was shelved. The bottom line was that Ashfield had been prepared to buy second-hand pirate buses for £2,500 each – many of which were promptly scrapped – but he shrank from spending £3,000 on brand-new Feltham trams.

Events in London were inextricably bound up with Morrison's efforts to bring all of London's transport – buses, trains and trams – into public ownership. Morrison said coordinating transport could only be achieved 'by the substitution of a single and simple form of public ownership for the complicated network of separate interests, private and municipal, which now add so greatly to the difficulties of the situation'.

Morrison spent months in tortuous negotiations with the various parties. In October 1930 he announced a new transport board. 'The new authority,' Morrison told the press, 'will have no tramway, tube or omnibus bias', and with one eye on the impending Royal Commission report, he added: 'Its transport policy will be determined by technical fact and public interest.'

Behind the scenes, Frank Pick took an active part in the negotiations over the London Transport bill and frequently lobbied Cyril Hurcomb in person. It has been suggested, wrote Hurcomb in a note that had been heavily influenced by Pick, 'that the bill might confer power upon the board to substitute trackless trolleys for tramways…I have always been inclined to favour this and I think the minister agrees'.[166]

Within days of the publication of the Royal Commission's report, the ministry included a new clause in the London Transport bill allowing the new board to abandon trams – without the need for a private bill.

'I consider it to be desirable that the powers of the board to abandon tramways… should be made clear in the bill,' wrote the civil servant in charge of the ministry's finance section. 'The main objects of the suggested clause are to facilitate the abandonment of tramways.'[167]

By March 1931 the negotiations with the Combine and other interests were virtually complete. The deal was that Ashfield would chair a new London Transport Passenger Board, and Pick would be his deputy. In effect this was the Combine takeover that Morrison had so strenuously opposed in the 'hands off the people's trams' campaign. And to add injury to insult the new London Passenger Transport Board would have unfettered power to 'abandon, either in whole or in part, any tramway system forming part of their undertaking'.[168]

The bill was generally welcomed, although *The Times* in its editorial pointedly recalled the campaign to save the people's trams. In parliament, Morrison admitted that the board would have the power to scrap trams. Morrison now acquiesced in a policy that he had described as 'sheer lunacy' only two years before.

'The hint that trams may go was received in ominous silence. The tram is cursed and condemned by every other class of road user, but it retains its grip on the affection of the Londoner as of the North-Countryman,' wrote the lobby correspondent of the *Yorkshire Post*.

Morrison's journey from tram fan to tram scrapper was not the major U-turn that it appeared. His support for the people's trams in 1928, reflected his conviction that public ownership, in the shape of the LCC, was superior to private enterprise. Fast forward three years and Morrison still believed in public ownership. But this time it was ownership by the state and not just a local council. Another factor that tinged his attitude to trams, was that Morrison, despite having sight in only one eye, was a keen motorist. Trams, people-owned or not, were the price of public ownership – they were to be sacrificed on the altar of state control.

After 24 August 1931 a new National Government took over from the Labour government and Morrison ceased to be Minister of Transport. The new minister in the National Government was a Liberal MP, John Pybus, who continued the plan to take London Transport into public ownership and successfully piloted the bill through most of its remaining parliamentary stages.

Meanwhile Ashfield was laying the groundwork for the wholesale scrapping of London's trams. At a chairman's meeting of the Combine's senior managers, held in November 1931, Ashfield floated the idea – in line with the Royal Commission's report – of replacing trams with trolleybuses when the track was worn out. Spencer said that trolleybuses were not suitable for busy routes, because of their smaller carrying capacity. The company's trolleybuses had seats for fifty-six passengers, plus five standing, while the Feltham had sixty-eight seats and room for twenty standing.

It was a well-rehearsed debate, and one that both men were familiar with. Trams were better at coping with rush hours because they carried more people. But this time Ashfield was ready with an answer. 'The time had come,' he said, 'to approach the manufacturers with a view to ascertaining whether they can design a vehicle, whether omnibus or trolleybus which would be equivalent to the tramcar in carrying capacity.' Pick was asked to set up a small committee to look into the idea together with the Combine's bus building arm AEC, the Associated Equipment Company.[169]

A prototype 74-seat trolleybus was delivered in early 1933. It was greeted with unalloyed rapture in some quarters. 'Another nail has been hammered into the coffin of the tramcar,' claimed the *Daily Mirror*'s motoring correspondent, who had been given an exclusive sneak preview as part of the Combine's public relations push to soften up the public for the change.

By now Ashfield believed that trolleybuses should replace trams. He explained his thinking to the Royal Society. Trams, he said, cause congestion and tramway terminals occupy valuable road space just where it is most needed. 'The solution of the tramway problem appears to lie in the direction of producing a trackless trolley vehicle of equal capacity to that of the tramcar, free from the rigidity imposed upon it by the necessity of running upon rails.' Much of Ashfield's talk was a rehash of the common criticisms of the tram. But it was significant because of who was saying it and the reference to the new larger trolleybuses.

In April it was officially confirmed that Ashfield would head the new London Transport board and that he would pocket the formidable pay cheque of £30,000 a year. Pick, his faithful lieutenant, would earn £10,000.

On the first day of July 1933 London Transport took over the capital's buses, railways and trams. Most of the senior managers came from the Combine. Responsibility for the trams was split between Spencer, who continued to run the Combine's old tramways in north and west London, and Theodore Thomas, the former manager of the LCC's trams who broadly took charge of the municipal trams.

In the first week of its existence, the new London Transport Board approved building 100 new diesel buses. These buses had fifty-six seats, fewer than the Feltham or the new trolleybuses, but crucially they each cost about £1,000 less than a Feltham. It was a sign of things to come.

Ashfield continued to take key decisions in his 'chairman's meetings', just as he did in the days of the Combine. The crunch meeting was held on 28 September 1933.

Spencer produced a plan for a programme of major track replacement in the north of London at a cost of nearly £160,000, including the flagship tramway on the Uxbridge Road. The meeting rejected the plans and told Spencer and Thomas to go away and produce a scheme for converting these tramways to trolleybus routes.

On some routes, the former Combine trams ran through onto routes equipped with the LCC's system of conduit electrification. The LCC's track was in far better condition than the Combine's. So the meeting decided that the report should also consider the 'desirability of not abandoning the existing conduit system despite the changeover to operation by trolleybuses'. Ashfield amended the minute to read 'not immediately abandoning'.[170]

At the next meeting on 12 October, Thomas came back with a plan for the wholesale conversion of trams to trolleybuses in north London. This was Thomas's report, and not Spencer's. Spencer did not attend the meeting. Nor would he ever attend another one. He resigned the next day.

Thomas took over Spencer's trams as well as his own. The new tram supremo told journalists that London's trams would gradually disappear. 'I do not think it would be right to anticipate the early disappearance of trams…as many are in good condition.' It must be obvious, he told reporters, 'that the outlying parts of London's tramway system must be changed to something more suitable'. In November 1933 London Transport announced that it was to replace 90 miles of tramways in north London with trolleybuses. It was the beginning of the end of London's trams.

Spencer received a golden handshake of nearly £6,000 to compensate him for his early retirement – he had another seven years to serve – and a position on the board of the North Metropolitan Electric Power Supply, a Combine company that had not become part of London Transport. Spencer's departure was lamented by his colleagues. 'If ever the history of tramways is written, Mr Spencer will occupy one of the most prominent places in it,' said one.[171]

In February 1934, Spencer walked up the first-class gangplank to board the *Winchester Castle* in Southampton. He was off to South Africa to head an inquiry into the future of transport in Johannesburg. It was a miniature version of the Royal Commission and he had been recommended for the job by Ashfield, who seems to have had a bit of conscience about the way Spencer had been treated.

The Johannesburg inquiry had unusual difficulties, because of apartheid rules. But influenced by events in Britain, the city was contemplating replacing its trams with trolleybuses. So, Spencer's experience made him a good candidate for the job.

The inquiry report closely reflected Spencer's views. He recommended a mixture of buses and trolleybuses on quieter routes and new trams for the busier routes. After some debate the city adopted the recommendations. The new trams, which showed a debt to the Feltham, would outlast those in London by a decade.

Chapter 23

A TALE OF TWO PRESSURE GROUPS

Thanks to the Royal Commission, the nation's roads would soon be rid of two impediments that caused the most moaning among motorists leaning on the bars of country roadhouses – trams and speed traps. There would be no speed limit and therefore no speed traps. And no trams. If motorists were the undisputed winners from the commission's report, the losers were pedestrians, who would find that speeding traffic made roads more dangerous, and commuters, who had the prospect of trams de luxe being snatched from their grasp and faced being relegated to buses.

The commission's pronouncements were not a done deal. The government had to accept its recommendations. Both the tram lobby and pedestrians had the opportunity to make their voices heard and overturn, or at least rein back, the recommendations. The buck stopped with the Ministry of Transport, ministers and civil servants. They were the key decision-makers.

However, it would be an uphill task. The pedestrians had to convince politicians that speed did kill. The tram lobby had to make the case that there was a place for modern trams on city streets. Both goals were achievable. As the 1930s wound on one of these groups – the pedestrians – would claw back some of the ground that had been snatched from them. But the tram lobby would lose almost everything.

At first the smart money must have been on the tram lobby to withstand the Royal Commission's onslaught. This was a powerful entrenched industry. Tramways were an important sector of the economy and a major employer. In 1931 tramways employed nearly 81,000 people and trams consumed 10 per cent of the electricity produced by the nation's power stations. The industry, both public and private sectors, had well-funded trade associations with permanent staff. These associations enjoyed regular contact with the ministry – giving them the inside track in the corridors of power. And two trade magazines provided influential support to the tram industry.

Both the pedestrians and the tram lobby had well-founded gripes about the Royal Commission's bias. 'They are motorists, who as a class object to the presence of rails in the streets,' the editor of one tram magazine told the American *Electric*

Railway Journal. To modern eyes the Royal Commission also had another bias. All its members were men, as were all the oral witnesses. This was an all-male event.

Two years earlier, Robert Cecil in the House of Lords had highlighted the commission's one-sidedness after the publication of its first report. It had taken extensive evidence from motorists but not from pedestrians. 'There did not appear to be any society for the protection of pedestrians,' he said. Tom Foley, a young Fleet Street sub-editor, read Cecil's speech and wrote to him, suggesting that they set up one. The result was the birth of the Pedestrians' Association.

The fledgling association mounted a deputation to the transport minister Herbert Morrison urging him to keep the speed limit. Ever the politician, Morrison told the pedestrians that it was unfortunate the association hadn't existed earlier so that it could have given evidence to the Royal Commission.[172] Morrison's crumbs of comfort counted for nothing: he still scrapped the speed limit.

Unlike the tramway associations, the Pedestrians' Association was run on a shoestring, financed by donations and subscriptions – the membership subscription was a shilling. But the pedestrians, who had several journalists on their committee, were well-versed in public relations, unlike the stuffy trade associations. The pedestrians were also more broadly based – they had women on their committee – as distinct from the all-male trade associations, which represented an industry, not passengers.

Predictably, the immediate reaction of tram managers to the Royal Commission report was to reject the charge of obsolescence. The post-publication soundbites contrasted the vitriolic anti-tram campaign with the attempts to modernise the country's tramways. 'In spite of…a most violent and grossly unfair vendetta carried on by a section of the press,' said Sunderland's tramway manager, 'the tramway systems of this country continue to extend and are in a most prosperous condition.' Burnley's recently retired manager accused the commission of having 'absorbed the Daily Mailean philosophy so liberally spread over the British Isles assisted by the builders and users of omnibuses'.[173]

The commission's report directly attacked the municipal tramways' core interest. For its part, the Municipal Tramways and Transport Association's initial reaction was to point out that towns and cities had recently spent £4 million on modernising their tramways. 'They would not have done that if they thought tramways were out of date.'

But the association soon retreated from this position. At the end of February 1931 the British Electrical Development Association wrote to the municipals to suggest a joint campaign to keep city transport electric. What the electricity industry wanted was to keep trams, where possible, and where it was not possible to replace them with trolleybuses – and not motor buses.

But when the association's council – its ruling body – met in March they rejected outright the idea of a joint campaign with the electricity industry, because the choice

In the years immediately preceding the Royal Commission's condemnation of trams, councils had spent large sums of money improving their trams. The foremost example was the LCC's enlargement of the Kingsway subway, which cost more than £320,000. (F. E. J. Ward/Online Transport Archive)

between trams, trolleybuses and motor buses was a matter for local consideration. The electricity industry was left to fend for itself. Instead, the meeting's minutes suggest the municipals were more concerned about negotiating a tax break to make it cheaper to scrap trams. In this they were successful.[174]

Why were the municipals so pusillanimous? Part of the answer lay in the influence of two men: Stuart Pilcher, the manager of Manchester's tramways who enthused about replacing trams with buses, and Owen Silvers, Wolverhampton's trolleybus champion. Pilcher was the association's president for 1930-31, the period when the Royal Commission published its final report, and his influence delayed and diluted the association's response.

Pilcher, often photographed wearing a natty bow tie, was an apostle of the new. In Edinburgh he converted the old cable cars to electric trams. He was subsequently one of the first municipal operators to run buses with pneumatic tyres. In Manchester he replaced a circular tram route with buses. The route had long stretches of single track, with passing places, so the tram service was slow. Buses took over in the spring of 1930 and Pilcher was able to claim that they were 1 mile an hour faster than the old trams.

Buoyed up by this success Pilcher became increasingly bullish about scrapping trams. 'Personally, I do not think there will be any tramways running in this country twenty years hence, or even within a shorter period,' Pilcher told the private-sector

Tramways, Light Railways and Transport Association in May 1931, regaling his audience with his success in replacing modern trams with buses.

His remarks produced a public spat between the municipals' president and the company association's president, Chris Spencer. Did Pilcher know what a modern tramcar was? asked Spencer. 'I have seen only one [tram] that could be regarded as modern.' Spencer of course meant the Feltham.

The Ministry of Transport's initial reaction to the commission's report was also lukewarm. The civil servant responsible for tramways noted: 'The recommendation that no new tramways at all should be constructed seems…to go too far.'[175] The ministry embarked on a post-publication consultation. In June it wrote to organisations that had given evidence to the Royal Commission asking for their views. The Tramways, Light Railways and Transport Association replied the following month. It disliked the report. Its central gripe was the burden of road maintenance. 'The tramcar…provides its own track at its own expense…and is… unfairly treated as was set out at length by Mr Spencer in his evidence.'

It took another six months and a further prompt from the ministry before the municipals even started to pull together a response. The lengthy delay reflected the internal dissension. Some members were happy to see trams go: others wanted to keep them. In December the association asked its secretary, Jabez Beckett, to draft a response. 'The strictures on tramways relating to obsolescence,' he wrote, are based on prejudice and not evidence. 'This point should be clearly brought out.'

Beckett also emphasised the unfair burden of road maintenance – exactly the point the private sector had made. The Royal Commission had claimed that trams were not unfairly treated because they only paid a licence fee of 15 shillings – compared to road tax for a double-deck bus of £96. Beckett, the former Accrington accountant, was in his element. He calculated that after including the burden of road maintenance, each tram paid £350 a year for its permanent way.

This seemingly uncontroversial draft caused an almighty row when the municipals met to finalise their response in December – almost a year after the commission report was published. Two council members tried, and failed, to have the whole section about road maintenance deleted. The minutes do not identify the members, but subsequent events point to a Manchester connection.[176]

In February 1932 the Association of Municipal Corporations – the organisation that represented all municipal authorities and not just those that ran trams – also rejected the verdict of obsolescence. 'Tramways are, and will continue to be, a useful and in some cases the only satisfactory means of passenger transport.' The town clerk of Manchester and a Manchester alderman tried to block this response. Pilcher later complained about the association making an independent response.[177]

Despite its initial scepticism about the Royal Commission's recommendation an acceptance that trams would disappear gained ground in the Ministry of Transport, aided by the municipals' glacially slow response and the knowledge that prominent municipal stalwarts like Pilcher and Silvers wanted to scrap trams.

The pedestrians tackled their task with considerably more vigour. The Royal Commission agreed with motorists that 'speed is in itself not dangerous provided the car is under proper control,' and it alleged that pedestrians caused more than 35 per cent of accidents.

One of the thousands of pedestrian victims was Bernard Moran, a clerk working for the Ministry of Pensions in Acton. Bernard and his wife Sarah had recently moved into one of the houses being built in Wembley, part of the interwar building boom in Metroland. In the early evening of 14 December 1930 they left their house. Arm in arm they started to cross the Ealing Road. They would never reach the other side.

A car powered around a bend in the road at close to 25 miles per hour. The driver braked and swerved but it was too late. The next thing he remembered was the sickening impact as his car hit the couple. Bernard and Sarah were both seriously injured and taken to hospital. Six days later Bernard, a well-liked employee at the ministry, died from his injuries. He was 44.

The driver was the Earl of Clarendon, the anti-tram member of the Royal Commission, who was on his way from Eton to his home in Hampstead.

The inquest was held three days later. Sarah Moran, who was still being treated in hospital, was carried into the inquest on a stretcher, which was placed in front of the coroner's table. She told the coroner that she had looked both ways and saw that the road was clear before starting to cross.

There was the usual conflict of evidence. A bystander said she was no judge of speed, but she didn't think the car was going fast. A more convincing witness, given his experience, was a bus driver. He said the road was poorly lit and the car 'was going too fast round a bend'.

Clarendon, who was legally represented, said he had turned off his headlight just before the accident. He denied that he took the bend too fast. He did not see the Morans until the last minute. 'They seemed to appear from nowhere,' he said. 'I instantly applied the brakes.'

On the flimsiest of evidence, the coroner told the jury that if a bystander had seen the car it was obvious that the Morans would have done if they had looked. The jury took the hint, came in with a verdict of accidental death and exonerated Clarendon from any blame.[178] Clarendon, who had been severely shaken by the episode, went home and wrote to his friend Wilfred Ashley to thank him for his help and support. Two weeks later Clarendon took up a new position as the governor-general of South Africa.

The next day's papers were universally sympathetic to the Earl. The *Daily Telegraph* firmly pinned the blame on Moran with the headline: 'The man who did not look'.

While the *Daily Mail* linked the Clarendon case to two other pedestrians who had been run over and killed. 'Three instances of pedestrians losing their lives through want of care were investigated yesterday.'

It was an all-too-common story. About half of road deaths were pedestrians. And as the Pedestrians' Association never tired of pointing out, it was easy to pin the blame on the victims. They could never give their side of the story.

Initially the pedestrians' influence in government was limited, with the ministry displaying the traditional antipathy of the civil service to the new kid on the block. The ministry's roads department, for example, blocked the association from having a place on the London and Home Counties Traffic Advisory Committee.

Most road deaths were barely reported: there were just too many of them. But one particularly horrific crash was a natural for the front pages. On Saturday 7 October 1933 a crowd had gathered outside Buckingham Palace to watch the Trooping of the Colour. Suddenly there was a cry of 'look out' followed by a terrific explosion as a car ran into the crowd, demolishing a gas lamp and knocking over a dozen people. Four people died, and the driver sustained serious head injuries.

Sensing the zeitgeist, the Pedestrians' Association and the Cyclists' Touring Club held a mass meeting to demand the return of a speed limit. The Archbishop of Canterbury sent a message of support, while the Mayor of Fulham sent apologies for his absence – from a hospital bed. He had been knocked down by a vehicle outside Fulham Town Hall.

'The main cause of this terrific loss of life and limb is driving too fast,' Cecil, the pedestrians' president, told the meeting, arguing that the ministry was more concerned with keeping the traffic moving than keeping the public safe.

The motor lobby was unnerved by the scale of the opposition and on the day of the pedestrians' meeting William Rees Jeffreys warned colleagues that pressure to bring back speed limits could become irresistible. *Autocar* smeared the Pedestrians' Association, alleging it was subsidised by the railways. It was fake news, and the magazine was grudgingly forced to retract the claim.[179]

Rees Jeffreys was right about the pressure to do something. It was irresistible. In January 1934 the government approved a new Road Traffic Bill, creating a 30-mile-an-hour speed limit in built-up areas.

It was a victory for the Pedestrians' Association. The Ministry of Transport now admitted that 'speed was the great cause of motor accidents', commented Cecil. 'The argument was overwhelming,' he said and he had been amazed at 'the effrontery of those who denied the obvious truth.' In 1935, the first full year of the new speed limit, there was a gratifying drop in road deaths, with 450 fewer pedestrian deaths than the previous year.

From a standing start, the pedestrians had proved that it was possible to take on the motor lobby and win. While the pedestrians consolidated their influence as the decade wore on, the tram lobby visibly crumbled. Towns and cities that modernised their tramways became increasingly isolated.

The press vendetta against trams continued, although it had diminished after reaching its peak in the 1920s. Unfair press criticism had been a regular item on the agenda of the Municipal Tramways and Transport Association. In May 1932 the topic was on the agenda, but the discussion was put off. In June the minutes record that the subject was considered. But nothing was done about it. The item never reappeared on the agenda. The industry's efforts to counter anti-tram propaganda had slumped from ineffectual to non-existent.

The acid test for the tram lobby came in 1932 with the publication of a report about freight. In January that year the main railway companies went to see John Pybus, the new transport minister in the National Government, to complain about unfair competition for freight from road transport. Pybus responded by setting up a conference of road and rail operators to look at the problem. Unlike the Royal Commission, the political balance of this 'conference' was scrupulously even-handed. There were eight members, four from the railways and four from the motor lobby. The conference was chaired by the impeccably neutral Arthur Salter, who had worked in the economics section of the League of Nations.

Salter concluded that goods vehicles ought to be paying more towards the cost of maintaining the roads. It was a unanimous report. It brought howls of outrage from road hauliers, who faced a three-fold increase in licence duty. Although Salter looked only at freight, it was inevitable that there would be some spillover into passenger transport. The report admitted that there would be 'an appropriate revision of the contributions to be made by…vehicles not within our terms of reference'. For buses the appropriate revision was upwards and one of the London General's 60-seaters faced an increase in road tax of one-half.

The prospect enraged the Combine's managing director, Frank Pick. In August 1932 London was in the grip of a heatwave, with the mercury reaching 95°F in the shade. Writing to Lord Ashfield, who was in Canada, the normally calm and measured Pick lost his cool. The Salter report was preposterous, he wrote, telling Ashfield that the motoring organisations would have to disown their representatives on the Salter committee. Pick became the leader of the motor lobby's efforts to undermine Salter and can claim to be a founder of the modern road lobby.[180]

On the face of it, the Salter report was good news for trams. The tramways' road maintenance burden gave buses an unfair advantage, as the municipals had pointed out as recently as January. So, increasing the tax on buses would help to redress the balance. But in September the municipals decided that instead of welcoming higher bus taxes, they should be 'strenuously opposed'. The association distributed 8,000 copies of a report attacking Salter to the press and MPs.

The two tramway associations set up a joint committee with the Society of Motor Manufacturers and Traders to fight the tax increases, reflecting their new-found interest in running buses. It was a watershed moment. The municipals had refused to join the electrical industry in a campaign to save the trams but they were happy to join the motor manufacturers and bus operators to fight off a tax hike for buses. The motor industry's charm offensive was paying off, in spades.

In December the municipals wrote to Pybus and briefed MPs complaining that higher taxes on buses envisaged by the Salter report would scupper plans to scrap trams. It was a remarkable volte-face. In less than a year the association had stood its own policy on its head. At the start of 1932 it denied trams were obsolete, by the end of the year it wanted to make it easier to scrap them. As the decade unfolded, the municipals would become increasingly sucked into the motor industry's orbit.[181]

In June 1933 the municipals' annual conference in Blackpool discussed the future of the tram. Pilcher's contribution was predictable. 'Trams may not be dead yet, but they are dying'. But others warned 'it would be a serious matter for the electrical industry if our traction loads were dropped'.

Cyril Hurcomb, who had listened closely to the debate, took home the message that operators outside London wanting to run trolleybuses instead of trams faced the same time-wasting and costly red tape that tramway promoters had to deal with – they needed a private bill. So, the ministry drafted legislation allowing tramways to convert to trolleybuses without one.

But plans for a seamless conversion were torpedoed by the Tramways, Light Railways and Transport Association, 'in view of the difficulties which would arise' – as the association coyly put it. Hurcomb's plans had fallen foul of the public-private sector rivalry. Many of the association's members ran buses, noted one civil servant, and they didn't want competition from municipal trolleybuses.[182]

Nevertheless, the ministry's civil servants talked up the trolleybus when they spoke to local operators. They were silent, and fume-free, and a lot of the tramway equipment, including posts and overhead wiring could be re-used.

The bottom line for the government was the impact on coal mines. The electricity that powered trams came from coal-burning power stations. For every seven trams that were scrapped, two miners were put out of work. But job losses in the pits could largely be avoided if trams were replaced by trolleybuses.

By the end of the decade, the trade associations and the industry trade journals had all been rebranded to reflect their new broader interests. They all dropped any mention of the word tramway from their titles. 'Tram' had become a dirty word.

However, millions of people still travelled by tram. And they faced being forced onto buses. This was a constituency that faced the greatest upheaval and it was also one that was, by default, excluded from any consultation. What did the travellers on the top deck of the Tooting tram think about it all?

Chapter 24

THE LONG GOODBYE

Middlesbrough's last tram set off on its final journey shortly before midnight on Saturday 9 June 1934. The local paper revealed with barely disguised glee that a Birmingham firm had bought the town's remaining trams to be converted into summer houses and hen runs. 'Death sentence after 36 years,' trumpeted the *Daily Gazette*, which added with gleeful approval that the 'thundering juggernauts to be silenced at last'.

Middlesbrough's trams had originally been developed by a private company. Three local councils bought out the company in 1921. It was a disastrous deal for the ratepayers. The councils had bought at the peak and they watched in dismay while the value of their investment plummeted as unfettered bus competition eroded the trams' earnings.

The debate over whether to scrap the trams – and what to replace them with – had gone on for several years. Eventually Middlesbrough decided to replace them with buses. The first route was scrapped on New Year's Eve in 1931. It was a case of 'fling out the old; bring in the new', recalled the *Gazette*.

Given the years of bad press the trams had endured, what happened on that night in June 1934 was quite extraordinary. Hundreds of people turned out to say goodbye to an institution 'and they cheered the old veteran to the echo as it rolled, rattled, swayed and shivered for the last time over the well-worn route'.

The trams might be dead, but 'they had a grand funeral. Nothing of the kind was anticipated,' wrote the *Gazette* reporter, evidently taken aback by the spontaneous outburst of affection, which jarred with the received wisdom in the newsroom that trams were widely loathed. 'Everything that happened…was entirely unrehearsed and completely unorthodox.'

'It was a right royal goodbye. The two miles of the route to the suburb of Linthorpe were thickly lined with people who cheered, in many cases ironically and in some, perhaps sentimentally, as the "poor man's alarm clock" clattered along for the last time.'

Similar scenes were repeated across the country as tramway after tramway closed. The last tram in Norwich was packed, with passengers crammed into every available space. Crowds lined the route and residents stood at their garden gates to wave the tram goodbye. 'To many the disappearance of the tram brought with it a pang of regret particularly among the older section of the community,' commented one flabbergasted reporter, desperately trying to rationalise the public display. When the last tram reached the depot – not long after closing time – the crowd sang *Auld Lang Syne* and pestered the driver and conductor for their autographs.

These occasions were sometimes riotous, with trams stripped of light fittings, destinations and even seats by souvenir hunters but they were normally convivial, sometimes excessively so. After the last tram event at Weston-super-Mare, the town clerk collided with a stationary wall while driving home. He was convicted of drunk driving and banned from driving for a year.

At York, where the council's trams were being replaced by West Yorkshire's private buses, huge crowds gathered to see the last tram being driven by the Lord Mayor. At the depot the tram was greeted by the tram workers' band. A bugler sounded the Last Post and the bandleader recited an unscripted ditty:

> Ashes to ashes
> Dust to dust
> The corporation won't have us
> The West Yorkshire's must.

The sentiment shone through the literary flaws. A director from the bus company hurriedly retrieved the situation, stressing the need for progress. The people of York 'would soon wonder how they had gone so long without the buses'.

Increasingly, councils organised official ceremonies for the last tram. It was one way of controlling the narrative, turning the sense of loss into a celebration of civic progress. 'The trams are dead, long live the buses' was the theme of the last day in Halifax. Invariably there was no end of civic dignitaries, from mayors to transport managers eager to talk to reporters, who had little time to ask ordinary people what they thought. As a result, one voice is almost entirely absent from the reporting of these events – and that is the voice of people most directly affected, the workers and the ordinary tram passengers.

Just occasionally, unscripted views emerged in the reporting. 'Since the buses took over, there had not been quite the same thought for passengers as in the old days,' said one woman. In Huddersfield travellers felt that 'it was almost like the passing of an old friend'. A more predictable reaction came from London where a local paper reported that 'motorists are particularly glad that the trams, which caused frequent stoppages to general road traffic, are abolished'.

In Nottingham the trams 'went out in a blaze of glory and public demonstration during the early hours of yesterday morning,' reported the *Nottingham Journal*. 'Remarkable scenes were witnessed along the whole route and despite the lateness of the hour, thousands of people turned out to play a part in what was indeed a

Scrapped trams being dismantled in Brighton in 1939. (Step Back in Time)

memorable and, in some respects, thrilling experience.' A corporation motor bus brought the official party, which included local dignitaries and Norman Hardie, the general manager of AEC, the bus and trolleybus builders and a leading light in the Society of Motor Manufacturers and Traders. The party was greeted with what the paper euphemistically termed 'expressions of regret at the passing of the trams, some more forcible than polite'.[183]

Why were vehicles that prompted such an outpouring of bile from one part of the population regarded with unalloyed affection by another section?

In an era before opinion polling, it was difficult to measure what ordinary people thought. There was a sense of loss. There was nostalgia. But did people want modern trams? The correspondence columns are a poor guide. It was the middle classes who aired their grievances by writing to the papers. And they were more likely to be bus passengers or motorists. Working-class tram passengers were less likely to pick up a pen after a long shift and less likely to question the inevitability of progress.

All that is certain was that a series of reporters who independently went to these events expecting to find people celebrating the end of the loathed trams found their expectations confounded.

Several towns and cities, including Aberdeen, Glasgow, Leeds, Liverpool and Sunderland, ignored the building pressure to scrap their trams and opted to modernise their tramways, laying new lines to serve suburban housing estates and

Last tram events became a great draw all over the country as ordinary people bade farewell to their old friends. The top deck of one of Cardiff's last trams in February 1950 was crammed. (Ian L. Wright/ Online Transport Archive)

investing in new trams. In Liverpool, the Ministry of Transport held a public inquiry into the city's plans to extend its tramways.

The class divide was evident at the inquiry. The AA and the RAC argued that buses were better than trams. To the tenants on the council estates trams were 'an absolute necessity' for them to get to work. But white-collar professionals disagreed. An accountant told the inquiry that his area had 'a very good class of resident and they preferred buses to trams. They would not use trams if they passed their own doorsteps.' Did he hate trams? he was asked. 'We definitely do,' was his reply.

Despite a handful of extensions, the country's network of tramways shrank throughout the 1930s. The private sector was particularly severely affected. Outside London private companies ran trams over 235 miles of road in 1932. Over the following five years 150 miles of these private tramways closed. The far larger municipal sector also dwindled, although the decline was less spectacular than the private sector's. Even so municipal tramways still closed at the rate of 60 to 100 miles a year. A campaign was reportedly organised to bombard councils considering scrapping their trams with postcards calling on them to 'do it now'.[184]

Glasgow built 150 of these Coronation tramcars, so called because the coronation of George VI in 1937 coincided with their launch. (Phil Tatt/Online Transport Archive)

Manchester was in the vanguard of this process. Stuart Pilcher persuaded his committee to replace trams with diesel buses as soon as the track became worn out, in line with the Royal Commission's wishes. And to speed up the process he deliberately ran the trams that caused the most damage to rails on routes he had earmarked for closure.[185]

By the mid-1930s the industry-based tram lobby had largely been silenced. Both private and public trade associations were now more interested in buses and trolleybuses. Much to the annoyance of Pilcher, who wanted diesel buses to replace trams, the coal and electricity industries mounted a vigorous campaign to keep transport electric. They distributed a sixpenny leaflet entitled 'What about your trams?'. The answer to this rhetorical question was that councils that weren't going to keep their trams should replace them with trolleybuses.

But the campaign had to counter powerful opposition. 'Petrol bus interests are working up as much prejudice as possible against the electric trolleybus,' warned Manchester's electrical engineer, in a letter to the Central Electricity Board.[186]

So it was left to individuals to defend the tram. In July 1936 the prospect of trolleybuses replacing trams on London's iconic Uxbridge Road prompted one resident, George Jackman, to try to harness the groundswell of sympathy for trams. He wrote to his local paper complaining about the widespread prejudice against trams and asking readers who supported fair play to contact him. The letter struck a chord. Jackman and his supporters wrote to MPs and councillors urging them to oppose this destructive policy.

From these beginnings the tram defenders set up the Light Railway Transport League to argue the case for modernisation. The league got off to a rocky start, with arguments between a faction whose main interest was historical and those who wanted to campaign for modern trams. The modernisers won, but by the time the league became active most of the key decisions to scrap trams had been taken.

The league publicised its cause by organising tram tours. For its London tour, the league hired a tram in May 1938 for an epic journey across the city from Purley to Waltham Cross. *The Times* was at its most sniffy. 'A 30-mile tramway ride is about the most uncomfortable way of making history.' A reporter from the *Daily Herald* was impressed by the diversity of the party. 'We want to save the tram,' said Jay Fowler, a 41-year-old printer from Cricklewood.

Despite these headline-grabbing stunts, the league was barely mentioned in parliament, unlike the Pedestrians' Association, and it had no discernible impact on policy. It wouldn't be the first pressure group to confuse publicity with political influence and its efforts seemed a bit scattergun compared with the well-focused lobbying of the pedestrians.

For much of the 1930s, Henry Watson, an engineer, ran a solitary campaign to save the tram. Watson had a long-standing interest in transport. But he became concerned that the 'scrap the trams' movement was based on flawed economics and that the holy grail of more mobile vehicles would increase road accidents.

Watson was much more than an ordinary member of the public. He was the author of *Street Traffic Flow*, a work of extraordinary scope and vision that was published in 1933. Watson foresaw a world in which private vehicles would be banned from city centres. Traffic would be monitored remotely by television – the BBC had only just started experimental television broadcasts – while traffic police would keep in touch by radio. It was a pretty fair vision of the way traffic is controlled today. The science magazine *Nature* praised its originality. 'So far as we know, there is no other book of like compass dealing with this extremely important subject.'[187]

Watson lambasted the 'bus mania' of the Royal Commission and its verdict that trams were obsolescent. 'There is a great deal of nonsense spoken and written about tramways by persons who know little about them…[and]…a tendency to exaggerate the merits of buses for handling heavy traffic,' he wrote. 'Popular ideas in this matter are frequently quite unsound.'

In May 1934 Watson wrote to the select committee considering London Transport's bill to replace many of the trams in north London with trolleybuses. The mutilation of the tram network was most ill-conceived. London Transport was wrong when it claimed that trolleybuses were 'an unqualified success' – the death rate for trolleybuses in Kingston was ten times that of London trams. The Feltham trams, he said, were efficient, popular and compared well with modern buses. He said there was a conspiracy among transport operators and newspapers to suppress facts that reflected badly on bus services.[188] His letter was passed on to the Ministry of Transport.

Watson also wrote to *Transport World*, the trade journal formerly known as *Tramway and Railway World*, highlighting the increase in road deaths after trams were replaced by buses or trolleybuses. 'Transport operators,' he observed, 'seldom tell the truth about these abandonments, though one might suppose that the effect… on the street fatality rate is of importance.' In this dispute, the journal was firmly on the side of the operators. It published his letter but rounded up half a dozen transport managers to rubbish it, led by Owen Silvers, the trolleybus apostle from Wolverhampton.

Watson's agitation caused some disquiet in the Ministry of Transport. The ministry was already well aware of his work and at least one senior civil servant thought he had a point. But a solitary campaigner was never going to change London Transport's established policy on his own.

So, Watson changed tack and joined the committee of the Pedestrians' Association, the most effective ginger group. The association had already highlighted the dangers posed by vehicles forcing their way through people trying to board or leave a tram, arguing for a ban in England like those in Edinburgh and Glasgow.

Now Watson hoped to persuade it to campaign against replacing trams with trolleybuses because it would increase the number of accidents. But the association declined to take up cudgels on behalf of the tram after the Ministry of Transport assured the pedestrians that 'more mobile units' were safer – without providing a shred of evidence. Watson resigned in disappointment.[189]

There was an effective public campaign against trolleybuses but it had nothing to do with saving trams. London Transport wanted to run trolleybuses down Tottenham Court Road and into Bedford Square, turning the elegant Georgian architecture into a giant roundabout, complete with ugly overhead wires. This cause célèbre had echoes of the struggle to run trams into central London and illustrated why the LCC eschewed overhead wires in the centre of the capital.

The Bedford Square scheme was a deliberate ploy by London Transport to see how far it could run trolleybuses into the city centre. The great and the good were soon up in arms and London Transport's bill attracted a record number of petitions against it.

The police were the most serious source of opposition. Herbert Alker Tripp was the assistant commissioner in charge of traffic at Scotland Yard and a member of the London and Home Counties Traffic Advisory Committee. Tripp steadfastly opposed the scheme and the select committee threw out the Bedford Square plan.

Tripp, who wrote books on transport planning, had a seminal influence on shaping Britain's cities. Road deaths, he wrote, had reached 'battle level', before making the evidence-free claim that scrapping trams 'will contribute in no small way to the reduction in casualty figures'. His thinking on building urban motorways influenced the County of London Plan of the town planner Patrick Abercrombie, who in turn influenced Colin Buchanan, the author of the classic 1960s work on rebuilding cities, *Traffic in Towns*.

Trams had no place in this brave new world. Watson's visionary work, in the meantime, was largely forgotten. Watson was a prophet too far ahead of his time. When the Second World War broke out, he was working as a sales rep.

Chapter 25

LONDON'S LAST TRAM

'If people had their way there'd still be trams,' grumbled sixty-year old old Bert Dagnall.

'Ah,' sighed his mate John Simpson, 'buses'll never compete with them whatever they say.'

The mood in the canteen at New Cross was glum. It was the early hours of Sunday 6 July 1952. London's last tram had clanked into New Cross for the last time. A grey dawn was already silhouetting the chimney pots. The wake was over. And now the workers in the canteen were sipping cups of tea and mourning the tram's passing, while a reporter from the *Daily Mirror* listened to their tales.

Like the one about the tram known as 'Beer Annie', because it was always breaking down outside pubs. Or the occasion when an unwary hot dog vendor set up his stall too close to the tramlines. After the inevitable tangle, a tram went charging down the Old Kent Road decorated with a garland of sausages.

And what a wake it had been. Thousands of people poured onto the streets to watch the very last tram. No one counted the numbers but the crowd was vast. 'Thousands of Londoners lined the streets between Woolwich and New Cross to give a tumultuous farewell to the last tram on Saturday night. All day the surviving trams had been crowded with cheering, singing people and at night there were extraordinary scenes,' reported the *Daily Telegraph*. The send-off for the last tram was a public demonstration comparable to the turnout for the cup final, or a royal funeral.

'The journey from Woolwich to New Cross of the last tram in London was incomparable. No triumphal car this, yet it had more glory in its dying than it ever had in its living. Its passage through Greenwich and Deptford was neither that of king nor of clown, yet majesty was affronted and levity confounded,' wrote George Gale, who had been sent to cover the event by the London office of the *Manchester Guardian*. 'It was Saturday night in South-east London and the last tram had become a pretext for a Cockney bacchanalia.'

Gale, widely believed to have been the model for Lunchtime O'Booze, *Private Eye*'s caricature of a Fleet Street drunk, and who went on to edit the *Spectator*, was no tram lover. Two days before the wake, Gale penned the tram's obituary notice. The tram, he wrote, with a typical Gale turn of phrase 'has become a period piece' but 'it never graced the period. Not even in its obituary notice should an apologia be written. The tram was monstrous.'

Like many reporters before, Gale found it difficult to square his personal loathing of the vehicles with the obvious affection that London had for its trams. 'As soon as the tram moved off,' he wrote, 'you realised that it was no longer an ordinary tram but had been made by the crowd at Woolwich into more than an object of affectionate derision or a scrap-album relic. It had become a festival queen, and as the festival was rowdy, beery, middle-aged and merry so was its queen.'

The ceremonial route took the trams past three Granada cinemas, which kept their neon lights blazing until the last tram had passed. The tram was followed by an advertising van carrying large banners proclaiming 'Granada says thank you to the trams for transporting millions of our satisfied patrons.'

The last tram was so delayed by the throng that it was an hour late arriving at New Cross. It was driven for its final journey by John Cliff, who defended trams on behalf of the Transport and General Workers' Union in the Royal Commission hearings. Cliff was now London Transport's deputy chairman.

Inside the tram shed at New Cross the newsreel cameras rolled as a visibly embarrassed Lord Latham, the chairman of London Transport, gave a brief eulogy. 'And so, in the name of Londoners and of London Transport, I say Goodbye old

The graffiti says it all: 'dear old buses', 'goodbye cheap fares' and a forlorn plea for the London County Council to give London back its trams. (Author's Collection)

tram.' Charles Latham, a former leader of the London County Council and a staunch political ally of Herbert Morrison, had taken over the chair at London Transport in 1947 following Lord Ashfield's resignation. He was one of a new generation of Labour politicians who believed social equality could be achieved through mass car ownership.

After the crowds had finally gone home to nurse their hangovers, the remaining trams were taken off to 'an awful piece of waste land in Charlton…where they burn trams to death. On a good day they burn five trams,' wrote Paul Jennings in the *Picture Post*. On a bad day it was impossible to burn a tram. If the wind was blowing towards the furniture factory next door, then the workers had to content themselves with stripping out the copper and leather and other useful materials. The Tram Age, he wrote, 'ended on this Wagnerian funeral pyre'.[190]

While Londoners were sad to see the trams go, one company rubbed its hands with glee. That was George Cohen, the scrap merchants, which owned that awful piece of land in Charlton and had the contract for scrapping the trams. Its profits for the year ending March 1952, when more than 300 trams were scrapped, topped £1 million. It was a peak year for burning trams. And it was a bumper year for Cohen's profits. The lucky shareholders pocketed a whopping 26 per cent dividend.

The Second World War had put London's tram replacement plan on pause. Most of its trams north of the river went before the war but south of the river there had been few changes. In post-war Britain the government exercised tight control over the allocation of steel to boost exports. The motor industry had challenging export targets to meet, which left shortages for the home market. There were waiting lists for almost all steel products, from cars and buses to Dinky toys.

After the war London Transport decided that it would replace its remaining trams with diesel buses and not trolleybuses. It had ordered 4,000 buses. But only 182 had been delivered by the end of 1947. It was only when the controls on steel were relaxed and the supply of buses improved that London Transport could resume scrapping trams.[191]

The Light Railway Transport League tried to take advantage of this hiatus, placing a series of adverts in south London papers pushing the message that the trams should be replaced with modern trams, and not buses. The threat to the trams did wonders for the league's membership, which peaked at around 50,000, while activists pushed thousands of leaflets through the letterboxes of houses in south London. It carried out a poll which allegedly found that 90 per cent of households in South London wanted modern trams and pressed the British Transport Commission, which since the post-war nationalisation push had been London Transport's holding company, to reconsider the policy.

The league scored one publicity coup when Walter Luff, Blackpool's tramway manager and the league's president, offered to lend London a tram so that people

Wimbledon's tram terminus in 1949. Steel shortages forced London Transport to put its tram-scrapping programme on hold. (John Meredith/Online Transport Archive)

could see what a modern tram was like. 'Would we lend them a tram?' Luff told the *Daily Mirror*. 'Of course, we would – the moment they asked too. And free, too. It's all good publicity for Blackpool, you know.' The offer doubtless caused some squirming in London Transport, but it ignored Luff. In July 1950 Latham announced a two-year programme to replace all London's trams, at a cost of £9 million.

The league also tried to salvage the Kingsway subway. After the last tram had run, Jay Fowler wrote to Latham asking him to keep a short section of line running through the Kingsway subway, pointing out that the last trams had drawn large crowds. Latham told him that people were just taking their last chance to travel by tram. 'The prospect of execution concentrates a man's mind most wonderfully,' was Latham's casually brutal dismissal.[192]

One tram fan couldn't be dismissed so cavalierly. And that was Queen Mary, who as Princess of Wales had opened the LCC's electric tramway to Tooting back in 1903. She had suffered her own bereavement earlier that year with the death of her second son George VI, one of the boys who'd been so keen to scamper up to the top deck of the Tooting tram. The Dowager Queen let London Transport know of her fond memories of the happy day when her late husband, George V, opened the first LCC electric tramway.

London Transport responded by giving Queen Mary a special presentation album, bound in leather, which included a photo of her family on the first electric tram to Tooting and a copy of the souvenir issue of the London Transport staff magazine, which was on sale for 2d. The Queen's reply was gracious. She liked the photograph and expressed an interest in reading the staff magazine.[193]

How far the Queen got with her perusal of the staff magazine isn't known. But Latham's introduction in the souvenir issue 'the passing of the trams' – echoing an old *Daily Mail* headline – emphasised the new. 'Now in 1952 the final replacement of trams by a more modern, more flexible and more manoeuvrable vehicle will be a landmark in the history of the capital…and a major work of civic importance.'[194]

Many other operators had organised last tram ceremonies. London Transport went one better. It had a week-long event. Trams carried the slogan 'last tram week' and passengers were issued with souvenir tickets. Long queues developed at stops with people wanting to have their last tram ride. Everyone wanted to get in on the act.

On the final day the Infantile Paralysis Fellowship hired a tram. Its tram was launched by Ethel Revnell, the film actor and star of the BBC radio show *Midday Music Hall*, who smashed a quart bottle of stout over its nose. Revnell, who was born in Clerkenwell, had fond childhood memories of trams. On the Farringdon Road, where she grew up, the number 17 tram travelled past her front door every few minutes. The hired tram's route from Woolwich to New Cross took it past 200 pubs and the

The tram hired by the Infantile Paralysis Fellowship, with Cockney film star Ethel Revnell on the platform hugely enjoying her last London tram ride. Beside Revnell inside the cab is Gerard Hoffnung, the noted artist and humourist. (Mirrorpix)

charity's fund-raisers tapped the drinkers for the substantial sum of £140 to help victims of polio.[195]

The last tram week extravaganza was organised in minute detail by London Transport's public relations team. The press office was at pains to control the message. The public naturally wanted to mark the retirement of an old and faithful servant, but London had to move with the times and get rid of an outdated form of transport.

At the same time, London Transport wanted to avoid any public disorder. The closure of the Kingsway subway was feared to be a particular flashpoint. The subway closed on 5 April 1952. London Transport arranged for 'a sizeable squad of police to guard the subway installations on the night of closing lest tramway supporters should attempt to stage a demonstration' reported *Modern Tramway* – the Light Railway Transport League's journal – because of 'the widespread opposition to their tramway policy'. In the event, the police were not needed and the closure was uneventful.

Coming up for air: a tram emerging from the Kingsway subway, shortly before the subway closed in April 1952. (Marcus Eavis/Online Transport Archive)

An editorial in the *Evening News* captured the tone London Transport had been striving for:

> Next Saturday a great sentimental farewell will be bidden to the last trams of all on the eve of their complete replacement by buses. Let us admit the validity of all the practical arguments against trams – arguments of economics and traffic control…and then confess with some pride that we cherish a quite illogical, utterly impractical affection for these now archaic, yet imposing and attractive vehicles.

The tram belonged to the past 'along with…beer at fourpence a pint'. Latham wrote to the editor to thank him. To Latham any fondness for trams was simple nostalgia. 'Those were the days,' he wrote, 'Or were they?'[196]

Various dignitaries, such as the mayors of the local boroughs, were invited to ride on the last tram, although women were banned, because of worries about public disorder. John Benn, whose grandfather had been the conductor on the royal opening of the LCC's first electric tram, was told there was no space for him. It wasn't true, there were spare places. But London Transport wanted to maintain a tight grip on the narrative. It seems it didn't trust Benn to stick to the party line in any interview.

In its press release giving details of last tram week, London Transport boasted that 'conversion of tram services to bus operation has already proved a big success on London streets', adding 'the absence of tram obstruction on the roads has transformed many traffic blackspots like New Cross'. The claim of ending traffic congestion should not be taken too literally – and all the more so because the press release was issued ten days before the tram depot at New Cross closed.

The day after London Transport issued this press release, Edgar Anstey, the head of British Transport Films, commissioned John Krish, one of its regular freelancers to go to New Cross and film Latham greeting the last tram. British Transport Films, like London Transport, was a part of the nationalised British Transport Commission. Its remit was to produce soft propaganda to showcase the great advances this modern country was making.

In the story that Krish told – and he told it on several occasions with minor variations – he said to Anstey 'if they're disappearing, we have to make a film about them'. But Anstey said no. So, off his own bat Krish made a documentary about last tram week. He asked a camera operator to come to South London and film trams for the week with the unit's cameras and, as Krish later recalled, some stolen film stock. It was one of the few occasions when the narrative spun out of London Transport's control.

The result of this guerrilla filmmaking, *The Elephant Will Never Forget*, was an elegiac tribute to the part trams played in the life of Londoners. Despite the film's unusual origin, it went on general release in 1953 as a quickie to be shown before the main feature. Said to be the most popular film ever made by British Transport Films, it was even screened at the Odeon's flagship cinema in Leicester Square, where it reduced some of the audience to tears.

From the opening sequence, the script, which was written by Krish, implicitly questions the official line of the replacement being a great success. 'Some people were glad to see the back of them and some of us were sorry they were going.' The 'us', of course, included Krish and the audience.

Towards the end of the film, there is some footage of the Charlton pyre. 'They burn them until there's nothing left but a charred skeleton,' ran Krish's script. 'You'd think they were afraid of ghosts.'

The unexpected popularity of the film spooked Anstey. Feeling under pressure from his superiors, he wrote to Krish to say that he wouldn't be getting another job from British Transport Films because it was time to get some new blood. Krish was 29.[197]

Krish went on to become one of the country's foremost documentary filmmakers. And there can be no doubt that he was one of 'us'. He used to shave in a tram driver's mirror.[198]

Chapter 26

THE END OF THE LINE

'A streetcar named defunct' proclaimed the *Economist* as London's last trams headed for the scrapyard. In an even-handed analysis, the magazine spelt out that Britain now only had ten municipal tramways, six in England and four in Scotland. 'The joint victory of the bus and the trolleybus is, in Britain, almost complete.'

It certainly looked that way. One of the consequences of the shrinking number of tramways was a shortage of home-grown tram manufacturers in postwar Britain. When Leeds invited tenders for fifty new trams, there were no takers. When Aberdeen asked Glasgow if it could manufacture some new trams for it, the answer was 'sorry, but no'. Anti-municipal trading laws prevented Glasgow's workshops from making trams for other cities. The campaign against municipal trading continued to cast a long shadow.

For a short while, a second-hand market in modern tramcars flourished. Leeds was one of the cities to take advantage of this market when it bought ninety of London's newest trams – the Feltham cars – in 1951. Leeds also ordered three modern trams based on the latest American research.

In 1930 the heads of the major street railways in America and the leading component manufacturers had set up a research committee, known as the Presidents' Conference Committee (PCC), to rethink the design of the tram. A lavishly funded team of top-class scientists and engineers set out to create a super streetcar. They had a laboratory and test track. The PCC car, as it became known, first took to the rails in Brooklyn in 1936. It was quiet, comfortable and with smooth rapid acceleration that didn't throw the passengers around. Here was a nifty little number that could successfully take on a bus, or even a motor car.

The new American ideas created a fresh flurry of interest in trams on this side of the pond but delays in negotiating licences and the war meant the technology was slow to spread to Europe. In 1951 Leeds announced that it was buying two experimental trams, billed as 'single deck and silent'. This was a substantial initiative. The council's transport manager went on a fact-finding mission to see PCC cars in European cities and the council floated the idea of buying 200 cars, enough to replace half the city's trams.

However, the future of trams in Leeds became a political football. Leeds, in common with other tram operators, was struggling with spiralling costs and falling passenger numbers, partly because of the end of petrol rationing in 1950. All public transport was affected, but tramways, with their large overheads, suffered more than bus operators.

The future of the trams became a key issue in the city's local elections of 1953. The Conservatives went to the polls promising to modernise the trams while Labour pledged to scrap them. Labour won.

The following month the two new trams took to the rails. In November the council laid out plans to scrap trams over the next ten years. The public was 'sick of travelling in obsolete tram cars', said the Labour chair of the transport committee. The cost of replacing them with modern trams 'was too heavy to be considered', he said. The city's last tram ran in 1959.[199]

Instead, Leeds and the government embarked on an even more costly programme of motorway building. The city was so proud of its achievements that the Royal Mail franked local letters with the slogan 'Leeds, motorway city of the seventies'.

The political division in Leeds, with Conservatives supporting trams, was a little unusual. Labour politicians were historically more likely to favour trams. Unlike buses, trams were more likely to carry working-class voters and they provided jobs for miners and steel workers.

The future of the tram in its Scottish strongholds was undermined by the unpopularity of Clement Atlee's postwar austerity measures. Even in local council elections, voters were out to give Labour a good kicking. Labour lost control of Edinburgh in 1949 and a Conservative-dominated alliance gained power.

With the change in political control, the future of Edinburgh trams became a hot topic. More than half a century ago, claimed the 85-year-old Norman Macdonald in a letter to the *Scotsman*, the chairman of London United Tramways had admitted to him that trams were obsolete. Macdonald, a lawyer and former bus promoter was the son of John Macdonald, the Road Board member, and like his father was an enthusiastic motorist who had inherited the paternal anti-tram creed. Here was an old man with an ageing mantra. Trams, he said were 'obsolete and obstructive' and in Glasgow – a 'tram-infested city' – the traffic delays cost millions of pounds a year. His views still carried some weight because of his prominence in motoring circles.

It was easy to portray Edinburgh's trams as obsolete. Most of Edinburgh's trams had been built in the 1920s. Since 1942 the council had spent more than fifteen times more money on new buses than it had spent on new trams. In 1950 the council decided to scrap a quarter of its trams. Two years later it decided to scrap the lot. The vote was on party lines.

Although many councils were considering scrapping their trams the stand-out exception, as the *Economist* pointed out, was Glasgow. In 1952 the city was still building new trams. Glasgow was in a unique and privileged position. Under the

Glasgow was still building new trams like this 'Cunarder' as late as 1952. (Roy Hubble/LCCTT Collection/Online Transport Archive)

Glasgow Corporation (Monopoly) Act of 1930, the number of private buses was severely restricted and the corporation ran most of the city's buses.

After the council elections of 1949, political control in Glasgow was balanced on a knife edge. On paper Labour had a one-vote majority. But this majority evaporated when a Conservative, Victor Warren, a former explosives manufacturer, became Lord Provost. Warren now had a casting vote.

Warren had long advocated scrapping the trams. 'There is hardly a person – certainly not a motorist and scarcely a pedestrian – who does not think that the days of the tramcar with its fixed rails in the centre of the city roadway are definitely numbered,' he claimed.[200] In April 1951 the council agreed to lift the tram rails in the High Street – a move that would be difficult to reverse – on Warren's casting vote.

Trams were not part of the postwar vision for Glasgow. The town planner Patrick Abercrombie produced a comprehensive plan for the region. His prescription for the city was much the same as his cure for congestion in London. He proposed massive road building and electrifying some suburban railways. Where railways were electrified, he said, 'care must be taken to avoid wasteful competition with road transport'. He recommended setting up a committee of inquiry.

In line with this recommendation, the British Transport Commission, the nationalised holding company, set up a committee of inquiry, chaired by a railway engineer. The committee had six members: five were railwaymen and the other one managed Scottish Omnibuses. The report recommended electrifying Glasgow's suburban railways. The quid pro quo for electrifying the railways was cutting back the trams so that their tracks ended at the council's border, because trains and buses would serve the suburbs better than trams.

It was the beginning of the end. Labour regained control of the council in 1952 but the tramways' finances, already in a parlous state, deteriorated even further after Pinkston power station, which supplied cheap current for the city's trams, was handed over to the South of Scotland Electricity Board, which put up the price of electricity. Glasgow's last tram ran in 1962.

The closure of Glasgow's trams, like the last tram in London, was marked by a cinematic tribute - *9 Dalmuir West*. This time it was filmed by John Krish's friend Kevin Brownlow and featured the work of women conductors and drivers. During the First World War, Glasgow, like other operators had employed women to replace men who had been called up. But unlike the others, Glasgow continued to employ women tram drivers and conductors, although they were not allowed to drive the corporation's buses until 1971. So, when the trams ended, women lost their driving jobs. On the final night the workers, and the city, had a grand old knees-up. 'Not till tomorrow will they realise what they've lost,' are the film's closing words.

Chapter 27

THE COMEBACK

On Monday 27 April 1992 trams returned to the streets of Manchester when the city's Metrolink opened for business. The local paper celebrated the return of the tram by organising a 'race' from Bury to Manchester town hall. One reporter took the tram, another the bus and finally one drove by car. The tram was the winner, with a journey time of 35 minutes. The bus took another 10 minutes and the car driver crawled in last with a time of 53 minutes. 'It should get people out of their bloody motor cars and open up the city again,' one of the passengers on the first tram told reporters.[201]

The Manchester comeback was part of a worldwide reversal in fortune for trams. For more than two decades the British tram had teetered on the brink of extinction. The return of trams to the streets of Manchester marked a turning point. But such was the obloquy attached to the idea of trams – a tribute to the corrosive persistence of the slogan 'obsolete trams' – that the publicity for this scheme eschewed the word tram and talked instead of light rail vehicles. Tram was a four-lettered word and there was a marked reluctance to call a tram a tram. Subsequent schemes also fought shy of using this word. So Sheffield had supertrams and Birmingham a metro.

The renaissance of trams around the world can be traced back to rising concern about our environment and more specifically the hazards resulting from air pollution. Motor vehicles pump out fumes for people to breathe on the streets where they live. Trams do not.

In the middle of a heatwave at the end of July 1943, the *Los Angeles Times* reported that 'a low hanging cloud of acrid smoke' had descended on the city. It was less than two years since the Japanese attack on Pearl Harbor and the paper's alarmist headline was 'City hunting for source of gas attack'.

The city's smogs became frequent and notorious. Unlike London's infamous peasoupers – dense winter smogs that were largely the result of burning coal in domestic grates – those in Los Angeles were different: they were summer smogs. In 1952 Arie Haagen-Smit, a Dutch-born biochemist, pinpointed the source of the smog. It was a chemical cocktail produced by motor vehicle fumes, which in warm sunny weather created a photochemical smog.

The oil industry's propagandists swung into action in a strenuous effort to trash this research and hired tame scientists to discredit Haagen-Smit. 'It is merely an unproved speculation,' one oil industry executive was able to claim, 'an interesting guess'.

Ironically at the same time as Los Angeles was enduring breathtaking smogs it was ridding its streets of an electric alternative to motor vehicles – its streetcars – squeezed off the streets across America by rising numbers of cars and the sharp-elbowed activities of motor manufacturers, tyre makers and the oil industry.

It was emissions from petrol engines that caused the Los Angeles smogs. Diesel fumes were a different problem. Back in 1932, John Owens, a senior scientist at the UK government's Department of Scientific and Industrial Research and a pioneer in the systematic measurement of air pollution, sounded an early warning about the hidden killers in exhaust fumes. The reaction of the vested interests was straight out of the propaganda playbook. The London General wheeled out a tame chemist who claimed that the diesel engine should 'cause no anxiety whatever as to its possible effect on atmospheric pollution'.[202]

By the 1950s cases of lung cancer were soaring alarmingly – they had risen fifteenfold in a quarter of a century. Traffic fumes were an early suspect. But after smoking was pinpointed as a major cause of lung cancer the spotlight of publicity shifted away from traffic.

Nevertheless, some scientists continued to warn of the dangers of fumes from diesel buses. In 1953, George Clemo, one of the country's leading chemists, warned that black smoke was 'murderous'. He told the British Association meeting in September of a ten-mile stretch of road near Newcastle which had eight schools alongside it. 'Hundreds of buses and lorries emit black smoke along the route all day long. It is impossible to state the extent of the damage to health thus incurred and probably only revealed after the lapse of years.' He was backed by Robert Parry, Bristol's medical officer of health, who told journalists that 'buses throwing out clouds of fumes' were certainly contributing to the increase in the city's cancer rate. 'It is a pity we got rid of the trams. There was no danger from them.'

It was a warning that went unheeded. That year London Transport decided to replace its trolleybuses with diesel buses. Local councils in London warned that the foul-smelling fumes of diesel buses would cause a rise in lung cancer. 'Diesel fumes may be a contributory factor to the increasing incidence of lung cancer,' said Islington Council, which called on London Transport to reconsider its decision.

At the time, concern focused on a trace chemical called benzpyrene, which was known to cause cancer in mice. The Medical Research Council was asked to investigate. Patrick Lawther, who headed the council's air pollution unit, carried out tests in a south London bus garage, with up to 200 diesel buses starting up and running their engines. The air inside the garage became chokingly smoky, Lawther told a meeting of the Royal Society of Health. But so far, he claimed, 'we have been unable to find any benzpyrene to measure.' When challenged, Lawther was forced to

Merton Bus Garage. In 1956 scientists monitored the exhaust fumes while 200 diesel buses started up. Despite choking on the fetid fumes, the scientists failed to detect any cancer-causing chemicals. (Topical Press/©TfL from the London Transport Museum collection)

deny that he was trying to whitewash diesel engines. 'A whispering campaign that has blamed diesel fumes for lung cancer was scotched last night by an authoritative denial,' reported the *Daily Mail*.

It was a view that Lawther maintained in the face of growing evidence to the contrary. 'Our earliest work on pollution from motor vehicles,' he wrote twenty years later, 'was to assess the suggestion that emissions from diesel engines cause cancer. We were comforted by our negative findings, but were (and still are) amazed to find how many were infuriated to hear the good news.'[203]

It was true that Lawther, who died in 2008, lacked the technology to identify the dangers of exhaust fumes. It was also true that he did not appreciate the adage that absence of evidence is not evidence of absence. By the 1990s modern technology was revealing a much more sophisticated view of the dangers of air pollution. One of the most insidious threats was invisible. Tiny particles known as PM10 and PM2.5 – a speck of PM2.5 is one-thirtieth the diameter of a human hair – travel unimpeded up our airwaves and lodge in the lungs. The latest research now proved that these particles also caused cancer. And the results were truly horrific. In 1994, *New Scientist* revealed that exhaust fumes were killing 10,000 people a year in England and Wales alone.[204]

Faced with growing unease about air pollution and the continuing need to cut traffic congestion, which hadn't been abolished by scrapping trams, transport planners around the world began to look again at the tram's advantages. In 1994 another Royal Commission, this time the Royal Commission on Environmental Pollution, waxed lyrical about the potential for light rail to persuade drivers to leave their cars at home and recommended that the government should put more money into trams.[205]

By the 1990s the political climate was changing. New environmental groups had begun to challenge the road lobby and the oil industry. Gradually the political influence of these previously unassailable industrial lobbies was being eroded. This shift in the tectonic plates of politics was given added impetus by the growing urgency of climate change.

In 2000, John Prescott, the ebullient deputy prime minister, trumpeted an ambitious ten-year plan for transport. It wasn't universally welcomed and some of Prescott's colleagues harboured reservations. Internal meetings at the department that discussed the strategy were attended by a 'Downing Street minder' who said little but 'glowered' when more radical ideas were mentioned.

One of the centrepieces of Prescott's integrated transport strategy was twenty-five new light-rail systems largely financed by the private sector including an extension to the tram network in Manchester and new systems in Leeds and Nottingham.

In London, the capital's transport operator developed a scheme for a cross-river tram, which would run from north to south through the centre of the capital.

Writing about the scheme in the *Spectator*, a former Conservative MP declared that trams were 'obsolete'. His views would not have been out of place a hundred years ago. 'Let me remind you why trams were abolished in the first place: because they were slow and noisy and expensive to build: did not mix easily with other road vehicles.'

After becoming secretary of state for transport in 2002 Alistair Darling initiated a review of the ten-year plan. Out went Prescott's expansive vision, and in its place Darling reverted to a more traditional approach, putting greater emphasis on road building to ease traffic congestion. Darling soon signalled this change of approach by stating that he wanted to see more investment in buses because they were cheaper than trams.

Blaming escalating costs, Darling axed most of the light rail schemes, including the expansion of the Manchester network and the Leeds supertram. Only the scheme in Nottingham escaped, largely because construction was so far advanced that it couldn't be cancelled.

The plan for London's cross-river tram limped on until 2008. One of the key arguments against attempts to build tramways through the centre of London in the early 1900s was that they would devalue properties on the route. In the public consultation the tramline was popular, ironically because people close to the route believed it would increase the value of their houses. Despite this public enthusiasm the plan was scrapped after the mayoral election of 2008 by the new Conservative mayor of London – and former editor of the *Spectator* – Boris Johnson.

In 2011 the government tried again, this time proclaiming a 'green light for light rail'. This plan, the brainchild of the Liberal transport minister Norman Baker, didn't survive the fall of the coalition government in 2015.

The tram's comeback in Britain has stuttered. Once tramways have been ripped up it is proving to be very difficult, and expensive, to replace them. The figures tell a dismal story. In the three decades following the Royal Commission's report in 1931 Britain scrapped nearly 2,000 miles of tramways. In the three decades following the return of the tram to the streets of Manchester, Britain has built 157 miles of tramway.

It has been a different story on the other side of the English Channel. Like Britain, France had scrapped almost all its trams. By 1970 just three tramways were left in the country. In 1985 trams returned to the streets of Nantes, followed two years later by Grenoble and then in 1992 by Saint-Denis, a northern suburb of Paris. Since these early openings the comeback had gathered pace as city after city saw trams as a way of improving urban transport. This century France has opened new tram networks at the rate of nearly one a year, the scale of transformation that Prescott envisaged in his ten-year plan. Why has France succeeded when Britain has lagged?

The urban living think tank Create Streets highlights two important explanations for this disparity: cost and delays caused by Britain's planning red tape. On average building a mile of new tramway in Britain costs nearly twice as much as in France. While the difference in delays is equally pronounced.

The French approach to planning is relatively streamlined. Take the example of the new tramways in Dijon. The council first approved the idea of tramways in 2008. Six months later there was a public inquiry, which approved the plan. After a few more formalities construction began in October 2010 and the two lines – a total of 12 miles of tramway – opened at the end of 2012.

Now contrast this with the sluggish progress made on extending the West Midlands metro into East Birmingham. Planning for this extension began in earnest in 2014. Three years later there was a public inquiry. Another four years passed before any construction started. And if all goes to plan, the extension should open in 2026. It is just over 1 mile long.

Birmingham may be a more extreme example of the delays built into Britain's planning process but it is indisputable that when it comes to building new tramways

Britain is in the slow lane. The fact remains that the cards are still stacked against trams, just as they were a hundred years ago. Since 1992 tramways no longer have the handicap of the old 18-inch rule, but they have gained new burdens that are equally onerous.

Back in 1929, Chris Spencer told the Royal Commission that tramways now had to lay nine inches of reinforced concrete to take the weight of modern traffic, instead of the six inches that were needed for horse-drawn traffic. Spencer's complaint was that trams had to pay to provide a smooth road surface for their most pernicious rival – the motor bus.

Today only the scale of the problem has changed. In Britain, tramways normally lay a concrete base of 600 millimetres – nearly two feet, or 24 inches – mostly to prevent heavy goods vehicles from damaging gas and water pipes buried underneath the tramways. In Europe some new tramways have as little as half this amount of concrete. Digging deeper holes and pouring extra concrete substantially raises the construction costs of tramways in Britain – all in the interest of providing streets that can take heavy goods vehicles.

Buried pipes and cables are a major problem for tramway builders. When the diggers start to rip up the road who knows what they will find? The companies' plans are often of little help. There may be extra pipes and cables, or pipes that aren't where they should be.

The rules and regulations governing tramway building are more than 25 years old and can be traced back to a shadowy outfit known as the Highways Authorities and Utilities Committee – a collection of utility company bosses and council road engineers. When a new tramway is being built, the default position is that all pipes and cables have to be moved. And it is the tram builders that largely have to foot the bill, by law. Under a piece of secondary legislation bearing the ironic title 'sharing of costs of works' tram builders have to pay 92.5 per cent of the costs, while utilities are more than happy to renew some of their leaky pipes at the expense of a tramway.

The cost of all this work is considerable. Construction of the first phase of the Sheffield supertram network cost £240 million in 1994, of which £60 million was for moving utilities. UK Tram, the industry body that now represents tramways says that moving utilities regularly costs up to a third of the cost of construction.

Britain's start-stop tram policy also increases costs. The lack of any rolling programme of tramway building means that each time a new tramway opens the engineers and planners behind it are disbanded. There is no continuity. There is no formal way of passing the knowledge they have gained to the next project. So tramway builders can't learn from their mistakes, they are condemned to repeat them.

Progress in Britain has undoubtedly been slow. However, as global temperatures soar, the urgency of tackling the climate crisis means that the reign of the internal combustion engine is coming to an end. Historically trams were once part of the problem, their electricity came from carbon dioxide-belching coal-fired power stations and contributed to climate change. But the UK's last surviving coal-fired power station, at Ratcliffe-on-Soar, near Nottingham, closed in 2024. Electricity is now more likely than not to be generated in power stations that don't rely on fossil fuels like gas and the government plans to phase out fossil fuels completely by 2050. So the future for electric vehicles – and trams – looks bright.

In November 2024 the Department for Transport's press office briefed journalists about its new 'integrated national transport strategy' – a choice of words that harked back to Prescott's ten-year plan. According to the briefing, trams will be an important plank in the new strategy and the department hopes to emulate the success of Dijon. Indeed, the civil servant in charge of developing the strategy spent several days in Dijon studying the French city's achievements at the end of 2024.

The future of the tram is in the hands of politicians, just as it has been for the past 150 years. After a period of consultation, the government is expected to publish its new strategy late in 2025. Will this strategy remove some of the road blocks that are holding back the tram's progress?

SELECT BIBLIOGRAPHY

PRIMARY SOURCES

The British Library has the papers of Robert Cecil (Lord Cecil of Chelwood).

The East Sussex Record Office has papers of William Joynson-Hicks (Lord Brentford).

Hampshire Archives in Winchester have the Automobile Association's records.

The Hartley Library at the University of Southampton has the papers of Wilfred Ashley (Baron Mount Temple) and Robert Waley Cohen.

The Institution of Civil Engineers has the records of the British Road Federation.

Living Streets, in London, holds the archives of the Pedestrians' Association.

The London Archives has records of London Transport and Combine companies, including the London General Omnibus Company, London and Suburban Traction, Metropolitan Electric Tramways, London United Tramways, Union Construction Company and Underground Electric Railways. The London Archives has the records of the London County Council.

The London School of Economics has William Rees Jeffreys's papers, including the records of the Road Board and the Roads Improvement Association.

The London Transport Museum has material relating to transport in London.

The Modern Records Centre at the University of Warwick has the archives of the Federation of British Industries, the Trades Union Congress and the Transport and General Workers' Union.

The National Archives has the records of the Royal Commission on Transport and the archives of the Ministry of Transport, as well as files from other government departments and the security services.

The National Tramways Museum at Crich, has the records of the Municipal Tramways Association (and its successors), the Tramways and Light Railways Association (and its successors), the Omnibus Owners' Association and British Electric Traction.

Transport for London's Corporate Archives has some rarer records from London Transport and companies that were part of the Combine.

PUBLISHED BOOKS

Abercrombie, Patrick, *Clyde Valley Regional Plan*, HMSO, 1945.

Abercrombie, Patrick, *County of London Plan*, 1943, Macmillan, 1944.

Bagwell, Philip, *The Transport Revolution from 1770*, Batsford, 1974.

Baker, Elizabeth and Philip Noel-Baker, *J. Allen Baker*, Swarthmore Press, 1927.

Barker, Theodore and Michael Robbins, *A History of London Transport vol. 1*, Allen and Unwin, 1963 and vol 2, 1974.

Barman, Christian, *The Man Who Built London Transport*, David and Charles, 1979.

Bernays, Edward, *Crystallizing Public Opinion*, Liveright Publishing Corp, 1923.

Bernays, Edward, *Propaganda*, Liveright, 1928.

Blacker, Ken C., *The Felthams*, Dryhurst Publications, 1962.

Brendon, Piers, *The Motoring Century*, Bloomsbury Books, 1997.

Brunner, Christopher T., *The Problem of Motor Transport*, Ernest Benn, 1928.

Davenport, Ernest Harold and Sidney Russell Cooke, *Oil Trusts & Anglo American Relations*, Macmillan, 1923.

Davenport, Ernest Harold and Sidney Russell Cooke, *Australian Finance*, Pelican Press, 1926.

Davenport, Nicholas (Ernest Harold), *Memoirs of a City Radical*, Weidenfeld and Nicolson, 1974.

Day, John R., *The Story of the London Bus*, London Transport Executive, 1973.

Donald, Robert, *The Electric Trust*, Friars Printing Association, 1902.

Dunbar, Charles, *London Tramway Subway*, Omnibus Society / Tramway and Light Railway Society, 1948.

Faulkner, Richard and Chris Austin, *Holding the Line*, Oxford Publishing Company, 2012.

Finer, Herman, *Municipal Trading*, Allen and Unwin, 1941.

Fulford, Roger, *Five decades of B.E.T.*, British Electric Traction, 1946.

Fyfe, Hamilton, *Press Parade*, Watts, 1936.

Gardiner Alfred, *John Benn and the Progressive Movement*, Ernest Benn, 1925.

Green, Oliver, *Rails in the Road*, Pen and Sword, 2016.

Grieves, Keith, *Sir Eric Geddes*, Manchester University Press, 1989.

Hamilton, James Muir, *Glasgow in 1901*, William Hodge and Co., 1901.

Harley Robert J., *Lord Ashfield's Trams*, Capital Transport, 2014.

Hibbs, John, *The History of British Bus Services*, David and Charles, 1989.

Higginson, Martin, editor, *Tramway London*, Light Rail Transit Association, 1993.

Hobbs, Andrew, *A Fleet Street in Every Town*, Open Book Publishers, 2018.

Holland, Patricia G., *George Francis Train and the Woman Suffrage Movement*, Books at Iowa, 1987.

Jeffrey, Keith, *MI6 History of the Secret Intelligence Service*, Bloomsbury Publishing, 2010.

Jonker, Joost and Jan Luiten van Zanden, *A History of Royal Dutch Shell*, Oxford University Press, 2007

Kennedy Jones, William, *Fleet Street and Downing Street*, Hutchinson, 1920.

Klapper, Charles, *The Golden Age of Tramways*, David and Charles, 1974.

London's Underground, *The Feltham Car*, 1931.

Lycett, Andrew, *From Diamond Sculls to Golden Handcuffs*, Robert Hale, 1998.

Mackay, John P., *Tramways and Trolleys*, Princetown University Press, 1976.

McKenzie, Frederick A., *The Mystery of the Daily Mail*, Associated Newspapers, 1921.

Morrison, Herbert, *An Autobiography*, Odhams Press, 1960.

Morrison, Herbert, *Socialisation and Transport*, Constable, 1933.

Morrison, Herbert, *The London Traffic Fraud*, London Labour Publications, 1929.

Munby, Denys, *Inland Transport Statistics*, Clarendon Press, 1978.

Oakley, Charles A., *The Last Tram*, The Corporation of the City of Glasgow, 1962.

Oakley, Edward R., *London County Council Tramways*, (two volumes) London Tramways History Group, 1989 and 1991.

Offer, Avner, *Property and Politics 1870-1914*, Cambridge University Press, 1981.

Pemberton, Max, *Lord Northcliffe*, Hodder and Stoughton, 1922.

Phillips, Timothy, *The Secret Twenties*, Granta, 2017.

Plowden, William, *The Motor Car and Politics in Britain*, Pelican Books, 1973.

Pound, Reginald and Geoffrey Harmsworth, *Northcliffe*, Cassell, 1959.

Pratt, Edwin A., *A History of Inland Transport and Communication in England*, Kegan Paul, Trench, Trübner & Co., 1912.

Roberts, Glyn, *The Most Powerful Man in the World*, Covici Friede, 1938.

Royal Commission on Transport, *Minutes of Evidence*, Volume 1, C. 55-138-91, 1929; Volume 2, C. 55-138-92, 1929 and Volume 3, C. 55-138-93, 1930.

Royal Commission on Transport, *The Control of Traffic on Roads*, first report, Cmd. 3365, July 1929.

Royal Commission on Transport, *The Co-ordination and Development of Transport*, Final Report, HMSO, Cmd. 3751, 1931.

Sleeman, John, *The Rise and Decline of Municipal Transport*, Scottish Journal of Political Economy, February 1962.

Smeeton, Cyril S., *Metropolitan Electric Tramways*, vol 1, Tramway and Light Railway Society, 1984 and vol 2, 1986.

Snell, Bradford C., *American Ground Transport*, a report presented to Committee of the Judiciary, Subcommittee on Antitrust and Monopoly, US Government Print Office, 1974.

Suthers, Robert B., *Mind your own Business*, The Clarion Press, 1905.

Suthers, Robert B., *The Truth about Trams*, Clarion Press, 1903.

Taylor, Henry A., *Robert Donald*, Stanley Paul, 1934.

Thompson, J. Lee, *Politicians, the Press and Propaganda*, Kent State University Press, 1999.

Thornton, Willis, *The Nine Lives of Citizen Train*, Greenberg, 1948.

Train, George Francis, *My Life in Many States and in Foreign Lands*, Heinemann, 1902.

Tripp, H. Alker, *Road Traffic and its Control*, Edward Arnold, 1938.

Watkins, Ann, *The Campaign to Save London's Trams*, 2010.

Watson, Henry, *Street Traffic Flow*, Chapman and Hall, 1933.

Webb, Sidney, *Municipal Tramways*, Fabian Tract 33, 1891.

Wilder, Robert H. and Katharine L. Buell, *Publicity a Manual for the Use of Business, Civic or Social Service Organisations*, Ronald Press, 1923.

Williams, (George) Valentine, *World of Action*, Hamish Hamilton, 1938.

Wilson, Geoffrey, *London United Tramways*, Allen & Unwin, 1971.

Wolmar, Christian, *The Subterranean Railway*, Atlantic, 2005.

Yearsley, Ian and Philip Groves, *The Manchester Tramways*, TPC, 1988.

NOTES AND REFERENCES

1. *New Scientist*, 19/26 December 1985, p79.
2. Bradford C. Snell, *American Ground Transport*, a report presented to Committee of the Judiciary, Subcommittee on Antitrust and Monopoly, US Government Print Office, 1974.
3. Letter from Queen Mary's office to Lord Latham, dated 14 August 1952, Transport for London Corporate Archives, LT000264/127.
4. Mathew Engel, *Tickle the Public*, Victor Gollancz, 1996, p69.
5. *Daily Mail*, 2 March 1901, p3.
6. Patricia G. Holland, *George Francis Train and the Woman Suffrage Movement, 1867-70*, Books at Iowa, 1987, pp8-29.
7. George Francis Train, *My Life in Many States and in Foreign Lands*, Heinemann, 1902, pp264, 268.
8. John Noble, *Tramways as a Means of Facilitating Street Traffic of the Metropolis*, 1865, p11; John Bradfield, *Tramways or Railways on Metropolitan Streets will be mischievous and dangerous obstructions and nuisances*, 1865-6; Noble, *Observations on Mr Bradfield's Pamphlet*, 1866.
9. Herman Finer, *Municipal Trading*, George Allen and Unwin, 1941, pp48-49.
10. Board of Trade, Tramways (Metropolis), 1871, Sessional Papers No 211, p26.
11. Select Committee on Tramways (Use of Mechanical Power), C. 161, 1877, p5; *Pall Mall Gazette*, 3 May 1878, p8.
12. London General Omnibus Company board minutes, 26 November and 30 November 1882, the London Archives (TLA), City of London Corporation, ACC/1297/LGOC/01/016.
13. *Economic Journal*, December 1901, p492.
14. Sidney Webb, *Municipal Tramways*, Fabian Tract 33, 1891, p2.
15. James Muir Hamilton, *Glasgow in 1901*, William Hodge and Co, 1901, p57.
16. *The Times*, 2 September 1902, p9.
17. *Morning Leader*, 27 September 1902, p4.
18. British Electric Traction board minutes, 18 September 1902, minute 706.
19. 'Municipal Trading in England and the United States', An address by the Hon. Robert P. Porter, Municipal Trading Committee of the London Chamber of Commerce, 1901.
20. Roger Fulford, *Five decades of B.E.T.*, British Electric Traction, 1946, p16.
21. Avner Offer, *Property and Politics 1870-1914*, Cambridge University Press, 1981, p237.
22. Robert Donald, *The Electric Trust; its History and Tactics*, Friars Printing Association, 1902.
23. *Truth*, 8 August 1901, p350.
24. *Railway News*, 26 April 1902, p654.
25. *Morning Leader*, 22 October 1902, p5; *Municipal Journal*, 24 Oct 1902, p869.
26. Robert B. Suthers, *The Truth about Trams*, Clarion Press, 1903, p1.
27. *Municipal Journal*, 7 November 1902, p916.
28. *Municipal Journal*, 14 November 1902, p931-32.
29. *Birmingham Mail*, 10 November 1902, p2.
30. *Birmingham Daily Gazette*, 8 November 1902, p4.

31. *Municipal Journal*, 22 May 1903, p487.
32. British Electric Traction board minutes, 7 November 1901, record payments totalling £300 to the association.
33. *Municipal Journal*, 7 April 1905, p343.
34. The Royal Commission on the Means of Locomotion and Transport in London (its official title), Cd. 2597, 1905, p50.
35. *Daily Express*, 4 September 1915, p4.
36. Piers Brendon, *The Motoring Century*, Bloomsbury Books, 1997, p80.
37. *Car*, 22 April 1903, p280.
38. *Daily Mail*, 5 December 1906, p6.
39. Reginald Pound and Geoffrey Harmsworth, *Northcliffe*, Cassell, 1959, p287. Geoffrey Harmsworth was Lord Northcliffe's nephew.
40. *Investors' Review*, 25 October 1902, p479.
41. *Daily Mail*, 9 December 1909, p6.
42. Hansard (HC), 25 May 1909, cols1088-89.
43. *Automotor Journal*, 14 May 1910, p516.
44. Memorandum from George Gibb, 20 November 1911, p4, Rees Jeffreys papers, RJ 2/10.
45. The London General helped to fund the campaign, through the Roads Improvement Association and the Commercial Motor Users' Association. London General board minutes, 31 October 1911, 6 February and 2 April 1912, TLA, ACC/1297/LGOC/01/034.
46. Letter from William Rees Jeffreys to the LCC, 8 October 1912, quoted in Road Board, Third Annual Report, HC. 222, 1913, pp71-76.
47. Royal Commission on the Civil Service, Fourth Report, HMSO, 1914, Cd. 7338, p76.
48. *Weekly Dispatch*, 30 July 1916, p4; Hansard (HC), 30 May 1916, cols2616-29.
49. Hansard (HC), 3 August 1916, col476.
50. London County Council, Report of the Highways Committee, 12 December 1918, pp3, 6, letters to the ministry dated 22 November and 11 December 1918; Hansard (HC), 24 July 1918, cols1819-20.
51. J. Lee Thompson, *Politicians, the Press and Propaganda*, Kent State University Press, 1999, p262.
52. *Daily Telegraph*, 10 November 1917, p6.
53. *Municipal Journal*, 16 November 1917, p1110.
54. Hansard (HC), 1 July 1918, col1374.
55. Rees Jeffreys' note on the history of the Motor Legislation Committee, Rees Jeffreys papers, RJ 2/3.
56. Memorandum from Albert Stanley, 13 February 1919, The National Archives (TNA), CAB 24/75/1.
57. Keith Grieves, *Sir Eric Geddes*, Manchester University Press, 1989, p78.
58. Hansard (HC), 17 March 1919, cols1761-62.
59. House of Commons Select Committee on Transport (Metropolitan Area), 1919, Cmd. 147, pp5, 9, 10.
60. *Commercial Motor*, 4 November 1919, p245.
61. *Evening News*, 5 November 1919, p4.
62. *Municipal Journal*, 24 October 1919, p1052.
63. London General Omnibus Company board minutes 6 November 1919 and 4 March 1920, TLA, ACC/1297/LGOC/01/036; Underground Electric Railways board minute 23 December 1919, TLA, ACC/1297/UER/01/004/008.
64. *Daily Mail*, 24 January 1920, p7.
65. *Daily Herald*, 10 August 1922, p5.

66. *Sunday Times*, 2 April 1923, p12.
67. Several chummy letters between Lord Ashfield and Wilfred Ashley are in the Broadlands Archives, BR 76/9.
68. Cabinet Conclusions, 17 March 1924, TNA, CAB 23/47/15 and 27 March, CAB 23/47/16.
69. *Scotsman*, 16 November 1928, p11.
70. London and Home Counties Traffic Advisory Committee, Omnibus Competition with Tramways, 1926, p10.
71. London and Home Counties Traffic Advisory Committee, Omnibus Competition with Tramways, 1926, p2.
72. Letters from Isidore Salmon to Ashley, 2 and 17 March 1926, Broadlands Archive, BR 78/3.
73. Henry Maybury, Talk to the Royal Institution, 5 March 1926, TNA, MT 6/3236.
74. *Daily Telegraph*, 23 April 1926, p3.
75. Harold Lasswell, *Propaganda Technique in World War*, Peter Smith, 1938, p206; Angus Fletcher, British Library of Information in New York to Foreign Office in London, 10 May 1929, TNA, FO 395/437.
76. Edward Bernays, *Propaganda*, Liveright, 1928, pp37-38.
77. Denys Munby, *Inland Transport Statistics*, Oxford University Press, 1978, p224.
78. *Daily Mail*, 24 March 1924, p8.
79. Hamilton Fyfe, *Press Parade*, Watts, 1936, p100.
80. *Record* (Journal of the Transport and General Workers' Union), November 1923, p7; Forward, 10 November 1923, p1.
81. London and Provincial Omnibus Owners' Association minutes, 12 February 1923.
82. Robert H. Wilder and Katharine L. Buell, *Publicity: a Manual for the Use of Business, Civic or Social Service Organisations*, Ronald Press, 1923, p103.
83. *Journal of the Municipal Tramways Association*, 1925, pp54-55.
84. Ibid, p257.
85. Quoted in Fyfe, op. cit. title page.
86. *Electric Railway and Tramway Journal*, 16 January 1925, p10.
87. *Sunday Pictorial*, 19 September 1926, p7; *Journal of the Municipal Tramways Association*, 1926, pp362-65.
88. Letter from Thomas Roles, Bradford Borough Electrical Engineer, to Walter Vignoles, 14 October 1930, TNA, MT 6/3235, part 1.
89. *Portsmouth Evening News*, 16 December 1925, p3.
90. *Derby Daily Telegraph*, 26 March 1926, p4.
91. Edward Bernays, *Crystallizing Public Opinion*, Liveright Publishing Corp, 1923, p57.
92. Andrew Hobbs, *A Fleet Street in Every Town*, Open Book Publishers, 2018, p5.
93. Timothy Phillips, *The Secret Twenties*, Granta, 2017, pp272 and 316.
94. Andrew Lycett, *From Diamond Sculls to Golden Handcuffs*, Robert Hale, 1998, pp44-45; List of MI5 personnel, TNA, KV 1/59.
95. Glyn Roberts, *The Most Powerful Man in the World*, Covici Friede, 1938, pp222-23.
96. Nicholas (Ernest H.) Davenport, *Memoirs of a City Radical*, Weidenfeld and Nicolson, 1974, p14.
97. Joost Jonker and Jan Luiten van Zanden, *A History of Royal Dutch Shell*, Oxford University Press, 2007, p277.
98. David Low, *Autobiography*, Michael Joseph, 1956, p162, quoted in Gill Bennett, *The Zinoviev Letter*, Oxford University Press, 2018, p101.
99. Geoffrey Jones, *The State and the Emergence of the British Oil Industry*, Macmillan, 1981, pp236-37; File on Paul Bichkov of Russian Oil Products, 22 September 1931, TNA, KV 2/2383.

100. Timothy Phillips, *The Secret Twenties*, Granta, 2017, p291. His source is 'Arcos Ltd.: A Chronological Note of Events', 14 May 1927, TNA, KV 3/15, p2.

101. Francis Delaisi, *Foreign Affairs*, October 1927, pp106-108.

102. The Shell advertising campaign ran from May to September 1922 It featured eleven prominent motor journalists who all vouched for the superiority of Shell's products. Three of these hacks, Edward T. Brown, James P. Holland and Edgar de Normanville, later wrote articles supporting Shell's campaigns against Soviet petrol, trams and railway branch lines. Brown later wrote astroturfing letters for the British Road Federation, which was partly financed by Shell.

103. Davenport, op.cit. p18.

104. Waley Cohen papers, MS 363/A 3006/1/3/30.

105. Lycett, op. cit., p46; Coroner's report, 4 July 1930, TLA, CLA/041/IQ/04/03/022.

106. *Manchester Guardian*, 20 May 1930, p13.

107. *Safety First* (Journal of the National Safety First Association), July 1925, p. iv.

108. *Daily Telegraph*, 1 December 1927, p7.

109. *Journal of the Municipal Tramways Association*, 1928, p61.

110. Ibid, pp63-65.

111. Frederick A. McKenzie, *The Mystery of the Daily Mail*, Associated Newspapers, 1921, p75-76.

112. Municipal Tramways Association minutes, memorandum of May 1925 following p1932.

113. *Yorkshire Observer*, 15 April 1925, p9.

114. Municipal Tramways Association minutes, 1924-25, before p133.

115. Hansard (HC), 21 May 1925, col795.

116. Municipal Tramways Association minutes, 1925-26, pp75-76.

117. London and Provincial Omnibus Owners' Association, minutes of the Executive and Parliamentary Committees 8 March 1926, circular following p67.

118. Cabinet conclusions, 10 March 1926, TNA, CAB 23/52/10.

119. Letter from Alfred Hacking, secretary of the Society of Motor Manufacturers and Traders to Jabez Beckett of the Municipal Tramways Association, 24 April 1925, Municipal Tramways Association minutes, 1924-25, pp99-100.

120. *Electric Railway and Tramway Journal*, 16 December 1927, p389.

121. Tramways and Light Railways Association minutes, 1919-29, meetings of 30 November 1923, p122 and 4 January 1924, p125.

122. Tramways and Light Railways Association minutes, 7 January 1927, p185.

123. *Yorkshire Post*, 13 February 1936, p3.

124. Torquay conference report, *Tramways and Light Railways Association Journal*, 1926, p3396.

125. *Electric Railway and Tramway Journal*, 19 September 1925, p145.

126. Chairman's meeting, 24 April 1930, TfL Corporate Archives, LT000503/014.

127. *The Tramways Light Railways and Transport Association Journal*, 1931, p4525.

128. *The Times*, 17 November 1925, p19.

129. Herbert Morrison, *An Autobiography*, Odhams Press, 1960, p138.

130. Letter from Ashley to William Joynson-Hicks, 5 February 1927, East Sussex Record Office, JIX/ACC9851/2/1/16.

131. Letter from Ralph Blumenfeld, 31 December 1927 to Ashley, Broadlands Archive BR 76/4.

132. *The Times*, 29 October 1928, p16.

133. *Daily Chronicle*, 28 January 1926, p9.

134. *The Times*, 8 February 1929, p14.

135. Trades Union Congress, notes to and from Walter Citrine's office, 28 and 31 December 1928, Modern Records Centre, MSS.292/654.2/3.

136. Hansard (HC), 19 February 1929, cols1053-58.

137. *Journal of the Municipal Tramways and Transport Association*, 1928, p237.

138. Maybury's comments were relayed to Cyril Hurcomb, permanent secretary, in a note dated 2 May 1928, TNA, MT 42/1.

139. Summary of progress by George F. Stedman, 7 July 1928.

140. *Daily Herald*, 25 July 1928, p2.

141. Letter from Robert Tolerton to commission members, 30 July 1928, TNA, MT 42/1.

142. Memorandum dated 1 May 1928, TNA, MT 42/1.

143. Royal Commission on Transport, Minutes of Evidence, 30 January 1929, p218.

144. Ibid, 15 February 1929, p337.

145. Ibid, 18 April 1929, p551.

146. Royal Commission on Transport, Final Report, The Co-ordination and Development of Transport, HMSO, Cmd. 3751, 1931, pp104 and 105.

147. Christopher T. Brunner, *The Problem of Motor Transport*, Ernest Benn, 1928, pp9 and 73.

148. Letter from Brunner to the Commission, 10 December 1928, TNA, MT 42/1.

149. Royal Commission, Minutes of Evidence, 1 February 1929, p314.

150. *Journal of the Municipal Tramways and Transport Association*, 1929, p124.

151. Draft report, 12 July 1929, TNA, MT 42/77.

152. Herbert Morrison to Arthur Griffith-Boscawen, 23 September 1929, TNA, MT 42/1.

153. Minutes of LCC's General Purposes Committee, 22 April 1929.

154. Letter to John E. Allen, 14 March 1929, TNA, MT 42/61.

155. Federation of British Industries, Special Committee on the Royal Commission on Transport, 7 August 1929, p2998, Modern Records Centre, MSS 200/F/1/1/87.

156. Sketch of the final report, dated 5 December 1929 in pencil (there are two other undated versions), TNA, MT 42/78; Letter from Clarendon, 9 January 1930 – wrongly dated 1929, TNA, MT 42/78.

157. Conclusions from meetings of the Royal Commission held in June and July 1930, TNA, MT 42/78.

158. *Daily Herald*, 27 September 1930, p9.

159. *Municipal Journal*, 16 January 1931, p95.

160. *Sunday Pictorial*, 13 January 1931, p5.

161. *Commercial Motor*, 6 March 1928, p90.

162. Telegram from Charles Matthews to LCC, 9 December 1930, TLA, LCC/CL/CER/02/035.

163. Letter from George Strauss to the LCC, 3 December 1930, TLA, LCC/CL/CER/02/035.

164. Board meetings on 3 April 1930 of the London United Tramways Company, ACC/1297/LUT/01/004; Metropolitan Electric Railway Company, ACC/1297/MET/01/007; London and Suburban Traction Company, ACC/1297/LST/01/003.

165. Minutes of the Development (Public Utility) Advisory Committee, 10 April 1930, TNA, T 191/1.

166. Cyril Hurcomb to Ernest Rowntree, 7 May 1931, TNA, MT 46/51.

167. Reginald Hill to Hurcomb, 11 February 1931. TNA, MT 46/51.

168. Clause 17 of the London Passenger Transport Bill as originally published, TNA, MT 46/51.

169. Chairman's meeting, 19 November 1931, TfL Corporate Archives, LT000503/15.

170. Chairman's meeting, 28 September 1933, TfL Corporate Archives, LT000503/020; For the state of the LCC's track see Martin Higginson, Tramway London, Light Rail Transit Association, 1993, p61.

171. *Electric Railway Journal*, 17 November 1933, p207.

172. Cecil of Chelwood papers, volume LXXXIII, British Library, Add MS 51153, 9 December 1929.

173. *Burnley News*, 21 February 1931, p7.

174. Municipal Tramways and Transport Association minutes, 1930-31, pp122, 164 and 176.

175. Ministry of Transport's observations, 25 February 1931, p6, TNA, MT 6/3236.

176. Municipal Tramways and Transport Association minutes, 1931-32, p122.

177. *Municipal Review*, March 1932, p113.

178. Coroner's record, TLA, COR/Me/1930/12/016/3.

179. *Autocar*, 1 December 1933, pp1027-29 and 22 December 1933, p1185.

180. Frank Pick was the first chairman of the British Road Federation, TfL Corporate Archives, LT000527/007, 17 January 1933; Minutes of British Road Federation, 11 January 1933, p7, BRF Archives, 1240/1.

181. Municipal Tramways and Transport Association minutes, 1933-34, pp272-73 and 1934-35, pp269-89.

182. Letter from Tramways Light Railways and Transport Association, 19 December 1934, TNA, MT 6/3235.

183. *Nottingham Journal*, 7 September 1936, p7.

184. *Commercial Motor*, 3 August 1934, p832.

185. *Tramways, Light Railways and Transport Association Journal*, 1932, p4830.

186. Letter to Sir John Brooke, secretary of the Central Electricity Board, 17 January 1931, TNA, MT 6/3235.

187. *Nature*, 30 December 1933, p987.

188. Letter and enclosures from Henry Watson to select committee, 22 May 1934, TNA MT 6/3255.

189. Minutes of the Pedestrians' Association Committee, 18 June 1935, 10 September and 19 November.

190. *Picture Post,* 5 July 1952, pp22-23.

191. Theodore Barker and Michael Robbins, *A History of London Transport, Vol. 2*, George Allen and Unwin, 1974, p339.

192. Letter dated 14 August 1952, TfL Corporate Archives, LT000264/127.

193. Correspondence between Queen Mary's office and Lord Latham on 12 and 14 August 1952, TfL Corporate Archives, LT000264/127.

194. *London Transport Magazine*, July 1952, p3.

195. IPF Bulletin (Infantile Paralysis Fellowship), August 1952, p14.

196. Latham to John Marshall, editor of the *Evening News*, 30 June 1952, TfL Corporate Archives, LT000264/127.

197. John Krish told this story several times, with minor differences. This mostly comes from an interview in *Perspectives on Documentary Filmmaking*, BFI, 2010.

198. Kevin Brownlow, Booklet with the DVD *A Day in the Life*, British Film Institute, 2010, p7.

199. *Yorkshire Post,* 4 November 1953, p1.

200. *Glasgow Herald*, 23 May 1936, p12.

201. *Guardian*, 28 April 1992, p3.

202. *Journal of the National Smoke Abatement Society*, Winter 1933, p17.

203. *New Scientist*, 9 December 1976, p585.

204. William Bown, 'Dying from too much dust', *New Scientist*, 12 March 1994, p12.

205. Royal Commission on Environmental Pollution, Transport and the Environment, Cm. 2674, 1994, p189.

INDEX